THE IDLER · NO. 43

THE IDLER

NO.43 BACK TO THE LAND

A COLLECTION OF ESSAYS ON THE ART OF LIVING

EDITED BY TOM HODGKINSON

IDLER BOOKS

MMX

IDLER BOOKS

P.O. BOX 280 BARNSTAPLE EX31 4WX

Idle Limited Reg. No. 5897340

A CIP catalogue record for this book is
available from the British Library

I

Editor Tom Hodgkinson
Typesetting Christian Brett
Art Editor Alice Smith
Proof Reader Sarah Day

The views expressed by the contributors
do not necessarily reflect those of the editors

The type used is Monotype Bembo Book designed by
Robin Nicholas and complimented with ITC Golden Cockerel Initials
by Richard Dawson from original designs first created by Mr Gill in 1929

Printed in Great Britain by the MPG Books Group, Bodmin and King's Lynn

ISBN-13: 978-0-9548456-1-2

www.idler.co.uk

That trade's proud empire hastes to swift decay,
As ocean sweeps the labour'd mole away;
While self-dependent power can time defy,
As rocks resist the billows and the sky.

from *The Deserted Village*,
Oliver Goldsmith, 1770

THE IDLER 🐌 NO.43
TABLE OF CONTENTS

Notes on contributors

Matthew De Abaitua's début novel, *The Red Men*, was nominated for the Arthur C. Clarke Award. He can be found at www.harrybravado.com

Ian Bone is the founder of Class War. www.ianbone.wordpress.com

Christian Brett is a typesetter, letterpress printer and gangmaster in charge of Bracketpress. www.bracketpress.co.uk

Graham Burnett is a writer and a permaculture designer and teacher. He is hoping to invest the fee for his article in a community apple press.

Pat Conaty is a fellow of the New Economics Foundation.

Leanne Cordingley and Andy Wright are co-founders of the Loop Project. www.theloopproject.co.uk

Stanley Donwood is an artist, whose recent show in Heerlen was looted by English tourists.

Warren Draper is currently replanting North Yorkshire; he has seeds in his pocket and mud on his mind. warrendraper@gmail.com

Simon Fairlie is editor of *The Land* magazine. He also sells scythes at www.thescytheshop.co.uk

John-Paul Flintoff is the author of *Through the Eye of a Needle* (Permanent Publications), and writes for the *FT* and *Sunday Times*. www.flintoff.org

Matthew Green is an artist and illustrator based in north London.

Jay Griffiths is the author of *Pip Pip* and *Wild: An Elemental Journey* (Hamish Hamilton).

N. M. Gwynne is a retired businessman and now teaches Latin, philosophy and medicine.

Clifford Harper is an illustrator whose work is the sole reason some people continue to buy the *Guardian* newspaper.

David Hockney is from Yorkshire. He makes images.

Tony Husband is a cartoonist who contributes to *Private Eye*, the *Daily Mirror* and many more.

Ray Roughler Jones is editor of *The Roughler* and Director General of Roughler TV.

Sarah A. King is an illustrator who lives and works in London, part of the Evening Tweed Collective.

Paul Kingsnorth is a journalist and campaigner. He has been deputy editor of the *Ecologist*, and is the author of *One No; Many Yeses: A Journey to the Heart of the Global Resistance Movement* (Simon & Schuster) and *Real England* (Portobello).

Gavin Knight lived in Odessa for two years and speaks Russian. He has written for *The Times*, *Prospect* magazine, the *Guardian*, the *Daily Mail* and many others. His book on inner-city crime will be published by Picador in 2011.

John Lawrence has illustrated over 150 books, including a number of private press and Folio Society editions.

Pete Loveday is an artist and creator of Russell.

Harry Mount is a journalist and author of *Amo, Amas, Amat: How to Become a Latin Lover* (Short Books).

John Nicholson, AKA the Baron, is an historian, model and real-ale connoisseur who lives in Bedford.

James Parker lives and writes in Boston, USA.

Tim Richardson is a garden and landscape critic. He is the author of *Sweets: The History of Temptation*.

Penny Rimbaud was born in 1943. He did not study at Oxford. He does not have a dog, a wife, a flat in north London or a house in Buckinghamshire. He has been a writer throughout his life.

Abigail Rorer is an American wood engraver and etcher. Her most recent book, *Mimpish Squinnies*, won the prestigious Gregynog Prize in 2009.

Lee Rowland is a psychologist and writer who taught scientific method at Oxford University, and now works with the Beckley Foundation.

Kieron-Rhys Johnson draws, cuts and designs.

Alice Smith is the *Idler*'s art editor. She's an illustrator, designer and collage artist.

Hugh Warwick is the author of *A Prickly Affair: My Life with Hedgehogs* (Allen Lane), and you can find out more at www.urchin.info

Notes on contributors

Stuart Watkins lives in Leamington Spa and has previously contributed to the *Radical Anthropology* journal, the *Socialist Standard*, the *Lancet* and Readysteadybook.com

Joanna Walsh is an illustrator and writer. Her website can be found at www.badaude.typepad.com

Boff Whalley is a fell runner, playwright, and a musician who has sold more records than John Prescott's had hot dinners. www.chumba.com

Joe Wilson is an artist and printmaker.

List of illustrations

Illustrator websites:

Neither Pete Loveday nor John Lawrence has his own website, but an adventure into the shiney-shiney machine will throw up a wealth of information. Some of which may be true.

AN IDLER'S DIARY

Tom Hodgkinson

THE ROMANS HAD A PROBLEM WITH EXHAUSTED SOIL AND climate change. In around 50 AD, the great writer on husbandry, Columella, introduced his series of books on agriculture with the following comments:

> Again and again I hear leading men of our state condemning now the unfruitfulness of our soil, now the inclemency of the climate for some seasons past, as harmful to crops.

He goes on to say that many think that the soil is exhausted by over-production. For Columella this is not actually the case: the earth, he says, is perennially fertile. The mistake has been manmade, and it is due to poor husbandry. The farms, he says, have been entrusted to slaves, 'to the worst of slaves, as if to a hangman for punishment'.

Today, we have handed over control of food production and the land to a tiny consortium of capitalists in the form of the supermarkets, and their Trotskyite lickspittles in the House of Commons (the House of Commons, mark you, which was founded in order to represent the will of the common people). Their primary concern is not health but profit. And everybody in the civil service knows that DEFRA is a department for dimbos in contrast with the perceived glamour of, for example, the Foreign Office, which attracts the brighter sorts. The intellectuals, too, have taken their eye off the ball, and very few these days profess much interest in farming, preferring instead to help the State cook up yet another hideous ideological experiment in social engineering to be carried out in our primary and secondary schools. Simply put, no one wants to get their hands dirty any more.

In the old days, according to Columella, the intellectuals and states-
men did not consider it degrading to take an interest in farming:

> It was a matter of pride with our forefathers to give their atten-
> tion to farming, from which pursuit came Quinctus Cincinnatus,
> summoned from the plough to the dictatorship to be delivered of
> a beleaguered consul and his army, and then, laying down the
> power which he relinquished after victory more hastily than he
> had assumed it for command, to return to the same bullocks and
> his small ancestral inheritance of four *iugera* [one *iugerum* is about
> three-fifths of an acre].

At around this time, the smallholding life had retreated, and food production was based on gigantic *latifundia*, slave-run farms with 80,000
staff or more. Meanwhile, the city-bound Romans were pursuing a life
of pleasure, and Columella attacks the decadent habits of his day:

> We spend our nights in licentiousness and drunkenness, our days
> in gaming or sleeping, and account ourselves blessed by fortune
> in that we 'behold neither the rising of the sun nor its setting'
> [a quote from Cato].

Yes, I know: it doesn't sound too bad. But in fact, this way of living is
not sustainable. So Columella urged Romans to get back to the land.
He acknowledges also that this is a very complicated subject, because
the conditions are so different on every farm: there are different soil
types and weather conditions, and indeed the weather changes every
year. Hence the profusion of books on the subject.

Columella was what we would now call a 'climate-change sceptic':

> I have found that many authorities now worthy of remembrance
> were convinced that with the long wasting of the ages, weather
> and climate undergo a change.

I mention the above in order really to show that it is time for all of us
to find ways of taking back the control of our food supply and of our

land from today's robber barons, the supermarkets, who steal from the poor and redistribute their hard-earned money to the rich (or in today's terms, 'customers' and 'shareholders'). These backwards Robin Hoods are helped in this project by the weak fantasists who sit in the House of Commons, that graveyard of ideologies. The land is our source of food, pleasure and beauty. We live on it; we live off it, and this is why we have partly devoted *Idler* no. 43 to exploring such issues. Chesterton remarked that the problem with capitalism is that there are too few capitalists. Most of us are slaves. So it is time to seize the means of production and free ourselves.

★

In *Idler no.43: Back to the Land*, we have gathered together an excellent group of essayists and contributors. The book opens with an interview with David Hockney, who discusses the great revolution in the way we looked at the world which happened in the Renaissance, and how that way of seeing appears to be crumbling at last. Hockney has also drawn a new self-portrait for this issue. Ian Bone of *Class War* and his ne'er-do-well pal Ray Roughler-Jones discuss idling for the working classes.

This issue's contributors include Harry Mount, Penny Rimbaud, Jay Griffiths, Paul Kingsnorth and Simon Fairlie of *The Land*, Britain's finest magazine. We investigate the Russian dacha system, the medieval guilds, life in the thirteenth century and that great scam we know as the Bank of England. We hope to provide food for thought and good ideas both old and new. We envisage a slow migration of people out of the cities to the country, and simultaneously a revival of husbandry in the cities and towns. It would not be difficult for a group of friends to get together, find a patch of land and put some apple trees on it and keep a few hens. Those parks and wastelands could be covered in happy, snorting pigs. We could get some life back into the city. Smash usury, brothers and sisters! Reclaim the fields!

★

FEBRUARY

To Sweden, where I give a talk as the guest of psychologist Samuel West. It appears that despite the comforts of IKEA, the Swedes are even more depressed than we are. There is the same ban on smoking that we suffer with, and Samuel tells me that the Swedes are gloomier than ever.

MARCH

My book *The Idle Parent* was released. Jay Griffiths gets it right when she calls it 'an act of family liberation'. There are good reviews in the *Sunday Times*, *Evening Standard* and the *Oldie*, and in the States, it is serialized in *Slate*, the online magazine. There are mean-spirited reviews in the *FT* and the *Guardian*, which both repeat the old lie that idling is only available to the moneyed classes (a lie which is always, I have noticed, repeated by the moneyed classes). For more on this, see this issue's interview with Ian Bone and Ray Roughler-Jones.

APRIL

To Simpsons-on-the-Strand for an *Oldie* lunch. I was very flattered to be invited, as Richard Ingrams is a hero of mine, having created both *Private Eye* and the *Oldie*, both of which would be in my top three magazines. When he introduced me to the assembled Oldies, Richard Ingrams patted my head in paternal fashion, which I thought was very touching. But I can't claim that my talk was a huge success: first of all, I antagonized the oldies with my scruffy dress. Everyone else had made the effort to dress up, and I was in jeans and untucked shirt with no tie. Then I accused the Oldies of being bad grandparents. 'You complain about being used by your children as a free babystting service,' I said. 'But why the phrase "free babysitting"? What happened to "playing with your grandchildren?"' Then I rambled on too long and a couple of Oldies heckled. I even saw one giving the internationally recognized 'Wind up' sign. After lunch, a lady told me that a group of women in the loos was complaining about me. Salvation was at hand, though, from the wonderful Barry Cryer. He'd enjoyed my talk: 'You were stirring things up!' We went to the pub with a few others and got pissed all afternoon. Cryer told a non-stop stream of jokes. Heaven.

JUNE

Issue 42 of the *Idler* was released. It's our first in the new format: a high-quality hardback book with 150,000 words of radical writing. I send out ten copies to newspapers such as the *Guardian* and the *Telegraph*, but not one mentions it. We do, though, get a mention in *The Bookseller*, so thanks to them. Despite the lack of publicity we go on to sell 3,000 copies, which in publishing terms is a healthy sale for a hardback book costing £18.99. Thanks to everyone out there who bought it and who continues to support our work. We rely completely on income from sales, as there are no ads and no other sources of income.

JULY

To the Port Eliot Festival, where Samantha Chalkley and I do our singalong. Over a hundred people pack into our tent, and despite the attempts of my 9-year-old son to subvert proceedings, everyone has a great time. We are booked by Viktor Wynd for one of his decadent London parties, and if anyone out there would like to pay us a handsome fee, then we will come to your party, too.

AUGUST

To Tapeley Park, the seat of the ebullient campaigning aristocrat Hector Christie, who invites me to give a talk at his 'Save Our World' festival. It's an opportunity to see what Hector is doing at Tapeley. He has made the house and grounds into a sort of experimental permaculture community, with beautiful vegetable gardens, piggeries and poultry. I was accompanied by the Whiggish cynic Toby Young, who was not particularly impressed. But I think there is something very positive there. Hector is indicating a new role for the aristocracy: to use the estates as productive entities which house a lot of people and act as a hub for debate and artistic activity as well. The aristocrats have been completely beaten up by successive Cromwellian parliaments over the last hundred years, so it is vital that they reinvent themselves. Hector shows one way of doing this. So thank you, Hector, and good luck to you, sir.

SEPTEMBER

To Soho for the Book Club Boutique, the literary salon run by those lovely alliterative ladies Salena Saliva and Rachel Rayner. I gathered together a fine selection of *Idler* contributors, including Penny Rimbaud (a rare appearance), the hilarious Dominic Frisby, a poorly David Bramwell, my brother Will, who brought along folk singer Sam Lee, and myself. It was a lively evening marred only by the heckling of a certain drunken poet during Penny's reading.

OCTOBER

To the South Bank for an event oganized by the New Economics Foundation. It takes place in an old warehouse, and there are stalls, bars, talks and music. I talk on freedom and work. The NEF, by the way, is agitating for a shorter working week, which would seem like a sensible idea from many points of view. Their idea is 21 hours, and that seems very sensible from very many points of view. The struggle to abolish wage slavery must come in two halves: first, improve conditions, hours and pay. Then break out entirely. This was how the medieval church abolished the slavery that had been a key feature of the pagan world, as you can read in N. M. Gwynne's fascinating study in this issue. Slaves were given more and more rights until they became completely free. So a four-day week could be our first step towards emancipation.

DECEMBER

To Mike's Café on Portobello Road, where I meet the excellent Ian Bone and Ray Roughler-Jones, for a conversation reported in this issue. I also visit Rough Trade and new bookshsop Lutyens and Rubinstein, as well as the senior buyer at Foyles. It appears that the independent-bookshop sector is thriving, as Waterstones crumble under the weight of its own avarice. I am planning to visit as many independent bookshops as possible in the coming years, and if any out there would like me to come and give a talk, please get in touch.

FEBRUARY

To Bridlington for an interview with Davd Hockney, also published in this issue. Then to Shaftesbury Avenue and the Apollo for the first night of Jez Butterworth's play *Jerusalem*. It is a superb portrait of a certain kind of rural life and also of the free spirit that hides in all of us. I can imagine local theatre groups doing it in the pub, and would urge everyone to buy a copy. It makes a good read as well as a good night out.

And let me leave you with the following lines from Oliver Goldsmith's 'The Deserted Village' of 1770. Goldsmith was a friend of Dr Johnson, and in a sense the Oliver James of his day, discoursing as he does against 'cumbrous wealth' and 'trade's unfeeling train'.

> Sweet smiling village, loveliest of the lawn,
> Thy sports are fled, and all thy charms withdrawn;
> Amidst thy bowers the tyrant's hand is seen,
> And desolation saddens all thy green:
> One only master grasps thy whole domain,
> And half a tillage stints thy smiling plain;
> No more thy glassy brook reflects the day,
> But choaked with sedges, works its weedy way.
> Along thy glades, a solitary guest,
> The hollow-sounding bittern guards its nest;
> Amidst thy desert walk the lapwing flies,
> And tires their echoes with unvaried cries.
> Sunk are thy bowers in shapeless ruin all,
> And the long grass o'ertops the mouldering wall,
> And trembling, shrinking from the spoiler's hand,
> Far, far away thy children leave the land.
>   Ill fares the land, to hastening ills a prey,
> Where wealth accumulates, and men decay;
> Princes and lords may flourish, or may fade;
> A breath can make them, as a breath has made.
> But a bold peasantry, their country's pride,

When once destroyed, can never be supplied.
A time there was, ere England's griefs began.
When every rood of ground maintained its man;
For him light labour spread her wholesome store,
Just gave what life required, but gave no more.
His best companions, innocence and health;
And his best riches, ignorance of wealth.

But times are altered; trade's unfeeling train
Usurp the land and dispossess the swain;
Along the lawn, where scattered hamlets rose,
Unwieldy wealth, and cumbrous pomp repose;
And every want to luxury allied,
And every pang that folly pays to pride.
These gentle hours that plenty bade to bloom,
Those calm desires that asked but little room,
Those healthful sports that graced the peaceful scene,
Lived in each look, and brightened all the green;
These far departing seek a kinder shore,
And rural mirth and manners are no more.

COMICS

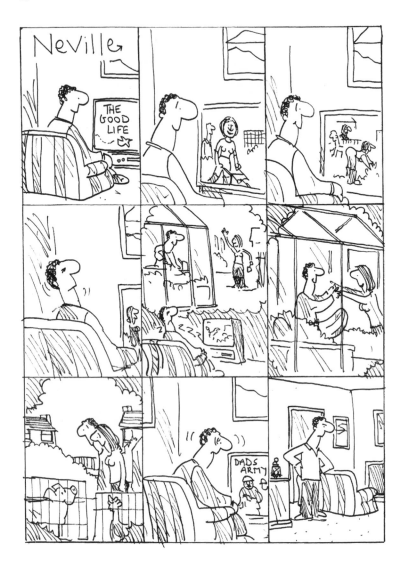

Tony Husband

15

Still, a few people thought it worth a go: In <u>1841</u> the Ripleys set up Fourierist Brook <u>Farm</u> in Massachusetts.

We started as a profit-sharing joint stock co. — Sophia Ripley

Trouble is, we now owe $17,445 — George Ripley

Author, Nathaniel Hawthorne quickly left.

*I have no quiet at all!

A new crop of blisters —the effect* of raking hay!

BLITHEDALE ROMANCE

Fourierist "La Réunion", Texas, went the same way after its ex-townie citizens failed to cope with droughts & blizzards.

Inspired by the writings of **Leo Tolstoy**

between 1910 & 1913, Mahatma Gandhi ran the **Tolstoy Farm** at Phoenix, South Africa.

I have serious doubts as to whether the struggle could have been prosecuted for 8 years ...if there had been no **Tolstoy Farm**.

In **1963**, Huw Piper Williams started **Tolstoy Farm** Washington. The founder abandoned the project after

Things got wild and different.

*quoted by T. Williams "The 60s communes hippies & beyond"

In "**The Restaurant at the End of the Universe**" (1980) Douglas Adams posits that in any case, we're descended, not from cave dwellers but

- **telephone** -
- **sanitation** -
- **Engineers** -

...Hey, I just invented hair straighteners!

cool!

So the problem persists: how to begin to plough our <u>half-acre</u> when all we can handle is a <u>hair-dryer</u>...

4. What Happened Next?

Piers Plowman: Left his half-acre to search for Truth —

John Ball: was hung, drawn & quartered in 1381, & his head stuck on London Bridge... villeinage remained.

The Diggers: Gave up their spades in 1651 after many skirmishes with landowners

Charles Fourier: Died in Paris in 1837, his funeral attended by over 400 mourners.

Brook Farm: burned down. The land is now a cemetery

La Réunion: recently re-opened as an artists' community — "It's going to be a lot of money but this is going to be permanent.*"

Tolstoy Farm (South Africa): reopened as a museum & community centre in 2006

Tolstoy Farm USA: Remained open continuously since 1963 and is now a collective organic farm

Huw Piper Williams: now runs an experiment in sustainable farming at Edwall, USA, for the last 30 years.

Ruskinland: John & Linda's plans include renewing the Ruskinland orchards, building up rare-breed herds of pigs and cattle and, of course, breeding Utopians: "we hope to be able to host many visitors who will draw peace and inspiration from Unellys and perhaps decide for themselves ways in which they could tread more lightly on the earth"

* Catherine Cuellar – La Réunion's (re)founder – Oak Cliff News, Texas

Joanna Walsh

SO MANY SPECIES DRIVEN INTO EXTINCTION, SO MANY OF YOUR FELLOWS ENSLAVED, CRUSHED, EXPLOITED, MURDERED, SO MANY FORESTS BURNED, SO MUCH SOIL POISONED, MINERALS EXHAUSTED, RIVERS POLLUTED, THE VERY CLIMATE DEFORMED IN YOUR RELENTLESS SEARCH FOR WEALTH AND POWER.... AND NOW, AS A LIFESTYLE CHOICE, AND WITHOUT MORE THAN A TOKEN RENUNCIATION OF A FEW OF THE MANY ENERGY-CONSUMING TOYS, YOU WANT TO PLAY AT AGRICULTURE! PART-TIME, OF COURSE.

PLEASE FORGIVE MY CYNICISM, O LORDS OF CREATION...

Pete Loveday

CONVERSATIONS

David Hockney

IT'S ALL ABOUT IMAGES

IN CONVERSATION WITH
DAVID HOCKNEY

Tom Hodgkinson

I T IS NOT EVERY DAY THAT YOU GET THE OPPORTUNITY TO meet a living genius, so I was thrilled when David Hockney accepted my request for an interview. I had read his book *Secret Knowledge*, a beautiful account of the use of the camera in art from the Renaissance to the present day. Art historians know that portraiture suddenly became more realistic around 1400 to 1500. What Hockney shows is that, in the fifteenth century, artists began to use lenses to project an image on to a piece of paper, which they then traced to get a realistic image. That's why Renaissance art looks so photographic when compared with medieval art.

It is Hockney's argument that the camera, in fact, far from being the only realistic means of depicting reality, is only one of many, and a rather boring one at that. It has come, though, to dominate the world. Its rise in the Renaissance comes with a new way of looking at the world: medieval art tends to look at objects from many perspectives; the camera has only one. It is fascinating to note in the book that Cubism, which was a revolt away from perspective and the camera-based view, has more in common with medieval art than with art from the 'realistic' period of the sixteenth to nineteenth centuries.

Hockney, who is 72, says that control of images gradually moved from the Church to the mass media. But now he thinks that the mass media is starting to lose control of the image. Could the image return to the people, in that case?

I sent Hockney a copy of the *Idler* and he left a message on the answerphone with the comment: 'It's all about images.' We fixed up a time, and so one cold February afternoon I arrived at York station. A few years ago, Hockney moved with his household back to Bridlington in East Yorkshire, home of his mother.

I was picked up at the station by Jonathan, who is helping Hockney with the computer side of his new work. Jonathan has a smallholding nearby with his wife and son. He spends weekends at home and the week at Hockney's. One current project, he tells me, is a reworking of the French painter Claude's *Sermon on the Mount* from 1656. They used a computer to clean up the original painting, thus revealing the colours and the light. Now Hockney is painting a new version of the picture for his upcoming show at the Royal Academy in 2012.

We arrive at Hockney's house after a drive of about an hour. Bridlington is a small remote town on the east coast of Yorkshire. 'We like it here,' Hockney had said on the phone. 'It's quiet. We are left alone.' His house is a thirties double-fronted detached red-brick villa. From the outside it looks like any other house in the street.

Inside the house is a stylish and witty jumble of dark colours, flowers, little signs, paintings and books. There is a double-height atrium and a gallery staircase, which lends the house a theatrical air. Jonathan shows me into the front room, which is packed with books. By the door there is a pipe rack with a sign above it that reads: 'Smoking Area'. Hockney appears in a paint-splattered pinstripe suit with braces and a green polo shirt. He has the glittering, piercing eyes of Picasso and the same sense of mischief: the first thing that strikes me is that his face seems permanently on the edge of cracking into a smile or a grin.

Hockney's partner John gets me a Corona and I sit on the chaise longue. Hockney offers me a cigarette – he seems to alternate between Camel Wides and Virginia Slims. I say thanks but roll my own. When I lose my lighter he gives me three of his with the easy generosity of the genuinely bohemian artist. There are two dogs, which are initially wary of me and leap back when I try to stroke them. But the male dog soon loses his shyness to the point where he jumps on to the sofa and starts trying to have sex with my arm. 'Get down, Freddy,' Hockney says. Then the dog knocks over my beer. I go to get a cloth, but Hockney waves me back to the chaise longue. He calls out through the door and John and another young man appear. They wipe up the spill and bring me a new beer. The whole atmosphere is enormously good-natured and convivial. You could be in the company of some jolly medieval monks: there is the same love of beauty and art, the productive atmosphere, the communal living, the intellectual curiosity, the division of labour, the interest in gardening and flowers, the hospitality and courtesy, the pleasure in food and wine. I suspect, though, that members of the Hocknickan Order are not required to take a vow of chastity.

Hockney explains that he lives here with his studio assistant, Jean-Pierre, and John, his partner of twenty years. He bought the house from his sister. Around the corner he has bought a gigantic 10,000-square-foot warehouse, just five minutes' drive away. He has a studio and a flat in Kensington but rarely uses it these days. 'I get too distracted in London,' he said. 'And to get a studio of this size in London, I would have to drive through half an hour of ugliness.' He is right on the sea, so he can get that feeling of open space that led him to move to California in the sixties. 'Was it the light that attracted you there?' I ask. 'Yes, and the sex,' he replies.

When they feel like a break, Hockney and John get in the car and jump on the overnight ferry to Zeebrugge, catching the tacky cabaret on the way. From there they drive all over Europe. Hockney can't stand airports or trains because you can't smoke. In the car, he can smoke, and they can drive wherever they like. One favourite destination is the spa town of Baden-Baden in Germany.

He says he likes my anarchic writings, that he hasn't voted for many years, and that he is not political although he is interested in politics. He believes that we need beauty. He says that we all need both to take more personal responsibility for our own lives, and to be more neighbourly.

He tells me with delight about the *Sermon on the Mount* project. He says that the original painting is very dark, but they discovered that it had been covered in soot from a fire. They cleaned it up on the computer. 'What attracted me was the sense of space in that picture.' I say that surely the subject matter was also interesting (I'm personally fascinated when artists return to medieval themes). And he says, yes, it is the great text on good ethics. He says he is not particularly religious but that he is very interested in religion. His mother was a strict Methodist. On his bookshelves is every conceivable sort of book: there is a lot of history and biography. There is Ted Hughes, Hardy, Evelyn Waugh.

I reflect that the rise of the camera in art coincides with the Reformation and a completely new theological attitude. We become more isolated after the Renaissance.

We go through into dinner and sit down in the dining room at an oval, polished wood table. The walls are painted dark red and there are heavy velvet curtains in the windows. Along the sideboard twelve candles have been lit, and a log fire burns in the grate. It is all very cosy and convivial. Hockney seats me at the head of the table and sits on my left. He continues smoking through the meal. He no longer drinks alcohol, and has a couple of alcohol-free beers instead. John serves up a delicious pigeon pie with mashed potatoes. We drink red wine.

Over dinner Hockney talks. He has an endless store of anecdotes and ideas, and speaks with great clarity, subtlety and humour. He remembers going to the cinema twice a week as a boy in Bradford, to see the Westerns. 'When I was thirteen,' he recalls, 'the man next to me put his hand on my cock. I've loved cinemas ever since.' He talks about the gay scene in seventies New York: 'We used to go to the bathhouses. It was very democratic: everyone's a prostitute and everyone's a client.' But they were wild, he says. 'My friend would say, "David, is this heaven or hell?" And I said, "If you're asking, it's probably hell."' AIDS killed many of his friends and put an end to that scene.

Hockney talks about his love for opera and tells me I must listen to it properly. He says that you need to put some effort into it, and then you are rewarded. Not everybody, though, gets the point: he tells a story of taking Billy Wilder to the opera. The show started at eight. 'Afterwards Billy said, "During the performance, at midnight I looked at my watch. It said eight-fifteen."'

Hockney says that, for fifty years, he has done exactly what he wanted to do every day, and that this is the essence of being an artist or a bohemian. It's not about the money, he says. 'If you can live that sort of life, you are rich. I mean, sometimes I have been working for other people, doing set design. But I have chosen to work with them.' He says he has only really been unhappy once, when his partner Peter Schlesinger left him, in 1970. 'It's only when you're unhappy that you realise you must have been happy before.'

He is interested in all the arts and says that he was rather dismayed by Mick Jagger's attitude to opera when he met him at a party in the sixties. 'He was very much performing the rebel pose, and sneered when I asked what he thought of opera. But surely as a singer, you would be interested in good singing?' And this is perhaps one thing that really marks Hockney out from most artists. He is interested in everything, whereas artists tend to be rather self-absorbed and often take absolutely no interest in other people's work whatsoever. Hockney is different; he is drenched in culture. He is also extremely well read.

I say that I have just had my first bespoke suit made, and Hockney comments on the importance of good tailoring. He says he has always had his suits made, and he advises friends that there is no point going to the gym or on diets to lose weight. 'It's actually a question of good tailoring,' he says. 'Anyone can look good in a properly fitting suit.' He says that never have people in general been so badly dressed, and he includes Tony Blair, one of his hate figures. 'I was appalled that he wore just a lounge suit to the Queen Mother's funeral,' he says. 'He was trying to be like an ordinary person. But an ordinary person would have had the manners to go out to Moss Bros. and hire a morning suit for an event like that.'

He shows me to my bedroom. On the landing wall is his famous portrait *Mrs and Mrs Clarke and Percy*: can it be the original? My room has a huge brass bed, two comfy chairs by the window and 'a *power shower*', as Hockney points out with some delight. He seems to take great pleasure in enunciating each word, almost as if he is mocking them. It is the same when he tells me about breakfast arrangements. 'Take anything you like. It's *self-service*.' To get his voice, imagine a (funnily enough) slightly less camp version of Alan Bennett. A copy of *Secret Knowledge* has been placed by the bed. On the shelf is a collection of Evelyn Waugh stories. I take it down to find that the dust jacket is marking a page right in the middle of 'Scott-King's Modern Europe', a coincidence, as I had read that very story just before Christmas. It is about a Latin teacher who, having witnessed the horrors of modern Europe, decides that to teach Classics is more important than ever. I don't sleep very well. I must have smoked about fifteen cigarettes since arriving; the room is hot and I am used to the cold, and my head is buzzing with everything I have seen and heard.

I come down for breakfast at half past eight. The kitchen has black-and-white-squared lino. It opens into a small courtyard garden, with pots and a barbecue. A couple of builders walk in and out. Jonathan comes in for his coffee. Hockney is sitting at the table on his iPhone, a black and white flat cap on his head. 'Morning!' I say. He tells me to help myself to toast and tea, which I do. The morning papers are spread out on the table. 'I'm drawing,' says Hockney. Sure enough, he is drawing the hyacinths on the kitchen table on his iPhone, with his thumb. Hockney is fascinated by the possibilities that are offered by the computer in terms of changing both how images are made and also how they are distributed.

After breakfast, Hockney drives me to his studio, which is around the corner. It is a vast warehouse on an industrial estate, with natural light that comes in through ceiling skylights. He shows me giant canvases of trees that he has been painting. He is going to paint them in each of the four seasons. There is also a giant reproduction of Claude's *Sermon on the Mount*, and along the walls are various new interpretations of the painting by Hockney. He says the beauty of such a large studio is that you can stand right back and take a good look at a large canvas. There is a scale model of the rooms at the Royal Academy which Hockney will take for his 2012 exhibition. I accept a cup of tea and a Camel Wide and we sit down to record an interview.

★

DH   The invention of *photography* was the invention of *chemicals* to fix
an image, meaning, it wasn't the invention of the camera. You can't
name the inventor of the camera, but you *can* name the inventor of
photography. Cameras are natural phenomena, really. But an optical
projection of the world, which is what a camera does, is not really the
way we see the world. Cameras just see surfaces, and we see space. I
think photography might actually have made us see the world as very
dull.

TH   And how would the world have looked in the medieval period?

DH   Well, I will point out that before that change [in the Renaissance]
you had very few shadows. Nobody painted shadows. Chinese,
Japanese, Persian, Indian; you name it, they didn't paint shadows. The
Chinese might have said, 'Well, everything's a shadow.' I ask: do we
see shadows? Well, we do and we don't. We can decide not to. In a
way, it was the arrival of shadows that made me see that maybe this is
optical, an optical technology, simply because it needed shadows. I was
surprised that art historians hadn't noticed that. Most art historians are
Eurocentric, they're very European-trained. I've always been interested in photography. A friend of mine was talking about art and
photography, and I said, 'Henry, is photography an art?' And he said,
'I always thought it was a hobby!' Very funny, and there is some truth
in it. Actually, for the early photographers, it was a hobby, wasn't it,
because you had to be quite rich to do it. The arrival of photography
slowly shifted power in the nineteenth century and created what
we had for most of the twentieth century, which is mass media.
Technology did it. And technology is going to take it away.

TH   That also coincides with the worst century there's ever been for
totalitarianism and bloodshed.

DH   You needed control of the media to be able to get away with what
Stalin or Hitler did, or Mao, and you could: in the mid-twentieth
century, if you controlled the media, you controlled all information.
By about 1930 it was possible to do that. Now we're moving out of
that time. It's probably now not possible.

TH   But isn't the information still coming via big American companies
like Google?

DH   Yeah. They *are* a bit frightening. I read your piece about it [*We*

Want Everyone: Facebook and the New American Right]. And I must admit, I wouldn't go on Facebook. If you want to keep your privacy, you have to be very careful. We do have a website, but I haven't done much on it, simply because I don't want to deal with people sending me things.

TH   I closed down the *Idler* forum because they started getting nasty.

DH   Yeah. I'm not sure that Internet democracy will be very good. It could be terrible, couldn't it? But there's a good and a bad side to everything; there's a minimum of two sides. There's always going to be a bad side and it depends how it's managed, I suppose.

TH   Going back to the transition from medieval to Renaissance and later culture, most of those medieval pictures that you show in the book are absolutely packed with people, and then around the Renaissance you get the focus on one person. I think also of the difference between Joshua Reynolds and Hogarth: Hogarth has little characters all over the place, very funny and clearly not done with the camera.

DH   Reynolds had a camera that folded up to look like a book, which is interesting, meaning it was hidden. He gave lectures saying that you shouldn't use it too much. He did it to get his likenesses, simply because it makes it easier and quicker.

TH   Had you really seen that isolation of the individual subject before? It seems to come along with the camera.

DH   Er, there are the Fayum portraits, which are about 2,000 years old. They found them in the desert sand and they are rather individualistic. The argument about the Renaissance has always been that it was humanism that did it. But my argument is that it is more likely to have been technology. For instance: the *Mona Lisa*. Why was it really interesting? Well, one of the reasons is that it is one of the first paintings to have very, very soft shadows on the face; the edges blended. He obviously saw that through cameras; Leonardo talks about cameras. People see it and think there's something very realistic about it ... but you know, there is the famous story of when the Jesuits went to China. They were fascinated by China, and realized it was a very advanced place. The scholars ran it. One of them painted the Empress of China. When she looked at it, she said: 'I can assure you, the left side of my face is the same colour as the right side of my face.' Very good.

TH I don't get it.

DH She was talking about the shadows. The left side is the same colour. She didn't see the shadows. It's interesting: you start asking yourself, do I see shadows? The first dramatic use of shadows, in a way, is Caravaggio. I'm pointing out now that Caravaggio invented Hollywood lighting. It's very close to it. And if you think about it, the lighting had to be the sun, because it would be the only thing that would be that bright. It's not talked about much. But if you look at a Caravaggio, you rarely see a scene lit like that in painting, only in films, later. Interesting subject, shadows. Interesting, yeah.

TH The camera is not reality because it's only a tiny millisecond.

DH I'll show you something. This is about the medieval world and the difference. I did this diagram twenty years ago. In pictures, we know: that's the world, that's the horizon, that's the vanishing point. The viewer is here, and the viewer is an immobile point. And that, theoretically, is at infinity. If the infinity is God, this and this will never meet. If this moves, then this moves. That's perspective as we know it. But in the medieval world, perspective is more often the reverse, meaning you could see both sides of the altar. The altar would be like that, not like that. OK, if you see both sides, that means you're in movement. You've moved. That means that infinity is everywhere; God is everywhere, including within you.

TH Rather than the Puritan's distant point.

DH We're stuck with this [the new way of seeing things].

TH It's the same in literature, because if you think about *The Canterbury Tales*, there are many points of view and many stories, all in one book. And compare that with *The Pilgrim's Progress*, which is one lonely journey through the world. It seems a similar thing is happening in art.

DH Absolutely, parallels, yeah. We've accepted perspective, and we think everyone else has got it wrong. But they didn't. They didn't get it *wrong*. Actually, there's no such thing. The Chinese use isometric perspective. It means that all the lines are parallel. They don't meet. Western perspective began with Brunelleschi in about 1412 in Florence. He makes a painting of the Baptistry. Ten years ago, I'd been thinking about this, and then I had a flash and it suddenly dawned on

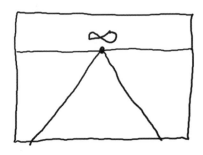

the viewer is an immobile point.
If the infinate is God. when the
viewer moves infinity moves. they
will never meet.

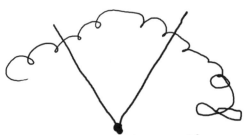

In reverse perspective the viewer
is now in movement. (They can see
both sides of the chair) and
infinity is everywere, including
the viewer. Isn't this better.
theologically.

Hockney explains perspective

me what he could have done. I realized he was supposed to have sat inside the Duomo in Florence and made this representation of the Baptistry which was in perspective. I point out that the Baptistry is an octagonal building. It does have sides. We went there, and set up a panel exactly the same size as his, and put it on an easel. And then, with a five-inch-diameter concave mirror, projected the Baptistry on to the panel. It acts as a lens and it will project back. You will point out that Brunelleschi wouldn't have known this. Well, he would. Florence in 1412 was perhaps the most advanced city in the world, certainly very up to date with technology. Brunelleschi was very secretive and he was an architect, and in a way, this is the architect's way of looking at the world. The vanishing point makes it *all the same time*, it fixes it, whereas a narrative painter is telling a story: time flows. So there's no reason why a narrative painter would have devised perspective.

TH   So the photograph is just a glimpse in time, and therefore much *less* real than a painting which is taking in a whole range of times and angles? [On the phone a couple of weeks later, Hockney talks about the use of perspective in crucifixion paintings. 'One of the first to use perspective was Masaccio's *Crucifixion*, 1420. The crucifixion is an odd form of execution, because there is no before and after, no action. So you can depict suffering. With perspective there are gains and losses: you lose the narrative flow, but you gain a better feeling of the volume of the body.']

DH   If you look at the medieval world and you look at the Chinese world at the same time, they have very sophisticated pictures ... I found this out in a film we did about the Chinese scroll. I was fascinated by the different perspectives. I asked a scholar of Chinese art why China declined so much from the seventeenth century, when it was very, very well advanced, to the mid-nineteenth century, when it wasn't. What had happened? And I was given two answers: one was that they'd lost their intellectual curiosity, which might have been the case; but the other was that there was superior military technology elsewhere, meaning more accurate guns and bigger ships, and so on. I immediately connected that with perspective, because when you set up perspective, you set up triangulation; with triangulation you can fire cannons more accurately, and that's what it was used for. The Chinese didn't have that technology; they'd rejected it, rejected it as not very human. Which is interesting, isn't it? They had rejected the idea of a vanishing point, because it makes you immobile. I think it was something like the eleventh century. They were very sophisticated people, and their art is. I tended at one time to think that it was all a bit the same, like many people. Until you really get into it, and then you find that it isn't at all. I got very interested in Chinese scrolls. You look at landscape in a different way: you *move* through it, like we do [in life]. In a way, one of my interests in this painting [*The Sermon on the Mount*] was its depiction of a very, very, very big space indeed. It's very clever: it makes you feel you go round the mountain. I was attracted to it. You'll see it, and then think about it later, and what you don't realize is that you start cleaning the painting in your head. The subject is the Sermon on the Mount; Christ and his disciples are stood at the top; people at the bottom listening ... but that subject isn't that obvious when it's very dark like that but the space is obvious, and the space is very big ... I'm attracted to big spaces. From all of Claude's paintings, this is highly unusual, because you have deep space on the left and right side, and what's in the middle is closest to you, which is rather like a reverse perspective might be, whereas in most of his other paintings, the deep space is in the middle and the things close to you are at the sides, like a theatre set.

TH   Would he have been commissioned to do this?

DH   He was a French archbishop ... he lived in Rome ... he was commissioned and then after about one hundred years, the picture finished up in Fonthill House in England, and there was a fire there. I'm assuming the fire made it rather dark. New technology allows us to clean it without touching the painting.

TH   And what about realistic imagery in Greek and Roman times?

DH   In painting, descriptions have survived of birds being fooled by the illusion of realistic paintings. In fact, one wonders whether that wasn't cameras, that kind of illusionism. The thing is, none of it has survived. Sculpture is a different matter. You can copy something two-dimensional on to two dimensions. You can copy it exactly. But you can't copy the three-dimensional world on to two dimensions; you have to interpret it in some way. That's always been the problem with depiction: how do you do that? There are always struggles in the depiction. There still are, they won't go away. For instance, when the Iraq War began I did a painting based on a Picasso painting called *Massacre in Korea*. Picasso painted that in 1951. I was a schoolboy. When it was painted, it was accused of being just communist propaganda, which I doubted, as a schoolboy. In his picture, some soldiers are killing, murdering, women and children. The soldiers look almost medieval, hints of chivalry, guns and things ... there's a child oblivious to it, picking flowers ... people missed it. I point out, Picasso might have been telling us something about *photography*. There couldn't *be* a photograph like this, because the photographer would have had to have been on the side of the soldiers. And Picasso is obviously not on that side. So it has to be a painting, and how different they are. I point out, perhaps Picasso was actually saying this. His painting is in kind of black and white, and he might have been pointing out that in 1950, for instance, the horrors of the death camps in Europe had been exposed, but you were just seeing photographs, mostly, of the survivors and the aftermath. You weren't seeing photographs of it *taking place*. Because that would have been harder: usually people who commit massacres don't like photographers. So there is another way of looking at them. Its subject could be photography. I actually made a version of it and I added a photographer. I called it *Problems of Depiction*, so people might figure it out. A photographer couldn't be there in that situation. It was used on the cover of the *TLS* with the title, *Problems of Depiction*. Then *The Times* rang me in California: 'Could we use this picture?' Well, OK then. Then there was a piece saying, was I suggesting that there was going to be a massacre in Iraq? They ignored my title. And actually, totally ignored the subject. I was amazed: they ignored what I said. I thought, well, they don't really think about pictures.

TH It's almost as if photography has actually made us more visually *illiterate* than your average man would have been in 1350.

DH The thing is, if you think about it, one hundred years ago, not many people made pictures. Two hundred years ago, very, very few people made pictures. Today, many people make pictures, with a camera. The more you make pictures, the more you might ask questions about them, and realize that you can deceive with pictures. You can show *this*, but actually that only happened for a fraction of a second. I make the point about the photograph of the young man in Ireland with the Molotov cocktail. You can feel his anger, you can. But when you see the next picture with the row of twelve photographers, you would have a very different emotion. Well, this is a performance. It's known that in war, the same pictures of children mutilated, for example, are circulated by both sides. I was told that during the Yugoslavian war, Dubrovnik had been attacked, and you see these pictures with smoke coming from it, but actually they were burning rubber tyres for the television. They're using pictures to deceive you, meaning that they are a weapon of war. So the more you know about pictures, the more you ask questions.

TH   Are you saying that this self-education process might happen now that people are taking more photographs?

DH   Yeah, because once you start making them yourself, you begin to realize what they mean in some other way. That's new, that there are millions of people taking pictures …

TH   And, as you said, distributing them.

DH   Now that's where we are entering very new territory. We are now going through another process. The church lost its power because of pictures moving into what we call the media. But now the media is losing its power because the pictures are now moving to everybody. Anybody can do it, anybody can distribute pictures, and that is a new era, in a way. And we don't know where it will lead.

TH   Is that potentially liberating, or are people still servile?

DH   There will be a good side and a bad side. Bound to be. There's a minimum of two sides. It can't just be one-sided: to say that it's liberating is just to see one side. There's bound to be a dark side. People will cheat to make the picture, by burning rubber tyres to create smoke, which looks terrific on television. Also, remember: cameras love smoke, they love fire. They love things moving. The movie camera likes movement. What we call 'action movies' is what movies always were. Some of the first movies were train crashes.

TH   The medium itself affects the content.

DH   That's it. You're bound to see more pictures of Rome being burnt than Rome being built, because that's inherent in the medium. To think that the camera is a neutral observer ... there's no such thing. A lot more questions should be asked. The *Daily Mirror* picture [of British soldiers apparently torturing prisoners, whose publication led to the departure as editor of Piers Morgan is now called the 'fake photograph'. But I pointed out that it's not really a fake *photograph*, it's a fake *caption*. It's very difficult to convince people that photographs are not really real. OK, so there are specialists in pictures, I'm one, I suppose: people who think about them, make them, think about the problems in depicting something, point of view, where you are, and so on.

TH   Now, Cubism takes off around the same time as photography is developed.

DH   Cubism was a rejection of perspective, and the first rejection for 550 years. In a way, it is saying, well, we don't see the world like that, we see it in glimpses, we put it together, we see with memory. Because we see with memory, we're all seeing something different, even if we're looking at the same thing. That's why cloning some-body ... would you clone all the memory in them? Can you? I doubt it. Meaning, you then wouldn't see the same things. But we tend to think we do. We don't ask these questions. We do have a visual culture, but it's not very critical.

TH   Wasn't that also the time that art became a rebellious and subversive activity, which it hadn't really been before?

DH   There's an opera by Hindemith, *Mathis der Maler*, and it's about Grünewald, who lived around 1520. It was written in the thirties, and the story is, how could Grünewald have been painting his pictures when there were big wars going on? In a way, there's a flaw in the story. The flaw is this: he's writing it in the thirties, and he's thinking of Grünewald as some sort of heroic lone figure ...

TH   Who was Grünewald?

DH   Grünewald was an elaborate picture-maker ... but Hindemith is making out that Grünewald was a bit like Cézanne, heroically work-ing in his studio. He wasn't like that at all. Grünewald was far more like CNN or CBS, meaning he had a vast workshop of people. In fact, the rulers always had artists around because they all needed pictures. It's interesting that the last person to set up a dynasty before photography was Napoleon. The thing is, we'd recognize Napoleon today from a silhouette, wouldn't we? Why? He only posed for one picture, but he had artists paint all kinds of pictures of his victories; you can see them in Versailles and the Louvre. He created an image without photography, just before photography, which is about 1839. Interesting that it was the French who did that. But he needed a lot of artists to do that.

TH   And Hollywood is today's equivalent?

DH   Yes, and Hollywood now needs 3D. But I came out of *Avatar* and I said, I want 5D! I want 6D. This here [gesturing around us] is minimum 4D. So what's 3D? Why bother with that? I wasn't that impressed with it, visually. In a way we're stuck with photography... it's still just photography. How do we escape it? Cubism was an escape, a terrific one. I've often argued that probably it hasn't been developed yet, simply because photography has become the big perspective picture. They should tell you then that perspective came from optics. The optical projection of nature is a perspective picture; it's coming from a mathematical point in the middle of the lens, isn't it? That picture dominates the world, now. It's a European way of looking at the world, which now dominates even China. Their old system doesn't do it: they've accepted the television and accepted the camera. You could also say of the Islamic world that it was invaded by images. It was a world that didn't have any, or have naturalistic images, but it was invaded by images by television. They had abstractions from nature. You weren't really supposed to paint human beings. There *were* such images – the Persians did it – but, technically, it wasn't allowed. Like Judaism, there was a proscription on images. So I don't know how they get round television, but they did. What is it? The Third Commandment? The Second Commandment? ['You shall not make for yourself an idol.'] Is it ever discussed? No, it never is, is it? One commandment, never discussed. I've often wondered why, and what the Archbishop of Canterbury would say about it. What would Tony Blair say about it? I don't suppose they've ever thought about it. Ever. It's going to change. We are in a big transition period, aren't we? When you become aware of it... You can see historical precedents... I can... the shift in power.

TH   Towards localism?

DH   Well, probably. You begin to see, is it the end of the mass market and the mass media? It probably is.

TH   What about the totalitarian state?

DH   China now wants to censor things. Can they? I don't know whether you can, technically. They've opened something that can't be closed. You might be right to question the technology. I'm not one to play it up. It's interesting enough that it's changing things, I'm fascinated by that. But people are not asking interesting questions about it.

TH   It still seems to fit in with an Enlightenment paradigm, that we're moving towards a manmade utopia where we escape from the constrictions of nature. And everyone is very pleased with themselves. With the technology, this word 'allow' keeps popping up in the blurbs. But I think: I'll do what I want! I don't need to sit around and wait until the technology permits me!

DH   Well, they're using the word meaning you couldn't do that before, and now you can. I follow it with great interest. What I'm following is that photography is going back into painting, and that's where it came from. Nobody could predict that photography could change so much. There's a certain historical period where it belonged. I've often thought that there might come a time when photographs will not look very realistic. We're not quite there yet, but it might happen. I could see how it could. I can see how it's possible. Not many people have thought about it.

TH   That's an amazing thought. A Chinese landscape might look more realistic to us than a snap.

DH   It's weird, but it is possible. The camera doesn't really see space, which is why landscape photographs are not often very interesting. Landscape is spatial and I'm aware that cameras just see surfaces, and we don't... I mean, the most interesting space of all is between you and me, where I end and you begin. That seems to me a lot more interesting than space out there. Although again I was reading very recently how a computer is helping astronomy. Now, the sky is enormous. However big a telescope is, it is only going to look at a tiny, tiny bit of the sky. If you're looking for things happening, how are you going to do that? Now, with millions of telescopes and computers ... it was about an exploding star. They were well aware that the star had exploded 160 billion years ago ... the deeper in space we're looking, the further back in time we are looking. Very hard to grasp. I'm assuming that things like that will lead us to higher things, when the mathematicians will say, there's eleven dimensions here, we just can't perceive them. Meaning we're not seeing what's there at all, which is a fascinating idea. Well, yes, we'd only *advance*, as it were, when we were more perceptive. It might make the world look startlingly different. Which would be exciting.

TH So you are saying that photography has *deadened* the world, in a sense?

DH Well, that's my view. Certainly I get bored looking through them after a while. Paintings are a lot more interesting. I lived in Hollywood, and I think it's now perfectly clear that there was a Golden Age of it. Remember, when movies first began, each screen was seen by a few hundred people. Today each screen is seen by one person; everybody has their own screens.

TH Our children spend a lot of time making little movie clips for YouTube and photographing each other and dancing.

DH They're making their own movies. Why would they want Hollywood? But one thing about Hollywood movies: you could *see* them, and you could *hear* them. They had very good lighting and very good sound. For instance, I'm going deaf. When we were very young – he must have been going deaf then – my father wouldn't go in the nearest cinema to us. We asked, why? He said, he always looked over the door, and he wouldn't go in the cinema unless it said, 'Western Electric Sound'. This was the Hollywood technology. And in the thirties and fifties, if the cinema didn't have that, the loudspeakers were indistinct. So he couldn't hear and he wouldn't go in, whereas we as children, we had good hearing. He didn't. But he didn't quite know it: he thought everyone was hearing the same thing, and he didn't like it when it was muffled. It would have been terrible. Loudspeakers did develop. It all relates. Hollywood was the only place that had all this technology at one time, and it had all the good technicians. They paid them well. That period is over. Your kids can make perfectly good pictures about dancing and music. They can make them themselves. That's why Hollywood wants to move to 3D. 3D is not terrific, not really. Therefore we are probably seeing the end of Hollywood, in a way.

TH But *Avatar* was a massive movie all around the world.

DH Yes, but I noticed that the publicity after a while was about how much money it was taking in. And I was disappointed in it visually. You couldn't see the creatures. You never actually saw what shape the creature was. And they didn't move very well. They were awkward-looking, and creatures aren't awkward-looking in nature. If they move they have a certain elegance. Even the elephant: when it moves, you are aware of its weight. I went to see *Jurassic Park* when it came out. The reason I went straight away was that I know dinosaurs don't exist, and this is a film made with cameras. How do they do it? It was quite ingenious, these great big creatures. But see it a second time, you begin to notice that the creatures don't really have much weight. The way an elephant moves: it has an elegance even though it is lumbering, a very heavy creature. I remember going to see Ridley Scott's *Gladiator*. When he got to Rome, he *descended* on Rome. I thought, yeah, when you go into LA, you descend on it. Whereas, actually, in Ancient Rome, everybody would have been looking *up*, not down. They would have arrived on foot or on a boat, and everything would be bigger. I thought, he's got it wrong. And I thought, well, that's because he's an English director who lives in LA, and that's how you arrive in LA. I notice things like that. I admit that most people in the cinema are in the cinema to see Russell Crowe as the gladiator. Me, with my critical eye, I notice things that other people wouldn't notice.

TH India has a very different kind of film with Bollywood. They've resisted Hollywood because they've had their own film industry. And so India is less Americanized than some other countries.

DH We've been in a period and that period is probably coming to an end. When you're in a transition period, it's interesting trying to see what's ending and what's beginning. An end is a beginning.

TH Facebook is a very American idea, and that is all over the world.

DH Yes, it is at the moment, but it might change. I point out, how do you get famous on YouTube?

TH I don't know. Lots of people watch your clip. Or, you don't.

DH At the moment, you might get famous because the press will pick it up. But when technology closes the press, how will you get famous on YouTube? Somebody I asked said, 'It's a very good question. There's always somebody else coming up.' You become aware that, in the future, if you want ads on television, TV will be one of two things: sport or disasters, because it has to be *now*. If it's *now*, you can't fast-forward the ads. Sport has to be now; you don't want to see the game from last week, because you know the result. The other thing is disaster. And of course there's a disaster every day somewhere in the world. So if you really want to know about disasters, you can know about them every day. But probably not many of them are near you and won't have too much effect. So slowly, that might die out. Meaning in the end you are only interested in what is local. Now, what is local might be horrible: you might have warlords, you might have lawlessness. I point out that the smoking ban is a lawlessness. You are going from what was a legally taxed industry and you're making it into an illegal industry which will therefore be tax-free, and it makes the country more lawless. Is that helpful? But that question is ignored. It was ignored by the medical profession because they didn't think like that. I pointed that out, but I am told, you're just an addict. I'm not, actually. Like the 'addicts' Clement Attlee, Baldwin, all these people who smoked. It didn't seem to harm them too much, did it? Did you notice that the man who devised the smoking ban, David Taylor MP, on Boxing Day went out for a walk, and dropped down dead, aged 63, from a heart attack? I had to laugh a bit, but I thought, well, if *I'd* have dropped dead, they'd have blamed my lifestyle. But they don't point out his meanness of heart, no they don't. There was another MP, Tony Banks, who was a vegetarian, non-smoker, teetotaller, exercise nut: died at 61 from a stroke. On the very day that his obituary ran in the *Guardian*, they also ran a piece saying that vegetarianism was good for avoiding strokes. I thought, well, maybe they've just forgotten about fate. I don't think fate's been cancelled, has it? But how do most people look at things? The medical profession talks constantly about the *quantity* of life, whereas, actually, most people go for *quality* of life. They choose it that way. Most people make choices but this [the smoking ban] is denying that choice, because they've allowed the medical profession to say there is this *one point of view*. Why not have a few?

They talk about diversity, but that doesn't include smokers, 9 million of them. What do you mean by diversity?

TH The more they talk about diversity, the more the vision of how we are supposed to live actually narrows.

DH Unbelievable. Politics is going to change. I've no doubt that our present kind of politics will be swept away. It might be swept away in ways we might not like, as well. I'm not saying it will be all good. I don't think it will, actually. Obama's election was probably the last one where television played a big part. Even in this one, for instance, when debates are televised, we read how every audience member had a party affiliation. They are terrified of any ordinary member of the public actually saying anything. But the Web provides that. Hillary Clinton might appear on TV as if she was with some ordinary people. But they were all highly arranged. On the Web, people would mock that, that night. Television didn't have criticism like that before but it can now. That's interesting. They were mocking it. I thought it was quite funny that they tried to manipulate the picture. When you read about TV debates here, it is all about how we can manipulate the image. I was reading about it just this morning.

TH All that fuss about Nick Griffin was all based around the idea that we are a free society and we have free speech. This guy is a bit unpleasant, so should we let him on? But meanwhile, people who want to engage in a debate about smoking or climate change, or whatever it is, are denied any sort of voice at all. Or barely given one.

DH There's not much debate about anything at all. Do any of the MPs represent me? Of all the new MPs there will be, how many smoke? Would they be given the job if they smoked nowadays? There are nine million smokers out there. They're now outlaws. But that could mean problems.

TH A smokers' army.

DH It won't go away. We're very naive. Take the Women's Christian Temperance Union which, in America, pioneered Prohibition. In 1920, they thought that the scourge of alcohol would be gone from the United States. The taverns were now closed; the working man would take his wage home to his wife on a Friday and have a glass of warm milk with his neighbour, and everybody would be healthy.

That's what they thought. Well, it wasn't like that at all. Organized crime was introduced to provide it. They simply handed over the distribution of liquor to criminals: that's what happened. Because that's what the real world is like. They denied the reality and thought you could impose it. They're doing it now, here. Same thing. Actually, I see it as just temporary, to be honest. The reason it is temporary is because there had been a lot of social pressure. 'Smoking is terrible, it's terrible for everybody.' I'm sick and tired of that. It certainly isn't. If you've lived as long as I have and seen what it was like before, you will know. People weren't dying off like flies just because someone smoked a cigarette near them. I simply doubt the medical people now. I've got to live, *now*, so I want it interesting, I want it pleasant, I want it my way. OK, I might not live as long as you say; but I don't care, really. If smoking knocks anything off my life, it's only at the end. You don't feel it. We're born and we're going to die. That's it. They think that now if you don't smoke you will live for ever, and it's absurd. Nobody took on the doctors, they were too frightened to do it. But I wasn't frightened. I'd argue with it. I'm still here, I'm OK. I'm still alive, feeling very lively, working away. I can't be socially intimidated so easily. I give lectures when people start going on to me.

TH You said in a recent essay that you can say what you want because you have no axe to grind. A lot of people are gagged because they worry they might lose their job, their mortgage.

DH Yes, a lot of pressure has been put on people. Now the only people who can ... are the hardcore ... and I'm one of them.

TH The government did seriously think that all you have to do is point out the dangers, create a smoke-free Britain, and everybody will spontaneously give up. They run ads non-stop on telly, as well, which we are paying for with our income taxes.

DH And we'll be paying a lot more because now you won't get the tax from the tobacco. Smokers pay for the National Health.

TH I always saw it as an attack on conviviality. For example, the pub. It's a shared space where you bump into people you might not have round for dinner, but it's nice to catch up and you meet people randomly.

DH In Bradford, we used to have thousands of pubs. There would be little alehouses on street corners. There were four pubs on each corner. The reason was that people had very small houses. If you wanted to escape, you could just walk down to the bottom of the street, and it was warm. Now, people have a bit more space, so you can see why some would close. But pubs aren't health clubs: alcohol is a terrible thing for you, really, but I'm not suggesting you ban it. I don't drink now, but I can see why people do. It's pleasant. In that sense I just feel very out of step with things. I don't care any more. I avoid the public. It's too aggressive for me now. I mean, York station, where I go to pick up people: you've got to be right outside to smoke. But there will come a time when [prescription drugs replace smoking]. I've seen in California, where the ads for prescription drugs are immense. It's not allowed in Europe. But when I pointed it out to Colin Blakemore, who is the head of the British Medical Research Council, he thought about it and said: 'That might be coming here.' And I thought, well I'm sure they're trying for it, the pharmaceutical companies, but it will be terrible if it does. If you think that's better than all the smoke-free stuff... there's a great big argument there. In California, there are ads for Prozac, painkillers, and for any drug, if there's something slightly wrong with you. It tells you what the brand is and you go to the doctor and say I need this, that and the other. They're usually painkillers, meaning something just to numb you. I've watched the demonization of sugar, and there is always something else. It's just bossy people, isn't it? There's a load of bossy people out there.

TH But it is sinister because it makes way for pharmaceutical companies to get in there with their products and make a lot of money. If you say sugar is bad, then the pharmaceuticals will come and say, we've got this sugar substitute.

DH They had saccharine and that was bad for you.

TH And margarine now turns out to have been not good for you, after thirty years.

DH Ha ha. I always ate butter. People have been eating it for thousands of years, so we can ignore that. It's delicious, isn't it? Don't you want pleasures, don't you want joy in life, what kind of life do you want? The way they go on, we'd all be living in a terrible clinic, and live to be two hundred. I feel out of step. But then I've always felt an outsider. It used to be that, if you were gay, you were an outsider. Now that's OK, but I'm a smoker, so I'm still an outsider. There's always something they'll get you on. What do I care? I don't really. But I will observe what's going on, from Bridlington. We do. I keep an eye on the Web. I look at things. I try and follow it. I'm fascinated. I'm interested that your kids make their little movies. Think about it: how do you get famous on YouTube?

TH The YouTube star only became a star when they went on big telly.

DH I don't watch *X-Factor*. But I read newspapers. So you read about Susan Boyle. And you're reading about that in a big paper. But there will come a time when the papers disappear. And then what happens? And how do you get famous on YouTube? You don't really, that's the point. And it might be then that nobody's famous, and that's where you're back at the locality, you're back at localism. Which is what it was before the mass media.

TH There were famous people, though, before the mass media. Fame did spread far and wide.

DH Slowly. There were, of course, leaders of countries, but they made sure they were on images; they were on coins. There were images made: think of Henry VIII. Henry VIII is one of the most famous monarchs simply because he was painted by a marvellous artist who made marvellous images. So we know what Henry VIII looked like, or think we do, and that's all from Holbein. Charles I we know because of Van Dyck. Henry VII, we don't know much. An image can't come into your head, but with Henry VIII it does. And it's Holbein that did it.

TH And Henry VIII was obviously the architect of the Reformation in England.

DH Yes, and you know what type he was by the way he stood. It's images, it's images. There's not that much discussion of images. There used to be. But there hasn't been much for nearly one hundred years, about the making of them ... they're just accepted as close to reality.

TH It does seem that people are going back to the old ways. It's like the idea that the market will outlive the supermarket. And people really are going back to digging their gardens.

DH Good idea. Yeah. If you start trying to think what will it mean, the end of the mass media, it's difficult, because it's been there a long time. I do follow Mr Murdoch. He's probably employing a lot of people to tell him what to do with the Web, I'm sure, but he's having difficulty seeing how to make it work. Probably it can't work at all, in his way, the old way, which is now dying.

TH Probably they should concentrate on making a very good newspaper. The other ones are cutting their costs and making their newspapers worse and worse.

DH Remember when William Wordsworth bought his copy of *The Times* in 1810, it cost one shilling. That was a lot of money. Very few people could afford it. That's what it genuinely cost to make, because it wasn't relying too much on advertising money. But newspapers were started just to give information, mostly to business people, about shipping: what ships were coming in, what ships were leaving, what the goods were on them and things like that. 'Shipping News', which was a big feature of *The Times* until about 1960. And that's what people bought it for. That information is going to cost money. Well, it will in the future. The price of newspapers was very low because really they got their money not from you buying it, but from the advertising in it. But now the advertisers are leaving it because they've got better ways to do it, so how will the newspaper pay? Well, if you want a newspaper with information, you'll probably have to pay a great deal more for it.

TH Which goes right against the idea that Google and so on promote, which is to make information free and widely available.

DH Remember that information isn't knowledge.

TH With the *Idler* we decided to do something of very good quality at quite a high price, to do exactly what we want and give up trying to get advertising. And it's been one of our best-selling issues.

DH *Private Eye* has managed without relying on advertising. It has a few, but not that many, meaning that they're not controlled by advertisers at all. They've kept the format for years and years. It's not altered much.

TH And you get information in there that you wouldn't get on the Internet, because you don't know what to look for. What do you type in?

DH Do you know the story about the Bettmann archive? It was an archive of 3 million photographs that are rotting on paper. Bill Gates was going to digitize them. Until they found that you couldn't. Somebody would have had to type in words that would bring them back. Every picture has to be looked at. The people looking at them had to be rather good at looking at pictures, to know a lot of words … and the kind of person who can do that is not going to spend their life looking at 3 million photographs. So it was not possible to do it. In the end they buried the pictures in a salt mine [where you can look at them now with an appointment].

TH That's very true. When you get your pictures back from Boots, you can show them to people and you don't need to write a caption under each one. But when you have these hundreds of pictures in your computer, you have to write a caption because you can't flick through them. It takes a lot of work and ingenuity to think of a caption for each one.

DH It was a fake caption in those *Daily Mirror* photos: if the caption had been 'People posing as soldiers' then the photograph is perfectly fine. They all need a caption, or you don't know who they are. Is that the enemy, or is it not? You know the famous picture by Capa in the Spanish Civil War … I'd always assumed it was staged, because it's highly unlikely that with a camera without a motor, you get something like that happening. On the other hand, he would have said: 'the picture was propaganda. It was for a cause, so what does it matter?' Which is a good argument, but we do tend to think that photographs represent reality. In LA, at the beginning of the Iraq War, there was a photographer who was fired for putting two photographs together, making a collage. They fired him, because they didn't want that, meaning that they believed in the photography that was, I was there, and it looked like this in front of me. Put two together, and they think that's gone. But they were fighting a losing battle, because the technology has let him do this. He could put the two together on his laptop and send the picture out, which he did. They spotted it because there was a repeat. He was simply trying to make a better picture. But they saw him as cheating. Really, when bullets are flying around, you don't have cameramen there without a gun. How could you? You tend to think they are there. I think it was the Spanish Civil War, the first time they redid things for cameras. Like people putting up the flag in the Iwo Jima, or people putting the flag on top of the Reichstag. A photographer got up there first. How come he was up there? It might be better if it all gets local again. Would it be worse? Could it be? I don't know. Could be more lawless.

TH   The scale of medieval warfare was nothing like the scale we have today. The story was that a peasant could be ploughing his field, and in the next field, a massive battle would be going on. They would meet at a certain time; they weren't allowed to fight on Sundays and Mondays, and so on. It was also less cowardly, because the knights themselves, the nobles, were the ones doing the actual fighting.

DH   They were at the front ... by the First World War, industry and industrialization had happened, so war was industrialized. The reason it went on for four years was because they were constantly making a new weapon. Let's try this out. And shooting all of Europe's youth. It was madness. There was a Victorian poet, Wilfrid Scawen Blunt, who described the First World War as 'the white man's suicide'. It had been industrialized, and by the Second World War, which was really the same war, it had been industrialized more. Now we're going to have cyber-war.

TH   But actually you can't do it. That's the arrogance of thinking that we can beat up the Afghans. The Afghans have a warrior ethic, whereas we are bureaucrats. They would rather die on the battlefield than of old age. You can't beat them. They're like Samurai or something. They are ferocious in battle, whereas we talk about 'doing the job'.

DH   Yes. But you should expect change, though, shouldn't you? It's the only constant thing.

★

We drive back to the house. Hockney takes me up to the small studio in the attic. Here Jonathan is working on a video piece. He and Hockney had been out with a video camera, driving slowly along a tree-lined avenue in the snow. Next to that film, a film plays of the same scene, but without the snow. Again, the idea will be to show four films, each simultaneously wandering slowly down the avenue, but each in a different season. 'Try that a bit slower, Jonathan,' says Hockney. 'Oh, that's nice. Very nice. Look at the snow on the tree. Like lace.'

Hockney shows me a short film which describes how he made his painting *Bigger Trees Near Warter* (2007), a huge (40 ft by 15 ft) painting (now in Tate Britain), but made in the small studio upstairs. It was done in panels, fifty of them, and the computer was used to make sure they matched up and to look at the thing in its entirety.

We go down for a coffee. Hockney discusses the medieval way of seeing: 'I think they may have had better eyesight,' he says, citing the workmanship of the miniature paintings.

Hockney says goodbye. I express my gratitude for his time and hospitality. He goes up for a nap. 'When you're ready, darling,' says John, and we drive back to York station at breakneck speed. John tells me how much he enjoys their forays into Europe, because he doesn't get much chance to hang out with Hockney in the normal hurly-burly of everyday life. He tells me that they sometimes go down to London, where Hockney has two flats and a studio in Kensington. But Hockney goes less and less, because, John says, people seem to sense that he is there and start calling. He also gets loaded with sob stories and requests for money. At the station John gives me a huge hug and kiss. I board the train and sit staring out of the window for five hours. Things seem to have brightened up. There is an intensity to what I am seeing. Trees look more alive. I feel that my eyes have been opened and that the world will never look quite the same again.

Stanley Donwood

TAKING LIBERTIES

A CONVERSATION WITH

IAN BONE

&

RAY ROUGHLER-JONES

Tom Hodgkinson

W
HEN IT COMES TO BEING A PROFESSIONAL IDLER, I
take my hat off to those two grandmasters of anti-capitalist
slack, Ian Bone and Ray Roughler-Jones. Bone is best
known for *Class War*, his provocative, aggressive, anarchist paper, and
his excellent biography, *Bash the Rich*, an account of a working-class,
bohemian life. Being working class for Bone is not about slaving in the
factories, but about pursuing a life of intellectual curiosity, pleasure
and freedom; in a sense, not working. Ray Roughler-Jones is Bone's
old friend, who I remember from my days working at the Rough Trade
shop in Portobello Road in 1990. Ray edits the *Roughler* magazine and
puts on all sorts of events in the W11 area, often working with the
actress Anna Chancellor, who starred in *Four Weddings and a Funeral*.
Another project is the YouTube channel Roughler TV. He has been on
the dole for about 40 years. Bone is publishing Ray's autobiography,
Drowning on Dry Land, on his indie publishing label, Tangent Books.
Another release on Tangent Books is *Hartmann the Anarchist: The Doom
of the Great City*, a story first published in 1892 and written by a 17-
year-old public schoolboy called E. Douglas Fawcett.

Anyway, I arranged to meet up with these two outstanding beacons
of the idling classes in Mike's Café in Portobello Road. 'Blimey, this

has smartened up a bit, hasn't it?' commented Bone when he walked in, well-dressed in a fedora and a nice wool overcoat.

★

TH   Now most people think of anarchy as violent and aggressive. But to me it is all about voluntary action and independence. I have been talking [with Warren Draper] about an anarchy movement – called 'Anglarchy' – that is rooted in English literature, Blake and Cobbett, very practical, and not about smashing up the bus stops. Although there may be a place for that. What's your idea of liberty, anarchy, freedom?

IB   Pretty much the same as yours: a world without work, a world of unlicensed pleasure. I certainly don't go for all that right-to-work bollocks. I see interviews with kids hanging around shopping centres, and all they want to do is sit on the wall all day and talk to their mates, and someone with a microphone goes: 'Wouldn't you rather have a job?' And they say, 'Yes, oh yeah, we'd rather have a job,' as a knee-jerk. But that's the last thing in the world they want.

TH   The recent marches and demonstrations in London: they were marching *for* jobs. They had banners saying, 'We want jobs.' And there's this thing called the People's Charter, which says, vaguely 'We want more and better jobs.'

IB   That's just bollocks. It's mostly people on the Left who have this ethos, but the feckless working class doesn't want 'more and better jobs'. The Left has an image of the Jarrow Marches. My granddad was an unemployed miner in Scotland in the thirties, at the same time as the Jarrow Marches. He was supposed to have had a job filling the pits in, but instead, there's a great photo of him playing cards and dominoes. The central question is, how do the working class become idlers, as opposed to those who can afford idleness, knowing others will provide their sewerage, drains, electricity, food, water and so on? There is a pivotal moment in Dave Douglass's new book where he writes about the return to work after the Miners' Strike, where many miners deliberately sabotaged the pits in order to take redundancy payments. This unseen, unheroic working-class struggle for *freedom from work* is seldom recognized or acknowledged, so idleness as a class issue is not taken up, because the Left has a different agenda, with its Jarrow heroism.

TH One of my enemy figures would be Tony Benn. He has this idea of full employment and the working classes riding off to the factory...

IB In the eighties the SWP organized the 'Right to Work' marches. Everyone had their little SWP bibs on. The kids who went on it were promised discos every night, sex, and all they got was Trotsky's Transitional Programme.

TH Do you ever hear that thing where people on the hard Left accuse anarchists of being bourgeois?

IB Fucking hypocrites – the SWP is entirely made up of people who used to be polytechnic lecturers wearing corduroy trousers ... what's their working-class composition? Virtually nil, now. But I don't really care about people's background: it's where you are now. What you can't do is do both: be politically anarchist and retain all the privileges of the previous life. For example, George Monbiot, who has done the classic thing: Monbiot is so keen on allotments that he has seven of his own. But it never occurs to him there might be six other people out there. Have you heard his thing: 'The Land is Ours'? Yes, the land *is* yours: you fuckin' own it, you cunt!

TH Yes, but Simon Fairlie and *The Land*, though: that really is a good magazine.

IB Oh yes, well, I like all the anti-Enclosures stuff, the history of English radicalism. The poaching wars. There were huge wars in the eighteenth century between poachers and gamekeepers, with huge gangs on either side.

TH How have things changed since you two first came to London thirty or forty years ago?

RRJ In Wales, signing on for us was a full-time job. The only people I knew who had jobs were people who were just about to have a court appearance. Nowadays, with the questions they ask you before you go on a medical, you can work out all the conditions to get on the sick ... 'bad back' used to be the only clincher ... now, with the Internet, you can authoritatively claim to have the symptoms of Ebola virus and they'll sort you out sharpish.

TH And when did you both take against work?

RRJ It's just that nobody worked, none of our friends worked.

IB No one ever worked ... in *Bash the Rich* there's a story about 'turning to the working class' but we didn't know anyone who was working! We were all on the dole so we started a Claimants' Union, a union for people on the dole. We would fight to get you all your entitlements. The classic line was: 'If they get you a job, we'll fight your case'! There were all the jokes about what occupation you gave when you were signing on: Father Christmas, snow clearer, and so on. One job I gave was 'Coronation Programme Seller'. 'What's that then, Mr Bone?' asked a puzzled clerk. 'Very long hours. On the day, you're up at five in the morning till all hours,' I countered – not mentioning I hadn't had the luck of securing such a position since 1953!

TH Is it actually responsible to be claiming dole from the State?

RRJ Well, the less money they have to start wars ...

TH Is it easier now, or harder?

IB It's just as easy. My son was sent for a job in Cashbusters in Bristol. How was he going to get out of it? I said, 'Well, first ask about unions. What sort of union is there?' Then the clincher – ask about paternity leave.

TH So you advise your son on how *not* to work?

IB Like a duck to water. He just didn't want to take a glorified debt-collection job.

TH Does the skiving thing go back for generations, do you think?

RRJ It's not exactly skiving. It's hard graft to be on the dole. They never leave you alone ... one time, we thought we'd better get a job. And we saw these dustmen in the pub in Swansea. They were always there at eleven in the morning. We thought we'd try that. We went down there. The interview was: 'What's your name? Right, you start tomorrow.' So we went the next day. Fireball XL5 was the name of our wagon. We said to the bloke in charge, 'Early finish, is it?' He said, 'Oh yes, you'll be finished by half past four.' We said, 'What about the eleven o'clock finish?' And he said, 'You've got to be here thirty years before you get that shift.' I remember running away from the depot.

TH So even the prospect of working till four thirty just for one day was too much?

IB Yes – we're fucking men of principle.

RRJ It's a tricky old life on the dole, because they don't leave you alone and they don't give you much money. So you spend the rest of the time trying to top up.

TH Little businesses and things?

RRJ Or whatever.

IB The critical problem for me has always been that capitalism needs a reserve army of the unemployed. What about the people who *want* to be unemployed? All these people who are broken-hearted because they can't get a job or are being made redundant ... so you might as well have people who want to be unemployed.

TH But capitalism wants the unemployed people who are desperate for a job, not the ones who enjoy being unemployed.

IB Remember the four-week rule in the seventies – if you were single and didn't take a job in four weeks they'd stop your money. A fucking disgrace.

RRJ It's tricky at the moment.

TH Are you on the dole?

RRJ I'm on the sick.

TH On the sick for what, though?

IB Bad back ...

TH I have one friend who has declared himself mad.

RRJ Then they leave you alone completely.

TH Won't you both be getting a pension soon?

IB I've never paid enough subs to get a pension ... I was on the dole for years. And I had a job as a community worker. I used to go in and read the *Guardian*, make some phone calls and go on the Internet. I used to sit there reading the Annual Report for hours. I didn't even *look* busy. You're supposed to look busy. Most jobs you could do the work in about an hour, to be honest.

TH So this is all about using your intellect to become master of your situation?

RRJ The thing is, I'm always busy. I can't stay in the flat after eight in the morning.

TH I meet people who have taken control of their own lives and their work and been creative, and created an autonomous life, and I wonder, why is it that so few people do that? And it's not actually a class issue.

RRJ People are frightened.

IB People have families, so it ain't such a good rate to be on the dole as when you've got no dependents … Even I had to work as a postie and a hospital porter for years when the kids were young.

TH Well, I've been in a nuclear family for ten years, and it can be hard to keep the energy up to stay freelance. Sometimes you think, this is too much hard work. Life might be easier if I just had to turn up in an office. And what did you do when you first got to London, Ray?

RRJ I didn't have a clue what I was going to do when I got here. I got a flat … I had a girlfriend at college, and she did what exactly what she wanted to do. She was *career-minded*. Her father was a professor and she had the work ethic. I didn't know what I was going to do. I went on the dole. And nothing much has changed since.

IB Ray was an accomplished shop-lifter in Swansea so was able to supplement his income.

RRJ I gave all that up.

IB Most people go round nicking big lumps of cheese, joints of meat and big Nescafé jars and hawk 'em round the pubs at lunchtime to get beer money, but …

TH So you were exiled from Swansea, Ray?

RRJ Yes. I nicked a suit with an alarm on, got chased by a security guard, who got knocked down by a car but still got up and nabbed me. All the security guards used to say, 'Morning, Ray.'

TH You had political beliefs behind this.

IB I didn't want to work either for the state, being an anarchist, or for some fucking capitalist company. I thought I'd never work officially, but I could do stints on the dole and survive on fuck all money with no possessions outside of a bin bag.

TH It's a gentlemanly existence, isn't it?

RRJ This is from my book: 'On the third day, they'd got us working in the bowels of some huge silo thing … a falling brick fractures my arm and crushes two of my toes. I was lucky. Who said hard work never killed anyone? The twat.'

IB A mate of ours, John, worked as a ticket collector at Ladbroke Grove station; stood as Class War candidate in the Kensington by-election in '87. He never checked any tickets because he would read

Class War or the *Sun* all day. After a while his Underground bosses said, 'We've been watching you for four hours, and you haven't checked one ticket. You've been reading a copy of *Class War* all day.' He brought a successful case saying he had been harassed. And then succesfully transferred to the sick for years claiming stress!

TH Have you ever gone into a job and tried to rouse up the workers to rebellion against the bosses?

IB Well, always. When I was in the Housing Association once, I eventually got the sack for breach of confidentiality. There was some fiddling going on, and I told the local paper. They quoted me, an anonymous source, but then put my name in!

TH I thought it would be a good piece for the *Idler*, to get a young man to take lots of crap jobs and, in a sense, just behave like a dignified human being and see how long you last. And say: 'I'm ethically opposed to that. I can't do it.'

IB Cashbusters … they're all working for debt-collecting agencies, pawnbrokers, call centres, charity muggers – all jobs offering mind-numbing boredom, and you don't even get the collectivity of signing on any more – it's all done from your computer.

TH My parents were in Fleet Street in the seventies, and the work-place was something completely different then. Clattering type-writers, shouting, smoking. People worked together and it was fun. They went to the pub together. Now we are separated by the computer. Before Wapping, the unions had ensured that there were some good jobs.

IB The printers, or rather the Union Chapel, ran the show and got their members on about a million quid a week … in the heyday of Red Robbo, fighting for jobs, the night shift at British Leyland used their engineering skills to build secret bedrooms on the factory floor where they could grab a crafty kip.

TH If there was something they didn't like in the paper, the Father of the Chapel would come upstairs and say: 'The boys ain't happy.'

IB All those big industrial jobs went. We went to a meeting called by Arthur Scargill … one of the miners' wives went through a litany of family deaths and illness from industrial diseases caused by working in the pits and then said: 'I'll fight to keep the pits open for my children

and my children's children ...' A lot of the miners didn't want to go
back. They were having a far better time on strike. They were meeting
lots of women. They were going all over the country ... they were
having a great time. There was an argument to say: 'Fuck the pits. We
ain't going back underground.' After they went back, a lot of them
systematically sabotaged the pits so they could take the redundancy
money. It's always the middle-class Lefties who claim that the working
class is desperate to fucking work. There's a whole lot of mythologized
hokum spun by the Communist Party around the Jarrow Marches and
South Wales Miners' libraries. And the proud working-class desire for
self-improvement ... In his top book, *The Intellectual Life of the British
Working Class*, David Rose shows that most miners detested the communists because they were arrogant and bullying. The most taken-out
book from Maerdy Miners' library was not *The Communist Manifesto*
but *East Lynne* a Victorian melodrama.

TH Can you generalize about what the miners did when the mines
closed?

IB Turn to heroin! No, get on the long-term sick. They ran pubs.
Many of them moved away and totally revamped their lives. After
25 years, few of them regretted moving from the pits, despite the nos-
talgic camaraderie.

TH Now what about the argument that says there is camaraderie in
the workplace?

IB Well, there is, and solidarity. But people will find camaraderie in
prisons or in the most desperate situations, you know. There *is* that
camaraderie, but you find other ways of getting it outside the world of
work. A lot of the miners found that difficult at first, especially with
Thatcher intent on destroying a sense of community through her 'No
such thing as society' speech.

TH The *Guardian* is the worst for this. The comments on their blogs
are by far the most mean-spirited of all the comment-makers. They're
the worst for calling for 'more and better jobs'. They're also the worst
payers in Fleet Street. And it's full of hierarchy.

IB Well, they're all Oxbridge, aren't they?

TH Well, I am too! But it is Oxbridge-dominated.

IB The editor's daughter is on the payroll ... When you see a young sprog in the *Guardian*, you know they're related ... Barnaby, Josh and Harry ... leave it out!

TH As an alternative to wage slavery, we want to do a 'Taking care of business' issue of the *Idler*, which will look at how to start your own small business. That is a realistic alternative. We are now running an online shop at the *Idler* as a micro-business.

IB For someone who is idle, you put in a hell of a lot of hard work.

TH As you can imagine, I've heard that comment a lot. Yes, we are quite productive. But at home, I work from nine to one and that's it, really.

RRJ If you are doing something that you enjoy, as he enjoys it, then you *are* idle.

IB It's like you said earlier, Ray: you are actually very busy.

TH Idlers *are* busy! You're more lazy in a full-time job. You just sit there waiting for six o'clock to come. Then you are too tired to do much beyond go to the pub or watch telly.

IB Do something to disengage your brain.

TH Jobs tend to be humiliating. You spend all day being told off and then you run to the tube. Then you can't wait for the tube journey to be over. Then you run home. What do I do now? Have a glass of wine and watch *Twin Peaks*.

RRJ The magazine I did, *The Roughler*, that was really hard work. It was a nightmare, and that was just a fanzine.

TH Yes, it is hard putting a magazine together.

IB The print costs have come right down. You used to go abroad to get stuff done, but you can get it done in this country now, cheap. The turnaround time is a hell of a lot quicker, too.

TH I've been looking at the pre-Reformation calendar. There was more fun. Cromwell ruined it and then Charles II reopened the theatres and the maypoles went back up.

IB Well, Charles II ... The Ranters were against him.

TH When were the Ranters?

IB Well, around the same time.

TH But Cromwell hated the Ranters and the Diggers and the Levellers as well.

IB Winstanley ... Ranters ... puritans ... fornication ... swearing ...

blasphemy – all that moment of liberation came out of nowhere.

TH   Now, do you think it is always only going to be small groups who break away in this way, like you guys, or the Ranters? Can you imagine mass liberty, or are people just too scared to take that liberty?

IB   A lot of them in jobs are doing what they want anyway…

RRJ Everyone's trying to be an entrepreneur all of a sudden …

TH   Yes, but take postmen as an example. I know two posties. One had a heart attack and one was off ill from stress for months. And that's supposed to be a pleasant job.

IB   'When I get fed up I can climb higher – in time for my heart attack when I retire' – that's an old number called 'Right to Work' our band used to do.

TH   All this ingenuity…

IB   Sabotaging the production line has been a staple of workers' fightback throughout history.

TH   Wouldn't it be better if all that ingenuity, energy and collective action was directed towards working for ourselves?

IB   Not if it's useless production or some chinless fuckwit fashion-designer entrepreneur. And don't get me started on fucking farmers' fucking markets.

TH   I don't get very far anyway in persuading people near me to boy-cott Tesco's … what sort of spirit do you see in people compared to the late sixties and seventies?

IB   There's very little fightback or imagination around at the moment. We are fed a diet of *Daily Mail* heath scares and panics: Don't go outside, you might get swine flu. Also in the eighties, if you went on a riot and weren't nicked on the day, you got away with it. Now with CCTV and telly coverage, you can get nicked months or years later. No fun in that.

TH   What about Climate Camp and all the rest of it?

IB   I think that's just middle-class wank turning into green careers on environmental quangos. Climate Camp is the new Cowes week.

TH   Well, what's happened to the working-class intellectuals, then?

IB   A lot of them have been bought off, writing opinion pieces like in-house bits of rough.

TH   Or they become stand-up comedians.

IB That's another lot – even the fucking comedians have all been to Oxbridge … Sorry to say it, Tom, but they're all fucking at it. Everyone from the protest movement to the journos are Oxford or Cambridge educated – Tony Benn, Tariq Ali, Ken Loach …

RRJ I interviewed Tony Benn. And I said to him, 'Tony, what about this story of Mrs Thatcher liking you?' 'Oh, that's in the past, we've got to forget about the past.'

IB I remember when Churchill died in South Wales. There were collections and some English villages raised thousands. Merthyr Tydfil raised half a crown, a couple of buttons. And some Green Shield Stamps.

TH But what's wrong with a good education?

IB Tony Benn, Ken Loach … I rest my case.

TH I wrote a chapter in one book about how anti-war marches were a waste of time. But my liberal publishers – who work with the organization Liberty – wouldn't print it.

IB One of the problems with the anarchist movement is that it's lost its libertarian impulse and its hedonism. It doesn't vigorously oppose restrictions on liberty. We believe in free speech – opposing Griffin going on *Question Time* was fucking ridiculous, with people saying: 'I believe in free speech, but …'

TH But a big part of the anarchist thing is to bust up racist marches, and so on.

IB Nothing wrong with a punch-up. I believe Griffin can have free speech but take the physical consequences if people don't like what he says. I used to admire Donald Soper on his stepladder at Speakers' Corner taking on all comers. Top geezer. There's a whole gamut of things … that's what I like in the *Idler*, that libertarian, English anarchy, an affection for place and roots. I love Frank Newbold's wartime posters: 'It's Your England … Fight For It' and Orwell's English socialist patriotism. A lot of anarchists are actually just boring leftists …

TH I like those creative things that actually add to people's lives, rather than the far Left whingeing. Which is also, in lots of cases, just resentment. And resentment is the wrong attitude.

IB Nothing wrong with a bit of resentment! Resentment and bitterness! The Yippees and the Dutch Provos showed you can be both bitter and funny. I can just imagine Monbiot on the train, saying 'Don't do that, Harry,' to one of his annoying sprogs who's annoying every other fucker in the compartment.

RRJ At dinner, the parents will stop the conversation so their child can interrupt!

TH We've been a bit guilty of that sort of thing. There's something wrong with my generation of parents. It's good to be ignored.

IB People give their kids ridiculous choices. Shut up and eat it! Would you like shallots? No fucking way.

RRJ If their mother and father are going out, the children should know they've got to behave ...

TH Some kind of horrible progressive thing has happened. The word 'parenting' is a new word.

IB They're treated as young adults. But they're not and you need to take decisions for them.

TH State schools are pretty awful, because they have been subjected to successive progressive ideologies. That's why at home we are rebelling by learning Latin, by rote. So we are learning *amo, amas, amat, amamus, amatis, amant.*

IB *Amabo, amabis, amabit, amabimus, amabitis, amabunt.*

TH The future simple! You remember it. You were probably taught well.

IB I did O-level Latin. It's so easy to learn.

TH That's why you have a good brain.

IB Because of the Latin?

TH Someone like Boris Johnson did Classics at Oxford. He has that bluff exterior but he is a serious guy.

IB There was a story in the paper this morning that a woman was suing her boss for sexual harassment at work, and he had sent her a rude poem by Catullus in Latin. He claimed that she couldn't possibly have known Latin, but she did!

TH The old ways.

IB The old ways! I went to visit a kid at Summerhill School once.

TH How did you find it?

IB Oh, fucking awful. Half of them are Japanese, strangely enough, and there was a big row about stabbing a pet rabbit ... They were having a debate about poor dead bunny but the young kids don't know what to think ... what are your views on stabbing a rabbit to death, aged three?

RRJ Piers Thompson [a friend with kids] said to me, which camp do you think we fall into, Ray? I said, there are two camps. Either you tell your kids what to do, or you ask them what they want to do. If you tell them what to do, that's tough love. If you ask them, then you're a twat.

IB On the train, Jane, my partner, has no patience with middle-class twats letting their kids run amok ... 'Stop these children coming up and pawing me ... Harry, Harriet and Josh ... you're going to get thumped in a minute.' She got off to a bad start, because their mater was reading the *Tatler*. Because she was reading *Tatler*, she thought everyone else had to look after her kids. After some strong words from Jane, the woman called the police ... everyone was craning their necks – class war on the 5.20 outta Paddington!

TH This new attitude makes having children doubly more difficult than it was before. The men are feeling emasculated because the women ask for so much help and, naturally enough, turn to the nearest person around. There's not enough help from the wider family group.

IB Also other people used to intervene with your kids. Children are indoors much more these days. The computer games but also the fear ... parents read the *Daily Mail* horror stories ...

TH Which are very rare instances.

IB The local papers like the *Hackney Gazette* are full of it ...

TH Even where we are, the mums are frightened. They say: 'You can't be too careful these days.' Although it may be changing: I just came back from a conference of teachers and social workers in Scotland and the theme there was that we have become too 'risk-averse', as the jargon has it.

IB I can remember hitch-hiking – no one does that now. So, Tom, you mix with a broad church of people, then? Social workers, Women's Institute? A life of ludic pleasure.

TH And hard graft.

IB It's hard work being playful all day. Don't you think the *Idler* will be sucked into the corporations and you'll be bought out and take the money and run off to Alex James's organic farm? It's inevitable …

TH   I think it would have happened by now. We have been doing it for seventeen years.

RRJ   When I get the dole now, they ask me what do I do, and I take up old copies of *The Roughler*, and I say, 'Can I use that computer?' and they say, 'Yeah, type this in,' and I show them my TV station, Roughler TV. Now, why don't they jump up and down and say, 'Look at this bloke, he's actually *doing* something!' Instead of saying, 'There's a job in this factory.'

TH   I was on the dole when I started the *Idler*, round here, and they did send me on a sort of dolies' business-training course for a week.

IB   You were on the dole and they sent you on a course to produce the *Idler*!

TH   Ha! But it's kind of unrealistic because they are asking these 17-year-old dolies to produce a business plan. There was the Enterprise Allowance Scheme. Can we not, though, find simple ways of working, which is making things and selling them? Women can make things at home.

IB   You want women staying at home?

TH   That's surely better than working at Asda, to have your own small business?

IB   What about the camaraderie and the saucy banter?

TH   I'd rather be at home making jam with a couple of friends than being bossed around by an idiot at Asda.

IB   Women at home … cottage industry … I'm going misty-eyed.

TH   The Women's Institute is coming back among young people. There are art students at places like Goldsmiths who are starting their own Women's Institute branches. It's creative.

IB   You really do see the good in everything.

TH   It *is* a good thing, though!

IB   Those organizations have always been around. The Women's Institute has been making jam at home for years, but you're saying it's a new trend.

TH   No, I'm saying that I'm into the old ways.

IB   The old ways!

TH It's the old ways that politicians hate. They don't have a sense of history, Left or Right. They are all Whiggish.

IB Or they make up versions of the old ways ... myths.

TH The yeomanry. Old-fashioned Tories ... You must have found with *Class War*, it made people realize that they were not alone.

IB Oh yeah. We would express the wish that the Queen Mother would die of cancer. And you would get an enormous postbag with people agreeing.

TH I think the over-60s are more radical than the young ones. How old are you two?

RRJ I'm 58.

IB 62. We know the old ways. How old are you?

TH Me? 41.

IB Ohhh! And he talks of the old ways!

TH Well, why do you think I've brought you together? So I can pay my respects and sit at your feet.

★

Ian gives me the last four issues of *Class War* and also a pamphlet written by Tom Vague about the radical history of Notting Hill. Ian asks me, teasingly, whether I was in the Bullingdon Club when at Cambridge. No, I say. I was playing in hardcore-punk bands and doing fanzines. Finally, we discuss schools.

TH I went to Westminster.

IB School?

TH Yes.

IB Fucking hell. They're all the same, Ray!

ESSAYS

Matthew Green

PROGRESS
AND THE LAND

Paul Kingsnorth

Y OU ARE A NIMBY, A REACTIONARY AND A ROMANTIC
idiot. You want to go back to a Golden Age, in which you can
play at living in prettified village poverty because you have
never experienced the real thing. You are a privileged, bourgeois
escapist. You dream of a prelapsarian rural idyll because you can't cope
with the modern, multicultural, urban reality. You are a hypocrite.
You are personally responsible for the misery of a lot of poor people in
Africa who need you to buy their beans. You need to get real. This is
the twenty-first century, and there is business to be done. There is
poverty to eliminate, an economy to expand, a planet to be saved. You
are not helping by playing at being William Cobbett or William
Morris. Snap out of it. Grow up.

These are some of the things you can expect people to say to you if
you dare to talk, today, about the land. Specifically, if you are foolish
enough to suggest that there may be anything positive about rural life,
about working the land, about land-based communities or about the
possibly simpler or more essential life it may represent, you can expect
to call down a firestorm upon your unsuspecting head.

I have written books and articles and given talks for a number of
years which have touched on these issues. I have told detailed stories
from all over the world about the struggles of land-based people
against the forces which would dispossess them. I have tried to explain
what makes those people so attached to the land, and I have also tried
to explain my own love of the countryside, my own work on the land,

my need get my hands dirty, and what I think we are losing as we continue to concrete over the fields and lose our folk memory of the soil.

Every time I have done so, someone has popped up with at least one of the lines above. Sometimes it is said in mockery, sometimes in anger. Sometimes I have sensed that the accuser feels some personal slight has been done to them. The phrases are so similar, so often, from so many different people, that they are clearly not the original thoughts of those who peddle them. This is received wisdom, passed down over generations; a curiously Pavlovian reaction. The assumptions behind it are clear: city good, country bad; city modern, country backward; consumption modern, production antiquated; 'progress' good, always and for ever.

This kind of thing is not new. Seventy years ago, in the viciously entertaining second section of his English travelogue, *The Road to Wigan Pier*, George Orwell provided a critique of precisely the same kind of nonsense. Orwell was a socialist, but he was an idiosyncratic one, and one of the many complaints he airs about socialism in *Wigan Pier* is its incessant, dehumanizing 'machine worship'. Orwell detected – it wasn't hard to detect – the extreme hostility of socialism towards the land and the people who belonged to it. The land, it was clear, represented the past. It represented reaction, smallness and stasis, inequality, feudalism and drudgery. In contrast, the urban, machine civilization which Orwell both loathed and was impressed by, represented a bright, shining, necessary future. Orwell's description of what happens when a challenge is issued to a 'vulgar machine worshipper' is worth quoting at length, because it could have been written yesterday:

> In the first place he will tell you that it is impossible to 'go back' (or to 'put back the hand of progress' – as though the hand of progress hadn't been pretty violently put back several times in human history!), and will then accuse you of being a medievalist and begin to descant upon the horrors of the Middle Ages, leprosy, the Inquisition, etc. As a matter of fact, most attacks upon the Middle Ages and the past generally by apologists of modernity are beside the point, because their essential trick is to project a modern man, with his squeamishness and his high standards of comfort, into an age when such things were unheard of. But

notice that in any case this is not an answer. For a dislike of the mechanized future does not imply the smallest reverence for any period of the past … When one pictures a desirable civilization, one pictures it merely as an objective; there is no need to pretend that it has ever existed in space and time. Press this point home, explain that you wish to aim at making life simpler and harder instead of softer and more complex, and the Socialist will usually assume that you want to revert to a 'state of nature' – meaning some stinking Paleolithic cave: as though there were nothing between a flint scraper and the steel mills of Sheffield, or between a skin coracle and the Queen Mary!

What is striking about this passage is that not only the arguments but also the language they are couched in have undergone little change in seven decades. What has changed is that it is not just socialists who adopt this line now, but people from across the political spectrum. Try proposing a 'simpler life' today; try suggesting that economic growth might be in some way not the panacea it is claimed to be; try questioning the value of the Internet or suggesting that we should scale back our material lusts in any way. Within ten seconds you will be accused of wearing a 'hair shirt'; another five will see you accused of wanting to 'make everyone live in caves'. Persist and you'll be compared to Pol Pot or – if the accuser has even less imagination – Hitler (he was a vegetarian, you know).

What is happening here, and why? Why does a love of or an attachment to the land or the countryside elicit such strong and negative reactions in so many people? I think that we can best uncover the origins of this attitude by taking a step back and examining the assumptions that govern the civilization we are currently living in. Every civilization has its founding myths, whether it likes to admit it or not, and ours is what we might call the progressive narrative. Since the Enlightenment, this particular version of the human story has been pretty much all-conquering, certainly in the West, where it originated, and increasingly in the wider world too. It is a story as simple and powerful as the religious myths which it supplanted and upon which it is parasitical.

Humanity, it tells us, started off grunting in the primeval swamps and will end up conquering the stars. Each generation will experience better lives than the one before, thanks to the machine civilization we have built to cocoon us. Soon this will allow us to abolish poverty, stabilize and manage 'our environment', extend US-style representative democracy to everyone on Earth and create a global civilization where everyone has access to Twitter, Starbucks and the Universal Declaration of Human Rights.

This is a caricatured but still reasonably accurate version of the progressive narrative. It tells us that things will always get better, and that if we work hard we can have everything. It is a powerful and appealing story. For this reason, it is embedded deep in our culture, and you can hear it rising, unexamined, from the depths every day, through the mouths of politicians, journalists, teachers, scientists – pretty much all of us.

Implicit in this myth, and essential to it, is the idea that progress requires an escape from the land. In the soil, in the woods and the fields and the moors and the mountains, lurks a dirty, frightening and very unprogressive barbarism. The countryside is the home of murky customs, superstitions, witches, inbreeding, fox-hunting and Tory MPs. Note how the word 'peasant', which in its literal sense simply means small farmer, has become a term of abuse. Karl Marx, the ultimate progressive (and a metropolitan social climber on the quiet), talked scornfully of the peasant populations of Europe, 'mired in the idiocy of rural life'. Revolution, he thought, would rescue them, by force if need be, from this slough of despond, corralling them into the factories, where they could be more useful.

The political left has always fetishized the modern, the mechanized and the urban. Traditionally, it was opposed in this by a conservative, often rural, right, which stood for king, country and the land (much of which they owned). Today, though, the progressive narrative has crossed political boundaries, broken them down and gleefully trampled upon them. These days, everyone from socialists to environmentalists to David Cameron is a 'progressive', and the future is urban, consumerist, fast-moving and mediated. There is no place for the land, for that might require us to slow down, look around us, understand where we are, see ourselves as part of a web rather than as detached individuals taking our pleasure wherever we can. It might remind us of where we came from and what we really are, and the consequences of that are too frightening to contemplate.

The progressive narrative propagates a number of fantasies about the way the world is, but one of the most pernicious is that everywhere is essentially the same. Places don't matter, individual human beings are free-floating entities, the same wherever they are brought up, un-attached to the land, consumers in a global mall – citizens of nowhere. This is the point at which the Left and the Right seamlessly meld into one. Leftists have long nurtured a vision of a world in which bound-aries are done away with, religion is dead and we are all 'global citi-zens'. Meanwhile, the neoliberal Right nurse their own dreams of a borderless world of free-floating capital, a 'global market' in which money is the arbiter of value.

Today, these two dreams have become one, though neither side will admit it. The longed-for One World is rapidly approaching, and it is a world of increasing subservience to the machine. It is also a world of Change, with a capital C. In the progressive narrative, change is the only constant. Continuity, stability, the simple act of standing still – all are looked on with suspicion. Attachment to place, locality, tradi-tion and culture are tantamount to fascism. Look at the election slogans of any politician anywhere in the world, allegedly Left or sup-posedly Right, and there it is: Change. A slogan we can all do business with. This, of course, is not new either. Marx and Engels pinned its inevitability down over 150 years ago in *The Communist Manifesto*:

Constant revolutionizing of production, uninterrupted distur-bance of all social conditions, everlasting uncertainty and agita-tion distinguish the bourgeois epoch from all earlier ones. All fixed, fast frozen relations, with their train of ancient and venera-ble prejudices and opinions, are swept away, all new-formed ones become antiquated before they can ossify. All that is solid melts into air, all that is holy is profaned, and man is at last compelled to face with sober senses his real condition of life and his relations with his kind.

Marx and Engels thought all this was rather good. Constant revolution suited them fine; what they were concerned about was who got the spoils. Today, that argument rumbles on, but the obsession with change is even more deeply embedded. Ethnologist Ullrich Kockel, Professor of Ethnology and Folk Life at the University of Ulster, has been studying land-based communities around the world for decades. In that time, he has come up time and again against the dogma of progress-at-all-costs and its corollary: a contempt for the land and its 'backward' people. In his recent inaugural address to the university he lambasted this worldview, which he sees not only in politicians and the media but in unthinkingly right-on academics who ought to know better:

> Any positive evaluation of the past, and any analysis emphasizing continuity over change is branded as indicative of reactionary politics, emotional regression, or both: an irrational scramble for shelter from the vagaries of the modern world. This diagnosis has become so commonplace and deep-seated that anyone daring to challenge it would find themselves immediately relegated to the same politico-cultural sickbed. Under no circumstances must one look for continuities (unless one wants to be seen as emotionally retreating into a fantasy Golden Age).

Change, in other words, is the only constant. From Barack Obama to David Cameron, progress – and its modern sub-narratives 'growth' and 'development' – is the only dish presented to us. And because we must all abhor stasis, we must abhor the land. For what is more stolid, unchanging and symbolic of the terrible, squalid past than mud, trees and rivers? And who is more likely to stand in the way of growth, progress and the machine than the foolish, reactionary, romantic dolts who persist in staying attached to it?

This is the attitude that has led, and continues to lead, to the destruction of land all over the world, and to the forced dispersal of people who remain attached to it. The cult of progress decrees that we should all become part of the mediated, virtual world of happy urban consumers. But some people persist in not being interested. Small farmers are not big consumers. Peasants are not much interested in voting. Tribal people would rather hunt and fish than let a PLC dig for bauxite under their ancestral forests.

And this is their doom. Consider Stalin's forced farm collectivization, or the slaughter of tribal peoples from Indonesia to the Amazon. Consider the tens of thousands forced from their homes by bulldozers in India to make way for dams to fuel the growing cities. Consider the North American Free Trade Agreement, which destroyed the livelihoods of Mexican peasants for the benefit of US agribusiness. Consider the ongoing concreting of countryside in rich countries such as Britain, where farmers still haemorrhage from the land.

All over the world, people are being forced from their land in the name of the machine. We rarely hear their stories. What we hear instead is an unceasing diet of progress-is-good-for-them propaganda, which differs little from Victorian lectures about the White Man's Burden and the need to bring civilization to the savages. Poor, unhappy peasants, we are told, long to leave their scrappy rural lives for the big cities. Our duty is to help them do it, by means of development and growth.

Stories that do not fit this narrative tend not to see the light of day. Some years back I spent time with peasant farmers in Brazil, who were part of the Movimento Sem Terra, or landless workers' movement. The Sem Terra are peasants without land. Often they have been forced from their land; sometimes they have left it to go to the cities, then changed their minds when they saw the reality of urban life. Now, the Sem Terra is the world's biggest social movement, and it is made up entirely of poor, small farmers whose wish is not for jobs in call centres but for land. They get it by force, occupying the unused estates of rich landowners. The successful Sem Terra I spoke to had never been happier; the land was where they wanted to be.

A similar tale can be heard in India. India, we hear in the media almost every day, is a thrusting, modern success story; a land of Microsoft and call centres and dynamism and growth. But more than all this, India is a land of farmers. The progressive narrative expects them to leave their pointless little farms and get with the urban programme. But many of them have other ideas. Vast farmers' movements have arisen in India in recent decades, counting millions amongst their number. They have invaded the offices of multinational seed companies, built bonfires of genetically modified crops and undertaken marches, hundreds of thousands strong, across the country. All this for the right to continue to farm; to continue to stay on the land, despite the efforts of the progressive classes to force them off.

Stories like this come in from all over the world, every day, if you know where to look. You may have read, for example, one of the gazillions of pieces in the mainstream media over the last few years about how many Chinese people are leaving the land and flooding into the cities. There were far fewer stories explaining how, in 2009, more people left the cities for the countryside than the other way around. In fact, to my knowledge, there were none. It's not the story we're supposed to be hearing. The continued existence, and often resistance, of land-based communities is a two-fingered salute to the dogma which requires us to believe that everyone everywhere, given half the chance, would throw down their hoes for a job in a Motorola factory.

All of this gives us, in the rich world, food for thought. In my younger days, I used to think that 'the system' could be smashed with revolution and resistance and the like – the time-honoured tools of the excitable political radical. I don't believe that any more. I don't really believe that the system can be smashed at all. But I'm pretty sure it is beginning to crumble by itself, as the myth of progress hits the buffers of reality. The economic woes that have shaken the whole machine over the past eighteen months are as nothing to the ecological woes that are unfolding, as the climate and the soil itself shiver beneath the force of our delusions. The world, it seems, cannot take much more progress of this kind. It has been calculated, for example (and by real scientists, not by troublemaking eco-hippies), that if the global economy grows at an average rate of 3 per cent for the next twenty years, we will consume, in that period, resources equivalent to all those consumed since humanity first evolved. Something, clearly, is going to have to give.

George Orwell, finally, concluded that 'progress and reaction have both turned out to be swindles.' He was right about that, and every year it becomes clearer. But what remains? To Orwell, the answer seemed a despairing one: 'quietism – robbing reality of its terrors by simply submitting to it'. But there is, it seems to me, another way. To put a spanner in the works of the progressive narrative, to foul up the machine in your own small way, the best course of action is simply to stand your ground. What really gets in the way of all this 'change', 'progress', 'development' and other euphemisms for destruction and profit is grounded people who know their place, in the physical sense, and are prepared to fight for it if they have to.

To belong to a piece of land, to know it and be able to work it, to walk it until you know what it wants, is a lifetime's work. To do such a thing, or even attempt it, is to slow down, breathe more deeply, spend less time in front of screens and more in the sun and rain. To get your hands dirty, to grow your own food, to provide for yourself and your family, to stand your ground, know your place – all of this is to commit an open heresy against the ossifying religion of progress. In an increasingly placeless, rootless world, the best way to resist is to dig – and the best way to rebel is to belong.

Alice Smith

IS URBANIZATION A TEMPORARY PHENOMENON?

Simon Fairlie

HERE IS AN ANOMALY. IN 2008, ACCORDING TO THE United Nations, for the first time in history, the number of people living in towns around the world outstripped the number of people living in the countryside. From China to Brazil, peasants are flocking into cities, swelling them to obscene proportions. Yet in some of the overdeveloped countries, especially the UK, people are moving in the reverse direction, and cities are shrinking. The trend is known in planning jargon as counterurbanization, the tendency of urban populations, over time, to return to the countryside that their forefathers abandoned. Since Britain was the pioneer of industrial urbanization, and is now pioneering the move back to the country (even though it hasn't got very much left), it is reasonable to ask whether urbanization might in the long run prove to be a temporary phenomenon; and if it is, is there any point in the bulk of the world's population making a return journey about as fatuous as that taken by the Grand Old Duke of York and his 10,000 men?

★

If you have the chance to address a gathering of people in London, you can test the force of the counterurban current in this way: invite the members of the audience to raise their arms if they live in the capital. Unless you happen to be a nationwide attraction, a forest of hands will wave before you. Now ask who expects to be living in London in ten years' time, and many, if not most of the hands will drop. Ask how many hope to be living in a leafier environment in ten years' time, and up they rise again.

Admittedly, some of these would-be urban refugees may have only recently arrived from the provinces, their spell in London being just a lucrative mid-life diversion. But others represent the tail end of a cycle that has rolled out over several generations. I myself am a case in point: early in the twentieth century, my grandfather left several hundred acres of farmland in central Scotland to try his hand as a writer in London. His son followed in his footsteps, spending the first 20 years of his career in Fleet Street, and the last 25 years within earshot of Capitol Hill. I too write from time to time, but writers are two a penny these days (although occasionally one earns a sovereign), and over the years I have more often earned my living from activities such as vinework, shepherding, dry-stone walling, smallholding and, currently, teaching people the lost art of mowing with a scythe. In short, I have gone back to the land – though not, alas, to the ancestral acres still farmed by my distant cousins.

Here in the country, you meet not those who hope to flee the city, but those who have already fled. The incomers have taken over all the more desirable rural housing and converted most of the shops, schools, rectories and barns into posh residences. Villages whose populations declined steadily throughout the latter half of the nineteenth century and into the first half of the twentieth are now girdled by a ring of modern villas and bungalows. The natives, identifiable by their local accent, are outnumbered and their offspring, unable to compete for housing with the influx, head for the nearest town or try their luck in London. Most of these incomers are retirees or urban commuters, whose engagement with the countryside may go no further than admiring the view. But the real work of the countryside, land management, is also increasingly being carried by counterurbanites. Millionaires from the city buy up farms and run them, sometimes, quite successfully. ('Merchants,' Adam Smith noted in 1776, 'are commonly ambitious of becoming country gentlemen, and when they do, they are generally the best of all improvers.') Smallholders, hippies, down-sizers and others who are consciously striving to 'get back to the land' buy up smaller fragments of subdivided farms. Nor is counter-urbanism restricted to the middle classes: there are plenty of East London accents in a West Country village these days; and the increasing number of black faces and rasta hats suggests that the counterurban urge is starting to infect Afro-Caribbeans, whose families might have gone full cycle from a shack in rural Jamaica, via a shanty in Kingston and a terraced house in Handsworth, to a rented cottage in the Somerset Levels, within four generations.

So pronounced is the phenomenon of counterurbanization in the UK that our cities are shrinking although our total population is growing. Admittedly, the decline of Liverpool, whose population has halved since the Second World War, is in large part attributable to the magnetism of the South. But that doesn't explain the decline in the population of London, which began in the fifties, and continued into the eighties. Since then it has crept back up, but London's population is still 12.5 per cent smaller than it was in 1951. More significantly, the recent increase in London's population is wholly attributable to immigration: 31 per cent of its current population are people who were born abroad. Without this influx, London's population would be barely half what it was in the fifties. That does not mean that everybody who left headed for the open countryside – though even those who decanted to suburbs and new towns were lured by a leafier environment. But it does suggest that a very large proportion of people who were brought up in London do not want to live there; and it bears out what can be witnessed during a trip on the tube – that the people who do want to live there are predominantly young, cosmopolitan and not yet settled.

★

This movement to reclaim the countryside has flourished in the face of persistent opposition from the establishment and the government. In the twenties, as the growth in private car ownership offered city folk easy access to the countryside and prompted the spread of jerry-built ribbon developments, Clough Williams-Ellis summed up the unsavoury face of counterurbanization in one damning sentence:

Having made our towns with such careless incompetence, those
of us who have the means to be choosers are calmly declining to
live in them and are now proceeding with the same recklessness to
disperse ourselves over the countryside, destroying and dishon-
ouring it with our shoddy but all too permanent encampments.

The newly formed Council for the Preservation of Rural England
rallied behind him, but worse was to come. Even those who normally
did not 'have the means to be choosers' were deserting the city.
Between the wars, with agriculture in the depths of depression, land
was cheap, and sharpsters such as Charles Neville, the founder of the
clifftop township of Peacehaven, were subdividing farmland and selling plots at prices that were affordable even to people of slender means.
Plotlands, as they were called, began to spring up all around Britain,
particularly along the coast – 'congeries of discordant huts and cara-
vans', the CPRE called them at the time, whose 'cumulative effect is
to produce a shoddy, unplanned and unsightly blight'. But to the
people who built them, sometimes bringing in building materials
piecemeal on the bus or by bicycle, these shacks offered a welcome
escape from the city at weekends, and ultimately a permanent home-
stead where they could stake out a rural lifestyle.

Upper-class conservationists, from the windows of their Bentleys
and their Palladian country retreats, viewed the prospect of the lower
orders colonizing the landscape with increasing alarm. As Dennis
Hardy and Colin Ward recount in their history of the plotlands,
Arcadia For All, this fear was a major influence in garnering support for
the 1947 Town and Country Planning Act, which 60 years later is still
the basis of the legislation restricting development in the countryside.
The first development plan rushed through after the Act was passed
was a plan for Shoreham Beach prohibiting the re-erection of plotland
shacks which had been removed for the war effort.

Since 1947, the government has relied on the Town and Country
Planning Acts to stem the otherwise irrepressible urge of lesser mortals
to go and live in the countryside. Anyone who can afford to buy a
labourer's cottage or a farmhouse or a village shop – in other words,
outbid a prospective labourer, farmer or shopkeeper – is welcome to

convert it into a marketable dwelling. But building a new dwelling, although considerably less injurious to the rural community, is, in the words of a succession of planning guidances, to be 'strictly controlled'.

Moreover, in 2000, the government decided that, as well as sticks to prevent people moving out to the sticks, there should be carrots encouraging them to remain in town. Its Urban White Paper, published that year, noted that, whereas 77 per cent of rural dwellers were 'very satisfied with the area where they lived', only 35 per cent of urban dwellers and around 50 per cent of suburban dwellers could say the same. The answer, the White Paper concluded, was not to find ways of accommodating more people closer to the countryside, but to make cities more attractive places to live. To this purpose, it enlisted the services of an Urban Task Force, headed by the architect Richard Rogers. The result has been a profusion of urban-regeneration projects, characterized by iconic structures of uncertain architectural pedigree, scantily clad with glass or stainless steel, boasting an undue complement of cosmopolitan restaurants, cappuccino counters and all-night bars. These environments may be attractive to flighty youth, but they offer little to mature individuals seeking a more grounded way of life.

★

Admittedly, the appetite for counterurbanization that the UK government is so keen to suppress has so far been less pronounced in other over-developed countries. In 2006, the EU commissioned the *First European Quality of Life Survey*, which examined 'Urban – Rural Differences' in matters such as wealth and happiness. On aggregate, people in the twelve richest EU countries were about five to ten times richer than people in the poorer countries of the EU and the three countries then applying for entry (Bulgaria, Romania and Turkey), and about 10 per cent happier. However, within the twelve richest countries, urban people were about 10 per cent wealthier than rural people, yet about 2 per cent unhappier. In the six poorest member countries of the EU, urban people were 30 per cent wealthier and 2 per cent happier; and in the three acceding nations, people living in towns were over twice as rich as people living in the countryside, but still only 3 per cent happier.

There are a number of conclusions we can reasonably infer from these figures:

a) The richer you are, the happier you are likely to be, though you need a lot more wealth to become a bit happier.

b) Someone living in the countryside is likely to be happier than a person of the same income living in the city.

c) In poorer countries, people are drawn to the city not because they will be happier there but because they may become richer, though that should lead to greater happiness.

d) Once people are richer – i.e. they 'have the means to be choosers' – then they may reason from (b) that they will be happier still if they move to the countryside.

If, as this survey and other evidence suggests, it is wealth and rural living that makes most people happy, then what is the point of towns? Of course, there will always be a sizable minority of footloose youths, cosmopolitan dilettantes and Johnsonian curmudgeons who prefer the pleasures of the metropolis – and most people enjoy paying a visit. But why do planners in the UK cram citizens unwillingly into cities that have long since lost their economic reason for existing? And more urgently, why do development agencies and policy makers in developing countries allow the peasantry to be coaxed or bullied into conurbations of gob-smacking unsustainability? Why don't they simply skip out the whole urban episode – the vainglorious march up to the top of the hill and down again – and instead concentrate on making people who live in the countryside richer?

★

In a recent programme on the BBC World Service, a reporter commented that peasants continued to flock into cities such as Bombay 'because the countryside cannot support them'. She did not explain why the countryside cannot support them, yet it is a reasonable question: India is self-sufficient in grain most years, it is the world's largest dairy producer and it is an exporter of numerous agricultural goods. If it can feed and clothe its citizens in town, why can't it feed and clothe them in the country?

The answer is that India's farmers, like most farmers in most parts of the world, are not paid enough to compete with the urban economy. This is nothing new. Over two centuries ago, Adam Smith observed that 'the industry which is carried on in towns is, everywhere in Europe, more advantageous than that which is carried on in the country.' The reason, he surmised, was that manufacturers and merchants could more easily combine in 'corporations' to protect their interests, establish monopolies and control markets.

> Corporation laws enable the inhabitants of towns to raise their prices, without fearing to be undersold by the free competition. The enhancement of price is everywhere finally paid by the land-lords, farmers and labourers of the country, who have seldom opposed the establishment of such monopolies … Both stock and labour naturally seek the most advantageous employment. They naturally, therefore, resort as much as they can to the town and desert the country.

Smith also added that this was not the case 'in China and Indostan' where 'both the rank and the wages of country labourers are said to be superior to those of the greater part of artificers and manufacturers.' But that has since changed, thanks, in more recent years, to a neo-liberal consensus whose application of the free-market policies that Smith advanced is strictly one-sided. Supermarkets, corporate grain dealers such as Cargill and biotech seed companies have as great a stranglehold over markets as any of the mercantilist corporations that Smith condemned, while the US pays subsidies to industrial farmers to plunder the soils of the Midwest. Meanwhile, in the name of free trade, the IMF's structural adjustment programmes and the globalization policies advanced by the World Trade Organization have forced the governments of developing nations to remove tariffs and other measures protecting local farmers, with the result that the price of what they grow is determined in Chicago. It is the same old story of the city sucking dry the countryside. The value of primary commodities slumps as the wages of those in the urban service and financial sectors soar; farmers around the world find themselves competing with each other in a race to the bottom, replacing human labour with urban-manufactured machinery and chemicals, until eventually it becomes more profitable for a peasant lad to sell chewing gum to passing cars at urban traffic lights than to stay in his village and produce decent food. The rural exodus, which in Britain was typified by the enclosure movement that was gathering steam in Adam Smith's day, is now repeated in the developing world at an altogether different level of magnitude, creating what Mike Davis has described as a 'Planet of Slums'.

★

Those tacitly or explicitly in favour of this exodus – for instance, the neo-liberal McKinsey consultancy, whose Vision 2020 plan for the Indian state of Andrha Pradesh envisages over 40 per cent of the rural workforce removed from their land by the end of the next decade – view it as essential for economic growth, for the creation of limitless wealth whose bounty will overflow and trickle down even to the dis-possessed. In an Oriental rerun of the American dream, our chewing-gum seller will scrimp enough to put his son through high school, his granddaughter will make it to university and work in the IT sector, and her son will run a property-development company from a villa outside Bangalore, before retiring to run a spice farm in the Nilgiri Hills.

Unfortunately, the chances of this scenario happening to any more than the few who strike lucky are negligible. Counterurbanization might be what the majority of Indians will eventually aspire to, but it seems unlikely that any more than a handful will ever make it. There will be no colonial proletariat willing to work for pitiful wages supplying consumer goods, cheap food and unsolicited phone calls to a billion bourgeois Indians, as the Indian and Chinese proletariats currently do for us. Moreover, the sheer scale of Third World megacities is so close to breaking the bounds of ecological sustainability at present that it is impossible to believe that they can ever sustain all their inhabitants at a level of consumption equivalent to ours – at least not without the discovery of a stunningly abundant and cheap source of renewable energy.

The cities of the world, so the Clinton Foundation claims, contain around 50 per cent of the world's population, but consume 75 per cent of the world's energy and are responsible for 75 per cent of greenhouse-gas emissions. In other words, townies emit three times as much carbon as country folk. This unsubstantiated but credible statistic flies in the face of the advice from the UK planning establishment that it is more sustainable for everyone to live in towns; and it casts a shadow of foreboding over the project to shift the bulk of the world's peasantry into conurbations. The vast majority of the people on this planet who do not exceed their carbon allowance or their permissible ecological footprint are peasants, who live largely from the renewable resources of their local environment. People working in fields produce energy people working on streets consume it. There is sufficient food grown in the world to feed everyone, and it is virtually all grown in the countryside, so why should there be any problem feeding people in the countryside rather than the town? We might have to persuade a few people in areas that can no longer produce sufficient food for their burgeoning population to migrate to sparsely inhabited areas such as the Midwest of North America, or New Zealand, but that shouldn't be difficult.

As things stand at the moment, it would be far safer and more rewarding for humanity to short-circuit the cycle of urbanization and counterurbanization and encourage people who currently live in the countryside to stay there. This can be done by one simple expedient: paying them a decent wage for what they produce: and that means paying bankers, media tarts, lawyers and all the rest of the tribe of urban charlatans who contribute comparatively little to the welfare of the human race a lot less.

Alice Smith

BRING BACK THE GUILDS

Pat Conaty

GLOBAL INVESTMENT BANKERS HAVE RECLAIMED THE divine right of kings and despite wreaking social, economic and global havoc, they continue to assert and are conceded these rights by an apparently servile state. Why?

Since the election of MrsThatcher, the level of UK indebtedness has increased at unprecedented historic rates and become overwhelming both for households and for government. Household debt for mortgage and consumer credit grew by more than ten times, from £46 billion in 1980 to £483 billion in 1996. Since then, under Labour, the aggregate indebtedness level has escalated to £1.46 trillion in 2009.

The bail-out of the global banking system has come at a cost to the tax payer comparable to that of the Second World War, and this cost is escalating. In borrowing yet more to pay for the banking debacle and the full costs of rescuing the 'gods that failed', government debt has escalated from under 40 per cent of GDP in 2007 to 66 per cent in 2010 and is forecast by the IMF to rise to 100 per cent in 2014. Credit Action has calculated that the average UK household burden in servicing this debt will rise from £58,370 in 2009 to £116,210 in 2013.

The creation of New Labour in 1995 was forged by the removal of Clause IV from the Labour Party constitution of 1918. This committed Labour to establishing a co-operative commonwealth and to:

securing for the workers by hand or brain the full fruits of their industry and the most equitable distribution thereof that may be possible upon the basis of common ownership of the means of production, distribution and exchange, and the best obtainable

93

system of popular administration and control of each industry or service.

Ironically, Clause IV has been achieved significantly *de facto* as the commanding heights of the economy have been brought into common ownership with the effective nationalization of most of the British banking sector.

Disappointingly, the stated intent of the government is to return to business as usual and to reprivatize RBS NatWest, Lloyds HBOS and Northern Rock as soon as possible. Is there a People's Banking alternative? A century ago, the Bank Panic of 1907 triggered radical social reforms including the People's Budget of the Liberal Government of 1909 – the first budget in British history with a focus on redistributing wealth and one that proposed a Henry George, inspired Single Tax on land to target unearned rentier income. A revolt in the House of Lords crushed this reform.

The long, forgotten debates about the social purpose of companies, investment and property rights that took place from 1905 to 1925 amongst Christian Socialists, trade unionists, Liberals, Fabians and social reformers are intriguingly relevant to our growing concerns about the future of work, rising world poverty and climate change. The focus of the debate was on how economic democracy might overcome what R. H. Tawney described as financial and corporate feudalism – then in the early stages of development.

Budget Cutbacks to Prop Up Socially Useless Global Banks

More recent history looks to be repeating itself. The adverse state of public sector finances due to the banking debacle has in Ireland already led to a system of structural adjustment which calls to mind the stringent regimes imposed by the IMF on developing countries in the wake of the Third World debt crisis. This public sector service curtailment to repay the taxpayer bill for global banking speculation is looming for many other EU countries, not least Britain. Civil unrest in Greece is a portent of much more to come.

The blackmail threats of the bankers to move offshore if their bonuses are jeopardised has not been faced down. The taxation imposed by Labour does not get to the heart of the problem. A Tobin Tax (named after the economist who proposed a tax on global financial trades in the seventies) could do more, but the more fundamental question is whether we need investment bankers? What added value do they bring? Nobel Prize economist Joseph Stiglitz thinks they are unnecessary and recent research indicates both their social and financial uselessness.

For example, the former IMF economist and investment-fund manager Dr Paul Woolley of the London School of Economics has appraised the utility of global investment banks, and his findings reveal that global capital markets have become profoundly dysfunctional over the past 20 years, due to a system of perverse incentives that have supported increasingly speculative behaviour. Woolley's analysis is supported by the views of Warren Buffett, the sage of Omaha and both the world's richest man and leading global investor. Buffett points to the rising transaction costs charged by global fund managers as an expanding 'croupier's take'.

In usurious ways, the bonuses and rocketing salaries of those in the City have been sucking the lion's share of value out of corporate bonds and other collective investments, which is destroying pension-fund yields. As a consequence, nine out of ten final-salary pension schemes have been shut to new entrants by employers and mounting deficits at the end of 2009 were £212 billion. For the alternative, money-purchase pension schemes, Woolley shows that the financial returns are much worse.

The underlying and unspoken truth of the private-sector pensions crisis is that it is a rip-off of colossal proportions. For a typical pension-fund yield of 5–6 per cent, Woolley shows that 1 per cent will be paid out to fund managers and corporate executives in share options, another 1 per cent will be paid out to brokers and the stock exchange in commission and fees for trading, and another 0.5 per cent will be paid to investment bankers for mergers and acquisition work to seek to increase returns on funds; additionally, up to 2 per cent will be paid to pension-fund and mutual-fund managers for their services to small retail investors and 0.5 per cent will be paid in stamp duty. One reason for the Bank of England's obsession about inflation is that, unless this is controlled, there will be no yield and the cover for the City of London's casino economy will be blown. The public would then have to consider direct investment in the real economy.

There is another facet to the social dysfunctionality of global capital markets. This is the growing gap between the rich and the poor in the USA and the UK that the casino economy has bred. When being accused of robber-baron behaviour a century ago, the world's then richest man, J. P. Morgan, condemned as excessive any gap in pay that exceeded a ratio of 20:1 between the chief executive of a firm and a shop-floor worker. In 1980, this pay differential had increased among large corporations in the US to 42:1. Today the differential is more than 400:1.

Jack Rasmus has shown that, in the US, trickle-up economics since 1980 have led to an annual income transfer of well over $1 trillion from roughly 90 million working-class families to the wealthiest households. Real earnings for 100 million US workers were less in 2007 than in 1980, when Reagan was elected. Financial analyst Jeff Gates has observed that the combined wealth of the seven wealthiest Americans exceeds the annual income of the world's poorest 2.5 billion people. Epidemiologist Richard Wilkinson and Kate Pickett's research has shown that the USA and the UK have the worst relative inequality internationally, and this correlates to a broad range of escalating social costs, including levels of violence, obesity, imprisonment, addiction and teenage pregnancy. One of the worst indices of social deprivation revealed by this research is that one in four UK citizens (and more than this in the USA) experiences mental-health problems, compared to less than 10 per cent in Japan, Germany, Sweden and Italy.

Another discrepancy related to the Anglo-Saxon reliance on the global capital markets is an increasing maldistribution of wealth between small businesses and global corporations.

For example, there are over 25 million American businesses. Of this total, the Fortune 500 corporations accounted for one third of GDP in 1955. By 2004, these 500 corporations accounted for two thirds of GDP. Trends in the UK are similar. Despite this lion's share of GDP, micro-enterprises and small businesses continue to be the engines of local and regional employment, not least because large corporations continue to hollow out, downsize and outsource work to save through subcontracting on pension, national insurance, taxes, social protection and other employment costs. The growth of self-employment internationally has been upward since the seventies in both OECD and developing countries. It provides four in ten jobs in southern European countries such as Greece and nine in ten jobs in India.

British small businesses (those with under 50 employees) account for 99.3 per cent of the UK's 4.5 million enterprises. They also account for 47.1 per cent of national employment. Indeed, self-employed people running the smallest enterprises (of, typically, just two people) account for 6.4 million in work – almost one in four UK jobs. Median pay, though, among the British self-employed is 20 per cent below their counterparts in the same trade in waged employment; they work the longest hours in the UK; and they have no holiday pay and negligible social protection in terms of sickness and pension provision.

While this bedrock of sole traders, artisans and small firms is locally owned and expanding in importance for both the British economy and for most national economies globally, their links to sources of long-term investment and low-cost capital is at best marginal and, for most micro-enterprises (under ten employees), non-existent. Witness the rising complaints of the Federation of Small Businesses about the lack of credit and support from the bailed-out banks, despite the increasing levels of injected equity, quantitative easing and loan guarantees generously supplied to the banks by taxpayers.

Ownership in global corporations is anonymous, institutional and changes continuously with non-stop hedging and other financial ebbs and flows. The share register of global corporations is comparable to an agglomeration of betting slips that are auctioned every day. Jeff Gates has reported that Amazon turns over its share register about every seven days.

The early twentieth century gave birth to the American Fortune 500 and the British FTSE100. Might they be replaced? How? The historic evolution of enterprise provides some important insights into why this reform is so essential for securing sustainable and self-reliant regional economies.

The Depersonalizaton of Business – The New Age Debate

The British debate a century ago about the nature of enterprise, private property and the equitable distribution of wealth was triggered by Arthur Penty, a Fabian and Christian Socialist member of the Independent Labour Party. As an architect, Penty recognized that professional partnerships operated like guilds to support and protect the work and position of high-earning lawyers, doctors, accountants and bankers, but there were no guilds for those working with their hands. Trade unions offered protection to some in large industries but, for craft workers and artisans, there was a gap. Penty was a leading supporter of the Garden City movement and he argued in 1906 that a 'restoration of the guilds' could help guide a deeper social-reform movement to emancipate labour and tackle growing social inequality.

Penty's provocative argument inspired A. R. Orage and Holbrook Jackson, and they used this idea to develop *The New Age*, a weekly review which, in 1907, they took over as joint editors. Together they attracted a broad range of responses to Petty's proposal and instigated an ongoing British debate on the social purposes of property that continued for almost two decades. Contributors and participants included George Bernard Shaw, Bertrand Russell, R. H. Tawney, G. K. Chesterton, Hilaire Belloc, George Lansbury and many others. Chesterton observed in 1910 that capitalism was increasingly malfunctioning, as it was creating fewer and fewer capitalists. From 1890 to 1920, a dramatic consolidation of corporate power was occurring in this Age of Imperialism as the City of London and Wall Street claimed and consolidated their dominant positions in the international capital markets.

Tawney pointed out the impact of the limited-liability legislation in 1855, and the Companies Act 1862 led to a revolution in the nature of business property. The new legislation paved the way for an increasing 'divorce of ownership and work', introducing a completely new form of modern property rights. Previous legislation had protected the property of the peasants, yeoman farmers, craftsmen and small masters. This pre-industrial legal system sought to ensure the livelihoods and safeguard the ownership of the means of production for these local enterprises.

Prior to the late nineteenth century stock-markets were relatively undeveloped, as shares were not easy to trade – apart from those established through a separate act of Parliament. The new legislation shortened by years the time needed to set up a share-capital company and made it far easier to raise capital for large enterprises, which enabled industrial corporations to expand both nationally and internationally. Prior to 1862, most businesses were operated as family enterprises or as partnerships with full liability for risks. Adam Smith championed the freedom to trade of artisans and mechanics, the inventors behind the Industrial Revolution. Limited liability introduced the concept of a business as a natural person with an almost unlimited range of rights on the one hand and a curtailment of social responsibilities on the other.

The net effect of the new legislation was to depersonalize enterprise and begin the radical separation between those working in the firm (owner managers and employees) and the shareholders – increasingly, anonymous and distant investors. This inexorably led to an elite rentier class of owners whose payments in dividends on shares and interest on corporate debentures could be earned while never visiting the business of which they were the owners. Such joint-stock businesses may be dated back 500 years in Europe, but they were the exception rather than the norm. Indeed, rentier mercantile corporations were what Adam Smith sought to free small business from.

Medieval Guilds and Mercantile Corporations

The expanding 'satanic mill' towns of the north of England, the long depression of the 'hungry 1840s', and the Chartist movement led to a growing level of advocacy for fundamental social change. Christian Socialists such as J. M. Ludlow and Edward Vansittart Neale from 1855 sought various methods to finance worker co-operatives. The guilds were looked to for guidance on reconnecting enterprise to moral purposes in the second half of the nineteenth century and an evolving set of social-economy arguments were advanced by John Ruskin, Thomas Carlyle, William Morris, the Arts and Crafts movement, Oscar Wilde, Ebenezer Howard, Edward Carpenter, and others. Ruskin's praise of the Gothic inspired generations of reformers. In

pointing to the moral-economy relevance of the guilds, he argued
passionately against the perversity of mercantile values because 'wealth
was life', not dead, barren money.

> A nation cannot last as a money-making mob: it cannot with
> impunity, it cannot with existence, go on despising literature,
> despising art, despising science, despising nature, despising com-
> passion and concentrating its soul on Pence.

From 1910, Chesterton and Tawney sought to develop these early
moral-economy ideas further, and drew somewhat separate but complementary lessons from the guilds for rethinking the relationship
between land, labour and capital.

Tawney cautioned against any romantic views. He pointed out that
guilds had been developed for urban workers and thus in the Middle
Ages provided services at most for one in ten of the population.
However, now, with the transition of Britain from a rural to an urban
society, a modern system of guilds might be the co-ordinated framework needed to tackle endemic social inequality, unemployment,
overcrowded housing and pollution.

The guilds are the vernacular and oldest form of business. As associations of urban craftsmen, they have operated in one form or another
in most pre-industrial civilizations. Their power and influence has
varied according to the powers of ruling oligarchies and the relative
freedom artisans could secure. In Ancient Rome, this was limited, and
craftsmen were allowed only limited powers to form burial societies,
under what were known as *collegia*. In Ancient India the *shreni* were
artisanal associations formed by dancers and mask carvers which
thrived in the Gupta period from 300 to 600 AD. In early Islamic
civilization the *warraqeen* operated as guilds for those involved with
paper-making, translation of texts, recorders of knowledge and book-
selling. Bodies similar to guilds provided support for craftsmen in
Ancient China, Persia and among the Yoruba in West Africa.

The Roman *collegia* were revived in the Middle Ages in different
regions of Europe. Indeed, the development of such early Friendly
Societies and fuller fledged guilds was fundamental to the revival of

towns and the development of trade. Medieval towns expanded primarily from markets sanctioned by feudal lords. The charter for a town allowed for self-management. To achieve this, a commutation of feudal duties had to be negotiated by the craftsmen in exchange for what became ongoing tax payments. In many areas of Europe, the achievement of this relative autonomy involved a struggle over decades and sometimes centuries. Artisans in Cambrai in Flanders fought from 907 to 1076 to secure their town charter. In 1107, the charter was repealed; it was then regained in 1127, again in 1138 and finally secured in 1180.

Just as feudal lords pledged their loyalty to each other, guild members in a town pledged an oath of fealty, agreeing in doing so to provide each other with social, economic and military mutual aid. Like all feudal organizations, status was based on an institutional hierarchy, and guilds were stratified in this way. There were vast differences among guilds in Europe, but in significant towns a division over time developed between major guilds and minor guilds. In the early Middle Ages there was a guild for each craft and a guild of guilds to co-ordinate and regulate the trade in the town. The early guilds involved a number of master craftsmen who together governed their specific guild but also appointed a guild official both to supervise and regulate the trade and to act as their representative in the guild of guilds. Through their respective trade officials in the Guildhall, co-ordinated efforts handled both the importing of food and raw materials into the town and the exporting of goods to other towns and to further away markets.

Each master was a freeman in the town or city, and this gave them the right to own or lease a shop (for both the production and the sale of goods) and to take in apprentices. However, unlike a caste system, masters were not allowed to give apprenticeships to their own children. Women members of guilds were rare (apart from in some areas of the clothing trades). Town freedom was linked to shop ownership, and a master could only own one shop. This restriction ensured that property acquisition was restrained and that micro-businesses involving under five people were the norm in medieval towns. The training period for apprentices varied but was of the order of seven years to learn the mysteries (the arts) of the trade and to produce a masterpiece.

Maintaining the quality of their goods was critical for the reputation both of the guild and of the town. The guild officials supervised the marketplace, fixed a just price for goods and sought to maintain a uniform, high standard through trademarks. All goods in the town had to be sold in the marketplace, and pre-emptive purchases and sales outside the defined marketplace were illegal. Food purchased for the townspeople was regulated to ensure that every household was ensured enough flour and salt for breadmaking. Guilds planned and managed the local town economy, but they were not the same as the political authority of the town.

The guild also regulated the working week and holy days (or saint days). Night work was illegal and weekend work was restricted to only a half-day on Saturday. Social services were organized to provide food and meals for the sick and to arrange funerals through the solidarity of guild members. In larger towns, almshouses, hospitals, sanitation and wells were developed by the guilds, as well as churches and chapels.

The demise of the power of the guilds occurred in several ways. Towards the end of the thirteenth century, a separation developed between what became known as major guilds and minor guilds. The major guilds were dominated by the professional classes: merchant bankers, lawyers and accountants. Revolts of the minor guilds against this loss of power to the major guilds took place at Rostock in 1313, in Zurich in 1336, in Hamburg in 1374 and in Lübeck in 1384. The king and upper nobility increasingly aligned with the major guilds to increase their control over towns and cities. From Paris in 1306 and in Cologne in 1371, this process led steadily to the royal control of many cities and towns.

There were two other causes of the decline of the guilds. The first was the introduction of Enclosures from Henry VII onwards, which increased the populations of the towns and led to a shortage of apprenticeships, an increasing number of journeymen (apprentices unable to become masters) and a rise of wage workers in a number of trades. The second was the putting-out system by merchants, who set up industries in villages with wage labour to bypass the guild regulations.

The rise of the nation state established capital cities as centres of merchant capital and forged an alliance between kings, princes and the major guilds who, in exchange for loyalty, were allowed to set and maintain their own pay and salary scales. This national alliance preserved a guild system for doctors, lawyers, accountants, surveyors, architects and bankers. For the minor guilds, under the Tudors, artisans lost this power and maximum rates of pay were set by magistrates from 1563 under the Statute of Artificers. Under 'Queen Betty's Law', the minor guilds were effectively abolished, as they lost their powers to combine and associate and these were not regained until Friendly Societies were allowed for sickness and funeral provision in the early eighteenth century, and thereafter when the anti-combination regulations were abolished in 1825. The king also took over international trade through corporations beginning with the Merchant Adventurers from 1407.

There was a vast difference between the medieval guild companies and the royal chartered corporations. The guild companies had some similarities to partnerships, but with more powers as each guild had a monopoly on their trade in each town. The word 'company', refers to the companion members of the guild from the same town. The word stems from the Latin 'con panis', meaning to take bread together (with reference to meals shared at guild meetings and at midday among masters, journeymen and apprentices).

Guild trade was based on fixed, just prices. Like any regulated system of prices, the determination was complex. However, the medieval guild regulations defined a perspective on property and trading that had a social aspect that is compelling. The guiding concept was the law against usury. This was codified by St Thomas Aquinas, based largely on Aristotle's views on money. Aristotle made a distinction between 'oikonomia', which involved the production of use values to meet the needs of households over the long term, and 'chrematistics', the manipulation of wealth and property to maximize short-term economic exchange value for the owner. Aristotelian ethics treats the latter as usury.

As Aristotle argued, money was barren and thus a consumable means of exchange that should not be manipulated in order to increase its value. Money advanced as a loan was repayable without any increase if the loan was secured. If the loan was unsecured and the investment was at risk in an enterprise, then the investor should share equally both the risks and the rewards with the business owner.

The just-price system sought to exclude usury and any additional sum not based on a work-related element. The guidance under the medieval canon law was complex, and it evolved from being strongly regulated during the time of Aquinas (1224–74) to becoming close to the market price, 'without deception', at the end of the Middle Ages under Cajetan (1469–1534). In general, and in the Aquinas view, the just price was based on three production costs: the cost of materials, the cost of labour (an assessment of time) and often an allowance for the level of skill related to the quality of the product.

The medieval system was also needs-oriented and this, additionally, related to the status of the producer. This is where the skill-related cost came into play, to ensure that the price was set to enable the producer 'to have the necessities of life for his station'. This involved a consideration and assessment of proportionality and formed the moral-economy perspective of the just-price system. As equity figured in this determination of price, 'sufficiency' was a guiding principle, as opposed to the free-market profit-driven efficiency of buying cheap and selling dear. Profit was acceptable, but only to mitigate risky ventures. Otherwise, any overcharging not related to an appraised cost was deemed to be mercenary and to constitute the deadly sin of avarice.

The guild officials sought to control key areas of abuse – having too much property (hence the restriction to one shop), buying raw materials that do not pass through the urban marketplace (the restriction against pre-emption), advancing money at interest, or allowing the trade and distribution tasks to pass to merchants. Because of the risks involved in trade between towns and cities, as the medieval economy developed, merchants established a specialist role in long-distance trade that was risky and involved legal forms of investment.

As Polanyi (a pioneer of socioeconomic theory who questioned the necessity of markets in functioning societies) observed, free-market pricing steadily undermined medieval just pricing as international trade increased. From the late fourteenth century onwards, this was conducted in England through chartered corporations based in London and Bristol with a monopoly over specific trade routes, whether this was the Wool Staple, the Merchant Adventurers, the Levant Company, and later the British East India Company and the Hudson Bay Company. The merchant houses organized the capital to finance this trade, and the growing profits from the corporations gave rise to merchant banking and international investment banking. Local banking developed separately through the goldsmiths and somewhat differently regionally during the Industrial Revolution.

The French socioeconomic historian, Fernand Braudel has argued against the perception of capitalism as a product of the Industrial Revolution and as thus competitive. This has been one form of capitalism, but the original and dominant form, according to Braudel, has been about monopoly, not competition, has exercised its power cunningly through merchant banking and has maintained its dominance since the thirteenth century with shifting government alliances internationally. Century after century, this power has grown, and the seat of power has shifted geographically from Venice and Genoa (1250–1510), to Antwerp (1500–69), to Amsterdam (1570–1733), to London (1733–1896), to New York (1897–2010).

Reviving Economic Democracy – Property and Improperty

It is the social purpose of guilds that make them relevant to the increasing interest in social enterprise today. The reconnection of productive property with social purposes is critical to this issue. But in the first instance, clearly understanding what property rights are is vital.

During the *New Age* debates, John Hobson, the liberal socioeconomic theorist of the late nineteenth century, and R. H. Tawney suggested a distinction between active property and passive property. Hobson described the latter as improperty (ie. lacking business proprietors and job owners). Tawney described a continuum forming a transition between property and improperty in this way:

i) Property in payments made for personal service.
ii) Property in personal possessions necessary for health and comfort.
iii) Property in land and tools used by their owners.
iv) Property in copyright and patent rights owned by authors or inventors.
v) Property in pure interest, including much agricultural rent.
vi) Property in profits of luck and good fortune 'quasi-rents'.
vii) Property in monopoly profits.
viii) Property in urban ground rents.
ix) Property in mineral royalties.

The first four are active property and linked to a proprietor, owner and worker. The last five are passive and linked to rentiers and distant owners. Property thus can be seen as a bundle of rights. As Tawney argued, economic democracy requires that the key ones, such as access to land and capital, must be reunited with producers. Clearly, from this list, the dependency of wage labour is apparent. Property rights are evident in the game of chess: the larger the pieces, from the pawn to the Queen, the faster and more flexibly the chess piece can move. The moves of each piece reflect the relative property share of each piece. Careful positioning spatially impedes and imprisons the opponent's pieces. Economic inequality in property, analogously, undermines freedom. Hence Plato's observation about proportionality; and how an income differential of more than five to one will destroy citizenship in a republic.

Tawney showed that to talk about rights without reference to bundles of property rights is meaningless and reflects of a lack of theoretical understanding and social economic analysis. Against a restricted focus on welfare economics and income redistribution, he argued for the need to focus less on poverty, and more on the underlying problem of wage slavery. To secure economic democracy and social justice requires access to productive property. He described British blindness and anti-intellectualism this way:

Englishmen are incurious to theory, take fundamentals for granted and are more interested in the state of the roads than in their place on the map.

For Tawney, the guiding principle of the medieval guild law is relevant, as it is centred upon the protection of active productive property. As summarized by St Antonio: 'Riches exist for man, not man for riches.' In the Middle Ages, there were two opportunities available, by securing productive property, to gain relative freedom and self-management: 1. to escape feudal dues and become a yeoman farmer and 2. to become a guild member and gain the freedom of the city. In advising Henry VII against enclosing land, Bacon counselled: 'Wealth is like muck. It is not good but if it be spread.'

Adam Smith and John Stuart Mill took a dim view of unearned income, and Mill sought ways to eliminate it. Smith championed the innovative mechanics of the Industrial Revolution. Mill went further and argued for the nationalization of land as a means to eradicate feudalism fully and to develop producer co-operatives to democratize business:

> The social problem of the future, we consider to be, how to unite the greatest individual liberty of action, with a common ownership in the raw material of the globe, and an equal participation of all in the benefits of combined labour.

To pursue this vision, Mill actively supported the passage of the Industrial and Provident Societies Act of 1848 to provide a legal framework for the development of worker ownership of industry and consumer co-operatives. Similar mutual legislation had earlier been passed in France. The playing field, though, was not level. John Stuart Mill had hoped that the new legislation would assist in the development of producer co-operatives, but lack of access to equity capital became an increasingly obvious constraint from the 1870s onwards.

Henry George was inspired by Mill's call for the nationalization of land to overcome the rack-renting of small businesses and tenant farmers. To achieve this, George proposed a single tax on land values. He also stressed that access to financial capital was as essential as access to land to liberate small business and to advance a co-operative economy:

> Abolish the monopoly that forbids men to employ themselves and capital could not oppress labour … remove the cause of that injustice which deprives the labourer of the capital his toil creates and the sharp distinction between capitalist and labourer would, in fact, cease to exist.

George was active in the Knights of Labor in the US, which was more of a broad-based social movement than a trade union. Founded in 1869, the Knights sought to revive aspects of the guilds by recruiting the broadest range of workers and small businesses into membership, including: homeworkers, craftsmen, industrial workers, miners, farmers and shopkeepers. They recruited workers in a decentralized way and from many diverse ethnic groups. The Knights had recruited over 700,000 members by the 1880s, and they organized workers and farmers across Canada as well. The only workers they excluded were rentiers, including bankers, stockbrokers and gamblers. A core focus of the Knights was on finding ways to end wage slavery by developing worker ownership and the development of producer co-operatives. The Knights also campaigned for women's suffrage, single taxes and land reform, banking and monetary reform.

Strikes in the 1880s depleted the funds and the local branches of the Knights, and they declined from 1890. Their efforts and ideas inspired Cardinal Manning in London and Cardinal Gibbons in Baltimore to develop a statement of Catholic social philosophy. This was first expressed in Pope Leo XIII's encyclical letter, *Rerum Novarum,* in 1891, which was influenced by Manning's advocacy with the Vatican. *Rerum Novarum* argued that ownership of the means of production should be spread as widely as possible among the general populace. Through the *New Age* debate and other books, G. K. Chesterton developed this vision of redistribution and, along with the Catholic Liberal MP Hilaire Belloc, they jointly argued for a decentralizing 'distributive state', in opposition to the bureaucratic risks of the welfare state advocated by H. G. Wells and Sidney Webb.

Tawney could see the merits of both arguments and with G.D.H.
Cole, he argued for a synthesis through a dynamic form of Guild
Socialism. This vision and argument was developed in the turbulent
period of industrial unrest prior to the First World War, and during
the war attracted growing support among intellectuals, trade unionists, Christian Socialists, some Liberals and many in the Independent
Labour Party. To implement the vision, in 1915 the National Guild
Leagues were set up and a popular journal, the *Guildsman*, was
launched in 1916.

Bertrand Russell, in his *Principles for Social Reconstruction* and *Roads to
Freedom*, became a strong advocate of Guild Socialism. He emphasized
the need for decentralism and complementary systems for co-
production and co-delivery that amalgamate organizationally and
democratically the interests of community, producers, consumers and
capital providers.

Cole and Tawney shared this view and argued that there were many
diverse organizational ways to reunite work with social purpose
locally and regionally. These included the development of worker
co-ops for the self-employed, guilds for the arts and cultural sector,
social investment funding from Trade Unions and the Co-operative
movement to buy out private firms, the further development of consumer co-operatives, the development of forms of municipal property
for recreation, allotments, affordable housing and social services, and
partnerships between local authorities and the Co-operative movement to provide energy and water services. In addition, at the national
level, larger industries such as railways, shipping, mining and steel
could be nationalized. This pluralist case made by Cole and Tawney
persuaded Sidney Webb to amend his previous singular focus on a
national welfare state and to draft and insert Clause IV in the Labour
Party constitution of 1918. The use of the term 'common ownership'
was inserted to allow for a diverse range of transferal of property and
ownership to achieve social justice.

There were four guiding principles underpinning the pluralist
vision of Guild Socialism: economic diversity, economic democracy,
economic wealth distribution and economic decentralization. For
Tawney and Cole, Guild Socialism was a mechanism for developing

democratic citizenship and transcending the limitations of representative democracy. Hence their emphasis on diverse local action to foster and develop both the spirit and the practice of economic democracy, the intent being to make democracy widely participative and a part of everyday life. This was the reason Mill strongly supported worker co-operatives. Gandhi made the case later very well when he argued that: 'Home rule begins with self-rule.' Democracy as verb, not merely noun.

For Tawney, economic democracy was the key. He argued that social justice was an evolving, historic struggle with three distinct stages. During the Reformation, religious freedom had been won, and then political freedom, from the English Revolution onwards. The third and crucial freedom still to be won was economic freedom. A key component in this struggle was the winning of freedom locally and the claiming of power from the nation state. Here Tawney's vision emphasized a radical devolution of power and the development of regional and local economic sovereignty for cities and towns:

> When Birmingham and Manchester and Leeds are little republics as they should be, there is no reason to anticipate that they will tremble at a whisper from Whitehall.

In the final framework for Guild Socialism, published in 1921, Cole attempted a pluralistic synthesis from the debates in *The New Age* and *The Guildsman*. He proposed a Guild Congress to decentralize power and to co-ordinate the efforts of diverse local and regional ventures, each seeking to meet citizen needs in a strategic range of ways. Cole advanced a theory of civic co-sovereignty, with the Guild Congress being a 'functional democracy' and acting as a national and regional counterweight to Parliament.

Within the Congress there were four broad types of guild groups: producer guilds, consumer councils and co-operatives, civic services (municipal) and citizens' organizations (voluntary sector). The Guild Congress, locally and regionally, was designed to complement the local-authority political system but woulsd differ in that it would be economically functional and extend beyond public services to bring together and involve the small-business and voluntary sectors. For example, Cole and other Guild Socialists developed plans for an Agricultural Guild for farmers and farm labourers. The distributive ideas informed the Land Settlement (Facilities) Act of 1919, which supported in the twenties an unprecedented development of small-holdings and the resettlement of rural areas.

Trade union interest in Guild Socialism was strong in the railway, construction and mining industries and, additionally, in the public sector among postal workers. From 1918 Guilds were established in the arts, clothing, furnishing, construction and farming sectors. Like farming, the construction sector is characterized by broad-scale self-employment. The largest National Guilds project was in the building industry. The co-ordinated programme was ambitious and involved a public procurement partnership with local authorities to build council housing.

In 1921 a hundred local building guilds were established and consolidated under the National Building Guilds. Finance was arranged with the Co-operative Bank and the Co-operative Wholesale Society. Housing constructed was paid for on a cost-of-production basis and the system worked well for eighteen months. However, the economic slump in 1923 and a reduction of subsidies from government for the housing built forced the prices below cost, and working capital diminished rapidly. At the end of 1923 credit facilities were exhausted and the National Building Guilds were forced to wind up. After the General Strike in 1926, interest in Guild Socialism and economic democracy waned.

Lessons from Guild Socialism and a Green New Deal

Guild Socialism inspired and was successful in the development of local authority services, with leaders such as George Lansbury in London. Municipal housing developed from the twenties as did social services, libraries, adult education, allotments and regional electricity boards. The Co-operative Women's Guild and many suffragettes advanced many guild ideas from 1912. In 1929 Spedan Lewis, the son of the founder, sold the family firm and worked with managers to convert the John Lewis Partnership into a Trusteeship company along the lines of three Guild Socialist themes: gain sharing, knowledge sharing and power sharing.

Until the thirties there was some hope that Labour Party ideas for nationalized industries would be developed on the basis of workers' control. The mineworkers were advised and supported by Cole but, after seven years of discussion with government, their plan for the joint control of the coal industry was rejected in 1926. In 1935 the nationalization plans developed by the Labour Party and the TUC dropped industrial democracy ideas, and the public corporations established from 1945 were not based on co-determination or co-partnership between management and labour. They were centralized, top-down and collectivist.

The Knights of Labor and the Guild Socialists were pathfinders of economic democracy. There is a growing interest today in associative democracy, first advocated by Alexis de Tocqueville in the mid-nineteenth century. John Stuart Mill advanced a similar concept of 'mutual liberty'. The balanced operational themes of mutual liberty are self-help and mutual aid. Mutual liberty was in essence the radical synthesis that R.H. Tawney and G.D.H Cole advocated. They both gave the concept a strong foundation by linking it to economic democracy, with a goal of overcoming the dependency of wage labour by ending the enclosure of land and capital.

Time is ripe for a resurgence of economic democracy. Responding to climate change requires a revival of regional economic self-reliance. The projected rise in unemployment to over 3 million in 2010−11 and the cutbacks in public services on the one hand point to an economic slump for many years ahead. To counter this, the need to retro-fit British housing stock to cut carbon, the need to develop sources of renewable energy, the need to redevelop local agriculture and sources of public transport all highlight the need to connect social investment capital in co-production ways that move us away from a mercantilist dependency on oligopolistic supply chains to regionalized short circuits that are democratically controlled. Jeff Gates outlines a broad range of modern job-ownership solutions that can be implemented to rescue 'Main Street from Wall Street' by creating an 'up-close' shared capitalism.

Since 1990 the number of social and ecological finance organizations (including social banks, credit unions, community-development loan funds and micro lenders) has grown across Europe and North America. Their assistance is vital to implementing an economic democracy agenda. Together with organizations in developing countries, they have assets of over €150 billion. In Europe, Triodos Bank, Ecology Building Society and Charity Bank are members of the International Association of Investors in the Social Economy. At the G20 summit in Pittsburgh in September 2009, a 12-point programme to reform the world financial system was advocated by the Global Coalition for Community Reinvestment – with support from groups in 79 countries. There is emerging interest in a Fair Trade Banking movement.

In the past six months there has been a growing number of suggestions for breaking up and de-merging the bailed-out banks, and to re-focus some of them on providing utility banking services. This is not sufficient. A key need is for regional and local development banking, as Cole argued in 1920. Social finance organizations over the past 20 years have developed sophisticated methods for local and regional investment. With some creative thinking, the Guild Socialist ideas could be revived and taxpayer funds in our nationalized banks could be redirected from the speculative global economy towards meeting the sustainable financing needs of the local and the regional. The Green New Deal arguments advanced by the new economics foundation could well be linked with a Guild Socialist strategy and the four Ds: democratize, decentralize, diversify and distribute.

Kieron-Rhys Johnson

ME AND MY ROSARY

James Parker

OCTOBER 2007: I'M 39 AND A HALF. THE COLOURS OF autumn are breaking like beacon-fires from tree-top to tree-top, reds and yellows in subtle or ribald shades crackling down from Vermont and Maine, through New Hampshire and into Massachusetts, where I live: Boston, to be precise. Nature's furnace burns, the elements rejoice, the air is pungent with acceleration and change, but I – apparently – am stuck. That is, I am stuck in myself. And all is not well with myself, or my Self, as I have come to view it. Suspended between anxiety and depression, between the fizz and the slump, oppressed by a sense of its own contingency but secretly suspecting itself to be at the centre of the Universe, my Self is in fact metaphysically diseased.

I carry on, of course – writing my column for the *Boston Globe* ('About the karaoke machine, that most prophetic of postmodern leisure devices, almost any number of intelligent-sounding things can be said ...'), reading aloud to the boy, embracing the wife – but break-down beckons. The season confers its auguries: a cold and merciless sky; dry leaves scurrying towards me, heaping themselves at my feet in what seems a sinister manner. Lacking the constitution for alcoholism, I nonetheless deliver myself desperately to evenings of whiskey-tippling. Now and again, in the company of dear friends, I feel like screaming. What would happen if I did?

It is at this moment, in the exact state of moral debility so derided by the hearty and life-embracing atheist, that I reach for the rosary.

How come? you ask. Why don't I just get myself on the Zoloft, like a sensible fellow? *Because.* Because I have a religious disposition, and the residue at least of a Catholic education, and being able – or so I feel – to trace a zig-zag line from my own collapse to the Fall of Man, I'm buggered if I'm going to start taking pills for it.

Still – the *rosary*? That clutter of muttering beads, Catholic claptrap clusterfuck, scowling recourse of old women in black mantillas? Dude. Why not just drink a bottle of frankincense and get it over with ... But you must understand that I came at the thing quite irreligiously at first, as your typical postmodern pagan, with thoughts of 'worry beads' and 'aids to meditation', like maybe this could be my new *practice*, you know? For chilling out the monkey-mind etc. I'd already tried the Deep Breathing, and the Counting To Four. Why not this?

In such a mood I purchased Garry Wills' *The Rosary*, an attractive and limpidly written little handbook with plates by Tintoretto and many cheering references to G. K. Chesterton. A nice book. A book I could deal with. John Paul II himself, as quoted by Wills, seemed to be giving me a New Age-flavoured thumbs-up: 'The West is now experiencing a renewed demand for meditation,' wrote the Pope in 2002, in an Apostolic Letter, 'which at times leads to a keen interest in aspects of other religions ... Much in vogue among these approaches are methods aimed at attaining a high level of spiritual concentration by using techniques of a psychological, repetitive, and symbolic character. The rosary is situated within this broad gamut of religious phenomena.' Techniques of a symbolic character. In vogue. Spiritual concentration. I could dig it.

Meanwhile, I didn't own a rosary. Where to obtain one? I asked at my local tobacconist's, fantasizing that somewhere in his pile of junk gifts and smut he might have a string of beads – but no. I went online, found a Catholic superstore with an Irish name, in a windswept part of the city. I wasn't going *there*. Then it came to me: the *botanica*. The sorcery-darkened little nook where they sell Santería knick-knacks – enchanted candles and icons and so on. I went in and spoke a bit of Spanish, and was handed my first rosary.

Guided by Wills, I commenced to mumble my way around it, fingers on the wooden beads – ten Hail Marys, a Glory Be, an Our Father, another ten Hail Marys ... Beautiful rhythms, particularly the Hail Mary – the even tread of its stresses, the inhalatory pauses. I didn't feel better, but at least I had these beautiful rhythms. Also, some sort of convergence of psychic materials seemed to be going on. In the New Year I got a New Job at the *Boston Phoenix*, as a staff writer, and my first feature was about the New Atheists, who were all the rage back then. I read Dawkins, and I read Hitchens. I read Harris. I read Dennett. What the fuck? Okay, so God's in His grave, fine, and all the saints are loonies, and Man has just fluked his way up the great Chain of Being – but then how are you supposed to get out of bed in the morning? Repelled, I began to attend Mass. Furtive and unshaven in the back row, with ears heretically pricked: that bit sounded alright, but I didn't like *that* bit ... And who were all these people? 'Hang in there,' said the priest one Sunday morning, watching me stagger out into the daylight.

When I was 24, in London, severely addled from a surfeit of raving and very low indeed, I had the notion that only something simple and violent and shuddering could cure me. A sudden access of strength from somewhere. A shock – not an electric shock but ... I could feel this deficit of energy, a slowdown or blackening of the circuits up in the brain there, as I meandered along Regent's Canal. Time wouldn't fix this, I thought: the remedy would have to be instantaneous, drastic, flooding the skull with light. Now in the Mass, 16 years later, I heard 'Lord, I am not worthy to receive you, but only say the word and I shall be healed ...' and was immediately in tears. *Only say the word.* A line from one of the New Testament's hard men, the centurion in the Gospel of Matthew. *Only say the word.*

I was reading the Bible, too. Mark's Gospel, mainly – a short book but an effective one. (You might say.) To be briskly and exactly acquainted with your own modernity, sit yourself down and read *The Gospel According to Mark*. And not in one of the reader-friendly editions, either. Find some mad old bulky Bible, King James Version, piously unexplored by its owners, and crack it open at the second book of the New Testament. And in the strength of the ensuing symptoms – the dim firings of indignation, the affronted reasonableness, the sense that some obscure but monstrous offence against good taste is being perpetrated – you will be able to measure your personal neurological distance from the origins of ... well, *what*? The origins of what?

Western civilization? The thing about Mark is how UN-civilized it feels, beginning with the backlit figure of the nutter John the Baptist as he comes roaring out of the desert, last of the Old Testament voices. *And John was clothed with camel's hair, and with a girdle of a skin about his loins; and he did eat locusts and wild honey; and preached, saying, 'There cometh one mightier than I after me, the latchet of whose shoes I am not worthy to stoop down and unloose...'* No nativity in Mark, no three wise men, just John in his wild-beast underwear – John, this sandpaper presence, a man before whom complacency is impossible. Five lines later, Heaven crashes in: with a gasp the surface of the river Jordan is broken and Jesus, newly baptised by John, hears his Father's voice like a pounding of wings.

And the miracles, those traditional obstructions to rationality, those deal breakers? Quite quickly I found I had no problem at all with them. The direct, unmagical, bouncer-ish manner, for example, in which Jesus ejected demons from the bodies of the possessed – alright, sunshine, out you go – and the additional rock-star detail that *all the demons knew his name*, were persuasive to me. The blind man, half-healed by the spit on Jesus's fingers, who says, 'I see men as trees walking,' before Jesus touches him again to complete the operation; the eerie reality of that, of the thin, stalking figures seen through blurred eyes ... Or was it an analogy, a description of some transitory state of merely vegetal awareness, on the way to seeing 'every man clearly'... Fact or metaphor? Flesh or spirit? Could it possibly be both? The Magi, that curious trio, make their offerings at the cradle-side of Christ. Then they go home. The road out, however, is different from the road in – it has to be. Herod is blustering in his tower, and must be avoided. *They departed into their own country another way ...* What immensities of transformation I felt in that short line. My critical faculties fell down before this stuff – fell, actually, to their knees.

(Elsewhere, they haughtily stood up again. 'Eternal life is like a big cake,' explained a priest at Mass one morning, to the group of children who had gathered near the altar to hear his sermon. 'If you don't eat all of it here on earth, if you just have a little slice, you can have the rest in Heaven.' I stayed away for weeks after that – until the realization that the church was still there, doors open, Sunday after imperturbable

Sunday, outlasting my peevishness as it appeared to outlast everything else, sent me gratefully back.)

My rosary sessions (daily-ish, with lapses) grew more interesting. Now, instead of just rattling through the beads-and-verbals, I was beginning to contemplate – or to attempt to contemplate – the sequence of 'mysteries' that have been traditionally attached to them. Gospel scenes, one for each decade of Hail Marys, upon which the rosary-sayer (the rosarifier? the rosarian?) trains his or her inner eye while repeating the prayer. Sensations of imaginative impotence overwhelmed me at first. I mean, how do you contemplate the Annunciation, the angelic irruption into the virgin's chamber and the pointing Golden Finger: 'It's YOU!'? But then next in the sequence is the Visitation: the pregnant Mary going visit her cousin Elizabeth, also pregnant, in the hill country. As Mary enters the house and offers a greeting, Elizabeth feels her baby (who happens to be John the Baptist) 'leap in her womb'. This I could focus on – motherhood, and things foreknown, and the primal thrust of joy *in utero* … A proper mystery.

So – years have passed, getting out of bed, into bed, round and round the circle of beads. And am I better, all fixed up? Yes and of course no. But I have a new way of going about things. A highly imperfect Christian, vain, lecherous and piggish, I find that the extra-worldly light by which I see my vanity and lechery and piggishness consoles me. Since my use or misuse of the rosary in a way preceded my religion, what I have to say about it will necessarily be somewhat half-baked. Somewhat? Let's make that *totally* half-baked. Hauled from the oven with barely a crust of completion on it. Still, if I'd let half-bakedness stop me I wouldn't be the award-winning cultural commentator and *illuminatus* I am today. So here goes.

...NATURE HATH IN STORE FOWL, VENISON, AND FISH, AND THE FRUITFULL'ST SOIL, WITHOUT YOUR TOIL, THREE HARVESTS MORE, ALL GREATER THAN YOUR WISH.

Sarah A. King

ARCADIA AND ALBION

John Nicholson

PART ONE

'A rose in Harlem'

THE EXHORTATION 'BACK TO THE LAND!' CONTAINS A RANGE of assumptions.

Obviously a change of behaviour is urgent, with or without the emphasis. We are encouraged to return, or revert, to a norm, our natural state. A restoration is to be effected. Implicit is our impending doom if we hesitate, for the course we are on is plainly fatal. We must repent, and that quickly, of the error of our ways. Nothing else will do. 'The land is the appointed remedy for whatever is false and fantastic in our culture.'

The call is not to go back to Nature but to the land. A moment's thought should tell you the two are not the same, although they are often confused. More about this momentarily. Before that it is necessary to point out a paradox. What are we to do when we get to the land? For there are contradictory impulses. On the one hand is a desire to somehow 'prove' oneself by submerging oneself in the processes of 'honest toil'. On the other hand the hope is to avoid all strenuous effort and go with the flow. The second version of harmony needs Nature more than the first. After all, there is an abundance of honest toil in cities.

Which reminds us of the nature of work in the countryside: the land. In pastoral images of peasants, the inevitable servitude of labouring to the demands of the seasons is ignored. There is little harmony in the driven, back-breaking work of the village labourer. Indeed, is this the attraction? During the Russian Revolution the simple test was 'Show your hands'. Those clearly not worn condemned you as an enemy of 'the people'. How marvellous for those students who, in the great wave of navrodniks which had poured into the countryside to show solidarity with the newly emancipated serfs, to now be able to display calloused paws and prove they did not belong to the intelligentsia. We do not have records of the response to the benevolent swamping of the rural labour market, but it is not unreasonable to think these recipients were not best pleased by the wave of wage-stealers, let alone those stupid enough to work for nothing but the moral benefits.

For we reach another paradox. Those who depended on this work were grateful for any imagination which could invent ways to lighten their load. Not for them the superiority of moral endeavour. They were going in the diametrically opposite direction. A similar phenomenon happened in the sixties when American hippies preached anti-materialism to the poor and dispossessed, who were only too eager to loot.

Any labour-saving device was welcome. The pastoral plough, pulled by beasts of burden, including men, gave way to machines powered artificially. The 'combine harvester' also replaced the work of many. That this 'freedom' was bought at a price – job losses – was not over-looked.

Before falling into the mistaken view of the countryside as pastoral, let us remember that, long before the Agricultural Revolution, labourers did not only rely on the sweat of their brow. A visit to any museum of rural life quickly dispels this notion. To be confronted by a wagon is to marvel not only at the expertise which made it, but more, by the scale of the undertaking. Surely it was made for giants?

This impression is reinforced as you look at the other exhibits. No primitive technology here, nor lack of skill. But the diversity extends in other directions. There were so many specialized skills: hedgers and ditchers, wall and fence builders, animal handlers who knew peculiar affinities (the best-known of which were horse-whisperers). Many more examples can be cited.

Nor was the countryside ignorant of machinery and metal. Two of its mainstays, the windmill and water mill, together with the black-smith's forge, relied upon mechanical metallic gadgets. It is no coinci-dence that 'mill' – as in Blake's 'Jerusalem' – was the first term for a 'manufactory'. Smiths were much more than the makers of artificial metal 'shoes' for horses. Indeed the decorative use in pubs of horse-shoes and brasses, of bits and apparatus, ought to produce the opposite effect to sentimental nostalgia for a lost innocence. Could there be a better symbol of the marriage between the natural, animal, primitive countryside and the practical, ruthless, iron world of technology than a horse shoe?

A new haymaking device was not merely an example of Improve-ment but, by accumulation, a proof of Progress. Man's mind was con-quering matter, dissolving time and space and unlocking (mechanical metaphor!) the secrets of the universe. By such tokens did propaganda permeate the consciousness. In rhetorical terms, the message turned up in all newspapers and magazines. A typical example comes from an American piece, 'The Moral Influence of Steam', which exalted:

> [steam] is now universally employed as the great motive agent in machinery, triumphing over time and space, outstripping the winds in speed, annihilating every obstacle by sea or land, and almost defying the organic influences which regulate the surface of our globe. Nor is it only over matter that it exercises this con-trol; for so wonderfully does it relieve the necessity of physical exertion, that it seems destined, in its future action and develop-ments, to disturb the moral economy of the world, by opposing that great law of the universe, which makes labour the portion of man, and condemns him to earn his bread by the sweat of his brow.[1]

Again it depends on your approach. What for some is the tyranny of routine can, for others, be the freedom of not having to think for one-self. Go to the land to get away from machinery, both physical and abstract? Drudgery, the daily grind, is not limited to the office. They await you in the countryside too.

The impulse was the same, to release power, energy, labour – call it what you will. A device could do the work of ten, of twenty, a hundred. What became of the unwanted ninety-nine, or how mind-numbing was the supervisory role of the one, was irrelevant. Saving labour also saved wages. Goods/food gushed off the assembly line, so profits went through the roof. Isn't this what everybody wants? The price of goods/food comes down, to be within reach of the many; the benefits are shared and spread through society. Here was Progress indeed.

According to this view, nothing is intrinsically wrong with the wish to save labour by substituting machines. Indeed machines are limited only in their scope and evoke the powers present in their situation. A healthier environment (e.g. the New World) would produce more efficiency and productivity (see below).

All this Improvement would create a newly freed group which could devote their time and lives to higher pursuits, a pastoral in which all work is done by robots. 'The head saves the hands. It invents machines, which, doing the work of many hands, will at last set free a large portion of leisure time from slavery to the elements. The brute forces of nature lie waiting man's command, and ready to serve him.'[2]

The logical extension of this – genetically engineered crops to ensure cheap, plentiful food – is an issue that recently produced alarm and put the spotlight on a process which, for two centuries, has been welcomed with open arms.

Ironically, we have reached the dream of the pastoral through the use of machinery. I promised to expand on the other urge to return to the land, not to labour but to relax, to shed the cares of civilization in preference of higher pursuits, the delights of the spirit. (We see a quest unites both impulses.)

★

PART TWO

And is there money still for tea?

THE DESIRED LIFESTYLE HAS LONG BEEN KNOWN AS pastoral. The genre has two starting points, the Bible, which like other holy books places paradise in a garden; and a literary form which dates back to the Romans. There is a bunch of pastoralists, such as Hesiod, but Virgil is customarily taken as the spokesman. Virgil itemizes the solid satisfactions of the pastoral retreat: 'peace, leisure and economic sufficiency'. He even named it: Arcadia.

He wrote a series of laments for one pleasant world being replaced by an inferior order. There was a shepherd, lounging, tootling on his flute. His neighbour passes by, evicted. The authorities were keeping a promise to veterans to rehouse them (shades of Homes For Heroes). The innocent small farmer had been chucked out and was on his way into exile. He chats to the flute-tootler. The best outcome they can hope for is that the tootler invites him to have a bed for his last night, and a supper, before he goes on his way.

The trope starts here.

'Beneath the apple bough' – Traditional

'A glass of wine and thou' – Omar Khayyam

'Come live with me and be my love' – Chris Marlowe

'Sod that' – Walt Raleigh

Despite Raleigh's bucket of cold water, dreams of an easy life in a rustic setting are ageless. Why? It is more difficult to understand why so many seek to achieve an Arcadian community. Traces remain in Britain in marks on the ground, the borders of plots, or ghost towns across the American West. What is remarkable about these myriad attempts is the similarity of their failure. How is it we never learn?

At one with Nature, the tootler hears the echo of his tunes. Nature is in dialogue with him. Let us examine this trope. For a start, there is guile in as much as a contrivance exists. The flute is a manmade arte-fact, a device for controlling sounds and forming them into harmony.

As with the rural reliance upon labour-saving devices so, we find artifice in Arcadia. Deep in the Essex countryside, off a side-road, is a turning into an open gate. No sign tells you anything. A rough track leads nearly a mile through fields until you reach a farm. Continue through its rutted yard, passing pens of animals and out the other side, where you find a pathway. A few yards along, the trees part to reveal a small two-storey cottage. Surrounding it is a paradise. Cultivated. The path wanders further off to go under a railway arch, a survival of a branch line to nowhere. Infinity beckons.

Here was held Camp Idle, to develop the notion that a concentra-tion camp was a misconstrued utopia. Backs to the land! Everybody do a day's honest work! Those taking the retreat/course were reminded of how an ideal can turn into its opposite. 'Working on a chain gang...'

The place itself presented a perfect emblem of Arcadia. Through the knee-high grass wove wide pathways to clearings where the obligatory tootler could lounge. To create these paths, machines and tools were used, bringing not just order but also making a contrast with the natu-ral grasses. To keep this paradise so perfect required endless work.

Constantly, the risk on which Arcadia rests was brought home. For paradise portrayed as a garden reminds us how a garden is an artificial construction, man-made. Paradise as a garden is the opposite of wilderness. It is Nature fashioned by Man, with mechanical aids. A garden is the opposite of Nature, which grows relentlessly and inex-orably. In four years an untamed garden reverts to a jungle, pure growth without intervention. The land triumphs over Arcadia.

Arcadia, the garden, wages war on two fronts. Not only against the city – a place of an alien order (simultaneously of disorder, chaos and disharmony) but also to keep at bay an equally terrible disaster, the wilderness. What is this force but the true face of Nature, the wild? Instead of gentle fecundity comes whirling devastation – weeds and murderous creatures. Both Arcadia's enemies are predatory, merciless.

By presenting Arcadia's riddle in this way we see the similarity between its threats, and much further. Beyond lies the real enemy,

Death. A place where Time stands still is a place where Death is vanquished. Even in the pastoral scenes depicted by Nicolas Poussin, Death still exists: the inscription on the tomb reads, *'Et in Arcadia ego.'*

Arcadia is best seen as a landscape of the psyche, an abstraction where the inhabitants enjoy insulation from disturbance, and incredible abundance. Escape to simplicity? As we have seen, real rural life is far from simple. Arcadia as the antidote for the ills of civilization? Leave behind the world identified with 'art':

> using this word in its broadest sense to mean the disciplined habits of mind or arts developed by organized communities. In other words, this impulse gives rise to symbolic motion away from the centres of civilization toward their opposite, Nature, away from sophistication toward simplicity, or, to introduce the cardinal metaphor of the literary mode, away from the city toward the country.[3]

No work and free food. That is what paradise meant in the folk culture of the Middle Ages. Bruegel painted this idyll as *The Land of Cokaygne*, where three figures lie in the countryside sleeping – or in a trance? Has a spell been cast over the land? Time is frozen. The food doesn't rot. Birds and other animals don't behave naturally and steal it. In the distance a ship has sails puffed by wind. Can movement exist when Time stands still?

Exactly the same dream inspired America's hoboes. Riding for free on freight trains, they sang of their version of Arcady, the 'Big Rock Candy Mountain':

> And the bulldogs all have rubber teeth
> And the hens lay soft-boiled eggs.

No authorities and food for free.

> There's a lake of stew, and of whiskey too,
> You can paddle all around it in a big canoe.

St Francis of Assisi talked to God's creatures, and his message was to share the simple life; he was wed to Lady Poverty. His followers, the Lesser Brothers and Poor Clares, preached this creed and set a bomb under the Church by reverting to primitive Christianity. We may gauge his appeal from his works *Little Flowers* and *Canticle of the Sun*.

Although Christianity may have weakened its hold, the appeal of a non-religious contemplative life continued in various guises. In *Candide* the hero settles for cultivating his garden and avoiding the buffeting of the world and Fate. In the mid-Victorian period, poets praised scholar-gypsies. Robinson Crusoe involuntarily went back to the land, having been shipwrecked and forced to fend for himself on a 'desert' island. Luck brought him company of a sort, rather like the presence of a pet. A native (all savages were cannibals) received lessons in civilized behaviour in return for becoming Crusoe's servant. The model would be applied across the world as the English civilized millions, freeing them from servitude to the land.

Arcadia peeps out from a deluge of Romantic paintings. As well as the rustic landscapes of Constable, we glimpse the governed country-side behind the squirearchy as the idle rich rearranged Nature to produce a sublime effect instead of harvesting food. Goldsmith's deserted village was submerged under spreading parkland. Arcadian harmony fell prey to the English nobility, keen to display its servile acreage in their portraits. Physically and socially isolated in their mansions, the idle rich were free to pursue pure, simple thoughts and pleasures.

In the grounds of the royal retreat, Marie Antoinette and her courtiers played at being milkmaids and had a toy dairy built for their games. Model Arcadians. Unfortunately for her, the real-life milk-maids failed to see the joke.

Poets did more than worship at the new altar of Nature, they sought to live the Arcadian life. One after another – Southey, Priestley, Coleridge – they were desperate to get to the pure new world to join a society living in Rousseauesque harmony until they would be 'cooked by a Cherokee, or oysterised by a tiger'. Wild beasts and cannibals were plainly the natural order.

For Coleridge, St Francis was a mentor:

If there be any whom I deem worthy of remembrance – I am
their Brother. I even call my Cat Sister in the Fraternity of universal Nature. Owls I respect & Jack Asses I love; for Alderman &
Hogs, Bishops & Royston Crows, I have not particular partiality;
they are my Cousins however, at least by Courtesy. But Kings,
Wolves, Tygers, Generals, Ministers, & Hyenas, I renounce them
all … May the Almighty Pantisocratizer of Souls pantisocratize
the Earth, and bless you and S.T. Coleridge.[4]

Sadly, the scheme flopped, but not the hope.

For Wordsworth, Arcadia was not limited to America or the Lake
District.

> Behold her, single in the field,
> Yon solitary Highland Lass!

There is a poignancy behind the lines. Why was she working alone?

> Will no one tell me what she sings?

Wordsworth speculates that her subjects may be 'Old, unhappy, far-off
things'. 'The Solitary Reaper' dates from 1805. Only a few years earlier
the clearances of the Highlands drove thousands off the land into exile.
Crofters and weavers starved or fled, many of them to America. That is
why the land was deserted.

The poet invites his readers to watch her, in their imagination and
through his eyes. He is also single, a passer-by. But, in the abstract,
hundreds, thousands, stand on the edge of the field staring. Yet these
viewers were not content simply to use their minds. Viewing plat-
forms would be set up, metaphorically, to accommodate the jostling
hordes. So we should turn the camera the other way to look from the
vantage point of the lass back to the tumult of her audience, brought
there by the poet.

Wordsworth so celebrated the Lake District as a rural oasis that, in
his lifetime, he saw he had created a monster which destroyed the idyll.
Trippers came in multitudes to enjoy solitude and calm. To take the

cure for the ills of urban living and civilization, crowds flocked from all over England's cities by train. Steamboats carried hordes of tourists on the lakes, villagers became dependent on serving the outsiders and so earned easy money, beyond anything they could hope for from their traditional pursuits. The Lakeland poet had ruined his Eden.

Arcadia, like oblivion, is not to be hired.

★

PART THREE

Step in, the water's lovely

HARD WORK OR IDLE, SIMPLE OR COMPLICATED, harmonious or mechanical, civilized or primitive, Arcadia or wilderness … Confused? You will be in the next episode.

A community based on the ideal of the countryside may be communitarian, sharing property and tasks, but it cannot be Utopian in anything but spirit. Utopia is regulated by the best possible rules and runs like a smooth machine, based not on Nature but on human reason. Paradise is the opposite, with no need for rules, since it is natural. Harmony prevails.

Robert Owen invented his model society from the impulse of Improving. His model factories show he had no thought of rural bliss. New Lanark, his model town – no village for him – would regulate the relationship between the urban and its surroundings, for Nature had become a sensible add-on, performing a beneficial function. New Lanark, like its derivatives, had modern conveniences at its heart, not rustic felicity. Utopias tend to be urban. Its citizen workers might acknowledge the surrounding land in as much as it supplied necessities such as food. Unlike More's Utopia, or its predecessors the monasteries, citizens left the land to the agricultural community.

For utopian communities, as conceived by industrialists, Reason's rule-book was enough. Look at any of their visionary settlements and there is the window-dressing of Arcadia, just as there is in suburbia.

These workers do not work 'the land' but tend to their assembly lines. They may glimpse Arcadia through the factory window, or lounge round the company sports ground and bathing pool. The walk from the factory to their homes is through insistent reminders of Arcadia. Flowers and trees abound. Who tends them? The workers delegated by the community. The verges must be trim. The paradox noticed in Camp Idle: Nature should be kept in order.

In the same way, human nature must not run wild. Many of these benefactors, pious nonconformists, abhorred the pub. Even a shop. Street in Somerset, although not laid out in a design, nevertheless is dominated by, if Clark's the shoe shop founded by a Quaker family. Inhabitants of Port Sunlight are rumoured to be; not exactly slow-witted – not worldly wise. Stewartby, near Bedford, offers a meeting house, a post office/shop and a swimming pool but no pub. Would-be alcoholics must travel to the neighbouring villages. Drunk in charge of your feet. In 2009 a stroll around utopian Bournville finds plenty of picture-postcard idylls, even a Shaker cottage. The obligatory public park and lake. The peripheral roads and throughways merit foot bridges. No solitary corner shop or 7/11. There's a police station but no take-away, not even a fish and chippie or Chinese. Presumably all these deliver to the inhabitants of Bournville? They can't all exist on nut rissoles.

Something is missing, unspoken. To what extent do these model towns still work in the way they were designed? A glance at Bournville gives the game away. Surrounding the factory are vast car parks, for the visitors but also for staff. How many of the workers walk to work? Or cycle? How many of the villas have cars parked on the kerb? Obviously garages had not been invented when the estate was built.

Is Bournville a suburb, a village, an estate? It is well inside Greater Birmingham, and a suburban rail service runs to its station, a few minutes' walk away. Suburbia was created by the train, it's supreme example being Metroland. Thousands commuted away from the city and office back to their semi-Arcadia. Today's suburbia is made by the motor car. 'Estates' became ubiquitous by the sixties. People who walked regularly or cycled were no longer the norm; such practices became a lifestyle choice. A 'semi' was the ambition; avoidance of the terrace at all costs. For this is England, so snobbery and class rule. Suburbia, theoretically the escape from snobbery and class, became their greatest practitioner.

There was no 'society', which was agony for some and bliss for others. Boredom was the price willingly paid for a respite from urban tensions. One simply did what the neighbours were doing, but privately; the husband to commuted back from the city to paradise and his bird in a gilded cage. The reality, that there were different tensions waiting, was overlooked.

> The English suburban residence and the garden which is an integral part of it stand trim and lovingly cared-for in the mild sunshine. Everything is in its place. The abruptness, the barbarities of the world are far away. There is not much sound except perhaps the musical whirr and clack of a mowing-machine being pushed back and forth over a neighbouring lawn and the clink of cups and saucers and a footfall as tea is got ready indoors. There is not much movement either: a wire-haired terrier lazily trotting around the garden in a not very hopeful search for something new to smell and the pages of a newspaper being turned and refolded by some leisurely individual in a deckchair.[5]

The Englishman's longed-for state, at one with Death.

Here is a perfect example of bringing nature into urbia, suburbia. But the English have devised many more ways to remind themselves of Arcadia even when they live in the middle of cities. The most obvious sign is parks. London is famous for its public parks but is much more obsessed by its greatest retention of pastoral, its river. Claims for Old Father Thames run through our history. Without the Thames, what would London be?

London is also world-renowned for its squares. These began life the other way round, empty of foliage, but then were reconceived as a foil to the surrounding terraces. The whole Regent's Park scheme illustrates variations on the theme, especially its village/estates. 'Avenues' in urbia consist of trees lining an ordinary street, but any tiny dwelling can bring Nature indoors with a potted plant; no longer the aspidistra.

Cut flowers in a vase, if nothing more is possible. Or a pet, an animal tamed and turned into a toy. A garden of any sort satisfies more deeply than the urge for a hobby. Back gardens are echoed in the Public Open Spaces which moat tower blocks. Above all looms the Garden City. Garden Cities might have begun with generous space but soon the specifications altered. Arcadia became a matter of ratios and densities.

To combat the charges against this packaging of Arcadia, especially suburbia, the aesthetic principles behind landscape gardening were applied to planning the new estates. These theories in turn were derived from Chinese practices and related to the sciences of divination. As translated into the English ethos, they seem to sum up all we now hold dear about our surroundings and our characters:

> To plan irregularly, to disdain formality, to contrive beauties that shall be great and strike the eye, but without any order or disposition of parts as shall be commonly or easily observed, to improve a scene according to the manner suggested by itself, and without regard to symmetrical arrangement.[6]

Carried to extremes we find that the planning for Bedford Park in west London in 1882 saved the trees and fitted the houses around them.

Some accusations against suburbia are oddly reminiscent of the terrace. Monotony, sameness, lack of individuality, drabness, dullness. A repertoire of architectural and landscaping antidotes has been invented. Alleys and courts, the hallmark of slums, returned in a new costume as lanes. Mews reappeared with fresh names. Lawns became interchangeable with verges, 'drives' and 'ways' twist, curve and undulate, anything to distinguish them from a street. Indeed the new pattern was for even more intricacy. If the joke was you got lost because the roads and houses all looked alike, now there were so many picturesque features, you lost track remembering them. Still a puzzle.

The new accusation was that estates were 'a passport to Noddyland'. One expert countered, 'As for Noddyland, any small, two-storied, narrow-fronted, detached dwelling possesses something of the proportions of a dollshouse. A treeless assembly of such buildings can hardly avoid a flavour of Toytown ...'[7]

This defence cannot hide the fact that suburbia had taken on the character of a child's game which can be manipulated into countless variations like a Rubik's cube, all adding up to the same result: a non-natural Arcadia.

If utopia and suburbia betray the flight from the city, has there ever been a true return to the land? Once there was a moment to break free from all this muddle. Lo and behold, a new Eden was discovered. A second chance to escape and start afresh with none of the old fetters.

The New World was so much more. Mankind's rebirth. Queue up to offer your paeans. A new dawn? A return to Eden, cancelling the Fall? Reunited at last? What more can you ask? (Answers on a postcard please.) The New World was a second chance. Here was another Eden, demi-paradise, ready to be inhabited, 'colonized'.

The early promoters promised that, in the New World:

> ... Nature hath in store
> Fowl, venison, and fish,
> And the fruitfull'st soil,
> Without your toil,
> Three harvests more,
> All greater than your wish.[8]

Here we see the extravagant claims: more food than you could possibly need, supplied without lifting a finger. The folk paradise was reborn.

Or was it? Was the land actually an empty howling wilderness full of demons? Wild beasts and wild men – there was little difference. Cannibals and Calibans. William Burroughs warned that the evil was already in the land, before the Indians, waiting. In that case the imperative to tame and civilize was even greater.

The millennial hopes for America dwarf any rhetoric about Australia, also used as a dumping ground for English dross. Indeed the contrast was consciously made. America would redress the balance of the Old. Americans possessed more vigour and vim, were physically, morally and spiritually healthier, with a healthier social and political order. How could this brave new world not ascend? America is 'the finest example of the struggle between civilized man and barbarous uncultivated nature'.[9] The virgin landscape was a source of spiritual therapy, a divine hieroglyph. 'The continent we inhabit is to be physic and food for our mind as well as our body.'[10]

At the end of the nineteenth century a different 'ascent', Aliyah, was made by Russia's Jews – to return to their land. Thousands of them 'came out of her, my People' and many of them walked all the way back to Jerusalem, their Holy Land. For centuries they had been seen as urban dwellers, incapable of any appreciation of Nature. Even their language lacked any vocabulary for birds, compared to the Native Americans' who had hundreds of words to describe grass. Now, suddenly, they would be farmers, cultivating the desert and making it bloom. Small theoretical communities, kibbutzim, settled and began their divine task. Arcadia in the desert.

If the theory that natural surroundings contained the inherent genius to stimulate invention (useful devices) held, then the opportunities offered by the New World clearly had unique advantages. By 1850, the very backwardness of the country – 'a desert continent' – had provided the 'transition from a wild and barbarous condition to that of the most elaborate civilization'. 'The progressive impulse' had been given 'an electric charge'.[11]

Hence the notion that America would harness machinery to its superior climate, both natural and social, and thus cleanse the system of the faults inherent in the Old World. The pure apple-cheeked farm girls in American mills (the 'nuns of Lowell'[13]) were contrasted with their pathetic drabs in Europe. America was Nature unfettered.

Simultaneously, America's eastern seaboard looked as though it would soon be built over by a megalopolis, stretching from Boston in the north to Washington in the south, while the case could be made for the western seaboard going the same way.

When faced with cities containing 36.5 million people (Tokyo), how can we believe it possible for more than a handful to 'repent' and go back to the land? If they did, then they would quickly blot out the countryside, just as trippers spoiled the Lake District.

Is there a way back to the land which we dare not admit?

The obliteration of civilization in terms of razing towns and cities, the urbanscape, and turning what remains into the ultimate assertion of the earth – back to rubble, to a primeval chaos of its components – is the ultimate restoration of the land. Can there be a better symbol of this impulse than Ground Zero, the site of the collapsed Twin Towers, the centre of the world's trade?

Is this the guilty thrill we dare not acknowledge, the hubris which we know is inevitable and inherent? How many times, before and since, have we been fascinated by the image on screen? Only the visual representation can be truly evocative of the punishment we desire, the humiliation of the over-reacher, the proud and mighty humbled, the works of man as nought. This, and not any thought of alien attacks, answers an age-old memory. This too shall pass. Only Earth abides.

The jumpers preferred 'death by ground', splattering themselves on the land, to being suffocated or burned by an enemy. They denied them that victory.

Earth to earth.

> The grave's a fine and private place
> But none, I think, do there embrace.[12]

1. Charles Fraser. 'The Moral Influence of Steam', essay in Hunt's *Merchants Magazine*, 1846.
2. Theodore Parker. 'Thoughts on Labour', *The Dial* magazine, April 1841.
3. Leo Marx. *The Machine in the Garden*, 9.
4. Richard Holmes. *Coleridge: Early Visions*, 82.
5. Arthur M. Edwards. *The Design of Suburbia*, 28.
6. Ibid. 156.
7. Ibid. 254.
8. Michael Drayton. 'To the Virginian Voyage', in *Poems Lyrick and Pastoral*, 1605.
9. George Perkins Marsh. Speech, Rutland County Agricultural Society, Vermont 1847.
10. Ralph Waldo Emerson. 'The Young American' lecture, 1844.
11. *Littell's Living Age*, reprint from *The Times*, November 1850.
12. Andrew Marvell. 'To His Coy Mistress'.

A POMACEOUS PARADISE

Graham Burnett

In orchards, we and nature together have created an exuberant and a
secret landscape – a treasury of genetic diversity and a repository
of culture. They are a wise way of sharing the land –
a positive gift to those who follow.

– The Common Ground Community Orchards Handbook

Adam & Eve went scrumpin/Adam & Eve went wild/Adam & Eve were
lovers/Adam & Eve had a child/They went scrumpin in the Orchards/
Scrumpin in the Fields/Scrumpin over Hedgerows/Scrumpin Head-
over-Heels!/Scrumpin in the Garden-Shed/Scrumpin in the Kitchen/
Scrumpin in the Bedroom/Scrumpin with a Mission!/Yes! Scrumpin!
Scrumpin! Scrumpin!/Scrumpin with a Mission!

– Dennis Gould, anarchist poet and pamphleteer

THE COOL-TEMPERATE CLIMATE OF THE UNITED KINGDOM
means that our traditional orchards produce some of the best-
tasting apples in the world. Ranging from the aromatic rich
complexity of Cox's Orange Pippin to the dry yet sweet/sharp nutty
balance of Egremont Russett, these are living celebrations of local distinctiveness and symbolize deep connections with our food-growing
past. The national fruit collection at Brogdale near Faversham in Kent
includes specimens of some 2,200 apple varieties that have been grown
in this country, and lists hundreds more: Norfolk Biffen, Kentish
Fillbasket, Chelmsford Wonder, Vicar of Beighton, Merton Knave,

137

Braintree Seedling, Crawley Reinette and Beauty of Bath. These are names resonant with flavour, historical context and regional variation; place-markers on the parish maps of our collective bioregional psycho-geography. Apples that tell stories of chance meetings, cross pollinations and lucky accidents; Newton Wonder, a variety said to have once yielded 1,840 lbs of fruit from one tree, is believed to have been discovered growing out of the thatched roof of a pub in Derbyshire. Flower of Kent is thought to be the variety which grew in Isaac Newton's garden in Woolsthorpe that in 1600 fell on his head and gave him the idea of gravity. Lane's Prince Albert – 'a lovely fruit which takes the highest polish of any variety' – was so named by Henry Lane because he planted it out immediately after cheering Queen Victoria and Prince Albert through the streets of Berkhamstead in 1841 ...

Today we live in an age where we are told that we have more 'choice' than our forebears could ever have imagined. Yet supermarket demands for uniformity, the capacity to be stored and travel well, and freedom from 'blemishes' have ensured that only some five or six apple varieties can now be found stacked on their sterile strip-lit shelves. Granny Smiths and Golden Delicious, textured like cotton wool and with less flavour, are air-freighted around the planet to be sold individually packaged in malls and motorway service stations the length and breadth of the country, but what now has happened to the Puckrup Pippin, the Red-ribbed Greening, the Scarlett Pearmain, Ball's Bittersweet or Slack-ma-Girdle?

Our heritage of small orchards is being excised from the landscape. Encouraged by EU subsidy grants, some two thirds have been grubbed out over the last thirty years to make way for rape fields, golf courses, superstores and housing estates as the priorities of industrialized agriculture and land speculation override the imperatives of tradition, resilience and self-reliance. Just as our town centres have become identikit clone-zones full of Tesco Metros, Starbucks and McDonald's, so too the patchwork tapestry that once made our countryside so bio-diverse and peculiar has been reduced to little more than an impover-ished monoculture – Welcome to Business-park Britain. Joni Mitchell once told us that they paved paradise to put up a parking lot. But not only does it seem that we don't know what we've got 'til it's gone, it's

also a highly precarious strategy given the uncertainty of global financial systems and the strong possibility that the age of cheap energy
upon which our food imports depend might soon be coming to an end.
Rob Hopkins, founder of the Transition Towns movement, likens the
short-sightedness of our current situation to the baking of a cake:

> Before the oil age all the major ingredients of the cake, the flour,
> eggs, and so on, were produced locally and only the icing on the
> cake was externally sourced. Our present economy has turned
> this on its head. For the great bulk of our needs we depend on
> supply lines which reach across the world and are dependent on
> an uninterrupted flow of oil. The tanker drivers' dispute of 2000
> showed how we are just three days away from supermarket food
> shortages.

However those of us who do appreciate our home-grown apples and
recognize their importance in the jigsaw puzzle that is twenty-first-
century food security can perhaps take some heart in the realization
that it's not the first time we've been here...

Our history has always been intertwined with the fortunes of the
apple and orchard. Although there is evidence that feral apples have
been around as long as peoplekind have populated these Isles, the
origins of our cultivated varieties appear to be the wild fruits found in
the isolated Tien Shan mountains of Kazakhstan. These evolved by
selection over many centuries from *Malus sieversus* into the comparatively sweet and succulent *Malus domesticus* preferred by wild pigs,
bears, donkeys and humans. Domesticated apples then travelled west
from the fertile crescent via the Silk Road before the Romans finally
brought them to Britain some 2,000 years ago as a more palatable
alternative to our sour little native crabs. During the Dark Ages the
arts of apple growing fell into decline, kept alive in a handful of
monasteries until the arrival of the Normans in 1066. With them came
new varieties such as the Costard and Pearmain, as well as a wealth of
European grafting, pruning and cider-making techniques. Amazingly,
there is no historical evidence of cider manufacture in the UK before
this time, although to my mind it's extremely unlikely that such a

wonderful source of refreshment and intoxication could have been overlooked. Fermenting into alcohol is what apples do – unlike wine and beer, they don't even require the addition of sugars or yeasts, those that occur naturally in and on the fruit being quite sufficient to set them brewing once fallen from the tree. Birds know this: fieldfares and thrushes that have temporarily lost the power of flight due to being drunk on rotting windfalls are a common autumn orchard sight. So too have itinerant seasonal orchard workers always known the trick of crushing a rotting apple – the blacker the better – in a clenched fist in order to extract a palmful of fizzing, crystal-clear instant cider. Enough palmfuls can actually get you quite squiffy, as I've found through personal experience, although my friend Charlie Tims warns me of the small danger of a toxin called patulin. This is found on the skins of some apples that haven't properly fermented and can have some quite nasty effects. I'm unconvinced that such health and safety risks would have stopped our ancestors deducing that cider brewing would also work on a larger scale however – the human race has always been noted for its ingenuity in working out new ways to get off its face, and I doubt that the Romans and Saxon Monks (however pious their public proclamations ...) would have missed this ploy.

The near-halving of the rural population caused by the Black Death and the War of the Roses saw another decline in the fortunes of the apple, reversed once again by the aspirational Tudors. The fashion for Italian Renaissance-inspired ornamental gardens saw an increase in fruit-tree plantings that were initially intended to supply the tables of the wealthy. Thanks to a combination of suitable climate, fertile soils and a supply of stock from Henry VIII's gardens at Teynham, market gardens and orchards spread across Kent, Essex, Herefordshire, Gloucestershire and Worcestershire, mainly for cider production. Apple, pear and cherry orchards continued to be extensively planted during the sixteenth and seventeenth centuries, although towards the end of the eighteenth century the quality of fruit crops declined once again, due largely to outbreaks of canker and to poor orchard management. The popularity of orcharding continued to fluctuate until the beginning of the nineteenth century, when the founding of organizations such as the Royal Horticultural Society, the National Fruit and

Cider Institute and the short-lived but influential British Pomological Society led to a more scientific approach to apple breeding, including setting up Woburn Experimental Fruit Farm and the Long Ashton and East Malling Research Stations in Bristol and Kent.

Much of the work carried out at these establishments was dedicated to developing the 'Malling' rootstock series that remains crucial to modern-day apple growing. Most fruit trees can be propagated either from seed or by taking cuttings. However, apples are like human beings in that each new tree that grows from a pip created by sexual reproduction is a fresh shuffle of the DNA card pack. Not only will it inherit many of the characteristics of its parents, it will also have many unpredictable traits of its own. This is great in terms of increasing bio-diversity and the richness of the gene pool, but only rarely will such fruits be directly useful or attractive to the tastes of peoplekind. From the point of view of a nursery, it makes more sense to propagate new stock vegetatively, that is, by cutting a scion of graft wood from the desired variety which is then grown on to produce a 'clone' of the original. In effect this means that the original Bramley apple tree, for example, was a successful variety grown from a pip by Mary Anne Brailsford in her Nottinghamshire garden in 1809, but every Bramley since then has been propagated by taking cuttings of living matter from that tree, or one of its descendants.

Unfortunately, most varieties that bear desirable fruit don't do well from cuttings, so need to be grafted on to suitable rootstocks. These are varieties selected for characteristics such as their vigour of growth, hardiness and disease resistance. Grafting is the process of joining the scion to the rootstock, ensuring maximum contact between the cambium tissue (that is, the layer of growing plant material just below the bark) of each so that they grow together successfully. This will create a new tree that has both desired fruiting qualities combined with optimum desired size and vigour. By choosing the appropriate root-stock, apple trees can now be grown in practically any situation. Malling (M) 27 rootstock will produce a 'dwarfing' tree suitable for a container or very small garden. It will require staking throughout its life, as well as frequent watering, weeding and feeding. Trees on this rootstock will begin to come into fruit after 2–3 years, reaching full capacity of 10–15 lbs after 4–5 years. M106, ('Semi-dwarfing' or 'semi-vigorous') is the most widely used of rootstocks and probably the best choice for the average-size garden. It is tolerant of a wide range of soils, producing a tree with an eventual size of 14–18 feet. M25 rootstock produces a very vigorous tree, suitable for a grassed orchard that will grow on as a full standard. These would typically be planted 20 feet apart, making a tree of 15–20 feet or more height and spread, eventually yielding 200–400 lbs per tree.

Enhanced by such advances in horticulture, the twentieth century saw two main surges in the popularity of orchards in the years following 1918 and 1945. These were periods when there were drives to repopulate the countryside, and when our vulnerability as a small island had been brought home to us by wartime blockades of imported food. The 'Land Fit For Heroes' scheme for returning soldiers from the First World War saw thousands of acres given over to orchards in a campaign to increase national self-sufficiency. Many were planted around my home town of Southend-on-Sea, including St Laurence Orchard, on what is now the northern outskirts of the town. Once managed by the Peacock family of Eastwood, this covered several acres and, along with other smallholdings in the area, expanded further in the post-Second World War era to supply much of the town's fresh fruit. Some older residents still recall the 'help yourself' barrels of windfall Bramleys and Pippins that were put out on Eastwoodbury Lane. However the end of austerity, combined with subsidies, new trade agreements and the rise of supermarkets and processed foods conspired to create a situation where it became cheaper and more convenient to buy apples that had been grown on the other side of the world rather than across the road. Farmers and growers either left the land or lost their livelihoods, and thus began the movement to grub out orchards en masse. Today only a tiny fragment, maybe an acre or so, of St Laurence Orchard remains, and even this was completely overgrown and forgotten until about four years ago.

Perhaps St Laurence Orchard does symbolize the lack of appreciation traditional apples (and by extension, locally produced food in general) currently receive in this post-industrial era of globalization with its cheap imports, fast food and sense of alienation from the natural world. But maybe, like the monks who provided sanctuary for the apple in their walled gardens during the Dark Ages, the dedicated enthusiasts and volunteers who now tend this and the many other orchard remnants across the land are also acting as guardians of these precious genetic resources. Perhaps their role is to keep them safe for a future when diversity and distinctiveness are once again valued. After all, the pattern of history suggests that, whether caused by human plague or plant disease, neglect or political expediency, it's not the first time the home-grown apple has had a grim prognosis.

It may be the necessity of adapting to climate change and peak oil that will bring about the relocalization of our food-production systems. Continuing to import 90 per cent of our fruit isn't sustainable if we are serious about cutting carbon emissions by the 80 per cent needed to prevent runaway global warming. Neither will it be possible if predictions about declining fuel availability are even half accurate. Increasingly we will need to think in terms of 'Food Yards' rather than 'Food Miles', rebuilding an infrastructure of farms, smallholdings, productive gardens and local markets as well as restoring our orchards. Or perhaps we will at last simply begin to tire of bland, watery Braeburns and Pink Ladies. Recent years have seen a popular reaction against the unnecessary industrialization, standardization and homogeneity blighting our diets, put into a context by Slow Food movement founder Carlo Petrini:

> Today, restoring food – debased along with its overseers, exploited as a tool of control and global power – to its central role in our passage through the world is an act of great political relevance. To some extent, it is a revolutionary act.

The renaissance of the real apple is part of this 'delicious revolution', as we begin to reclaim diversity, flavour and autonomy into our daily lives. St Laurence Orchard is one of many throughout the land currently being restored and recognized as an invaluable community asset, in this case by Growing Together, a charity supporting people with mental-health needs through horticulture. Project Manager Ron Bates explains the beneficial connections that orchards can make between people and nature:

We've been working here to implement a management plan that's been drawn up to increase biodiversity. We've put in lots of wild flowers to diversify the flora. We've also put in a lot of new fruit tree plantings, quite a long list. They're not the standards, these majestic old things that we've already got here, they are going to be smaller, easier to maintain. It's an amazing environment. It's an ecology. We've got the first indicators, such as these holes in the old trees that are used by woodpeckers and later by starlings, robins, all sorts of birds. For the first time, this year I heard whitethroats here. So nature is always changing, it's an ongoing process. And we come and help to manage it – giving people skills in pruning the older trees, looking at their shape and space. Joining in with the harvesting ... Offering the experience of a place that is very tranquil. It is literally a breathing space; people enjoy coming here and working here. The locals keep an eye on it, and there's apple days, invitations to blossom days, bug days. We've had teaching days; we brought down Andrew Tann from Colchester, whose family have had Crapes Fruit Farm since the 1920s, the same era that this orchard was planted. He's run workshops on pruning and grafting skills. People and nature maintain and use this space, giving it life and meaning.

Schools, local authorities, parish councils and community groups are also creating new orchards in previously underutilized spaces. Eve Libertine, one-time vocalist of the anarchist punk band Crass, has recently published a series of hand-printed cards to help raise funds for a community orchard in Stoke Newington, north-east London. Butterfield Green consists of 34 half-standard fruit trees, including apples, plums, cherries, pears, peaches, quinces, medlars and hazelnuts, planted in an area of public open space between a main road and park during the winter of 2007. It is managed and maintained by the Shakespeare Residents Association in partnership with Hackney Council and Growing Communities, a local social-enterprise project dedicated to growing food in urban areas. There have been tree and orchard care events, including Apple Days, ground preparation, planting, mulching, pruning and grafting demonstrations, school events and bird and bat watching. Each tree has been 'sponsored' by a local resident who assumes responsibility for its watering and aftercare, and fruit harvests are free to local people. Project co-ordinator Maggie Chattaway explains the social benefits: 'The orchard is proving popular locally and has had a bringing-together effect on the local community, involving all sorts of people who have never been involved in growing things before.'

Charlie Tims is an artist who creatively and profitably engages with 'The Invisible Orchard', that huge range of fruit trees unnoticed in public spaces or ignored in private gardens. As part of the recent Power of 8 'West Acres Green' project envisaging how people might feed themselves in future cities, he began the Local Apple Trading Initiative. 'Your Apples, Our Press, Your Juice' posters were put up around the streets of Islington, offering 'an opportunity to make use of all the waste apples lying in your garden. You can even bring apples lying waste in parks or the street.' LATI offered to buy these at £1 for five kilos; they were then pressed by Charlie into fresh juice for resale at £2 a bottle. He also offered a mobile pressing service, the outputs of which were fermented into 'Murgatroyds Cider', 'produced from a blend of unique West Acres Green varieties, including Red Verge, Curbstone Brawler and Old Scrapper'. I had the honour of sampling a bottle and have to say it was one of the most distinctive scrumpies I've ever tasted – dry, tart, but very quaffable, with a definite urban edge! Another urban artist, Vahakn Matossian, has begun an ambitious project to map and network all of the fruit trees growing in public places in London. This is being made available online to encourage guerrilla gardening and city scrumping:

Yes we live in a sometimes harsh urban sprawl, but nature is all around us … We're not saying that every Londoner can get all the fruit they need from the city streets right now and through the year, but a load of the fruit from the trees that do bear goes to waste unpicked … Fruit City is not just a map of trees, but an initiative to wake people up to the nature on their doorstep. To re-engage folks with the wild and goodness around them and to get local community orchards planted.

The consistent champions of our orchards are Common Ground, an organization founded to promote local distinctiveness and explore the links between people, nature and culture. On 21st October 1990 they launched the first Apple Day at Covent Garden, once the largest fruit and vegetable market in London. Including cookery demonstrations, games, wassailing, apple identification, juice and cider making, gardening advice, and of course many hundreds of apple varieties, Apple Day is a celebration and demonstration that variety and richness matter, and that it is possible to affect change in your locality. It has been marked in each subsequent year by people organizing hundreds of large and small local events across the UK and beyond.

It's vital that, while we need to protect and promote our orchards, they should not be seen as static museum pieces. Nor should they become part of the ever-burgeoning 'Heritage Industry', to be 'experienced' like just another theme-park attraction. Rather, we need to reinstate them as living, evolving ecosystems, inevitably changing and adapting to meet the needs of an ever-shifting future, with economic as well as cultural and environmental importance. In 1989, Julian Temperley and Tim Stoddart founded the Somerset Cider Brandy Company, based at the Burrow Hill Farm orchard in Kingsbury Episcopi. This was granted the first ever full cider-distilling licence by HM Customs, and they now manufacture a cider brandy made by distilling the fermented juice of cider apples. Swirled gently in a glass and sipped slowly, it evokes seasons of mist and mellow fruitfulness, reminiscent to me of the photographic orchard portraits of the late James Ravillious. There are still many commercial orchards in Essex, where they enjoy a relatively warm and dry climate. Andrew Tann continues to make a good living growing over 150 varieties of apples in his 15 acre orchard near Colchester. Most of these are sold direct by mail order, with different mixes of apple varieties available from August to January. In October and November his cold-packing shed smells like the sweetest place on earth. Nottingham-based permaculture designer and proprietor of Cool Temperate Tree Nursery, Phil Corbett, has been experimenting with the idea of 'coppice orchards', using 'own rootstock' trees to combine the fruiting yields of traditional orchards with the timber production of conventional woodland management systems. Martin Crawford, founder of the Agroforestry Research Trust in Dartington, south Devon, reminds us of the need for longer term planning, as well as perhaps broadening our definitions of what an orchard means:

> In the face of climate change, not all varieties of apples will continue to thrive well in their indigenous homelands. They may well be good varieties and some will adapt to changing conditions better than others, but gradually their optimum locations are moving northwards as climate zones shift. So Devon apples will soon be of more value in Wales, whilst apples from north-west France will be valuable in Devon. A forest garden is a kind of underplanted orchard – you start with fruit and nut trees, and with careful design and placement, shrub crops and perennials are grown beneath – all can be useful edible plants. Forest gardens are more than this though – they are aesthetically beautiful places which can reconnect people with nature in the same way that a wild forest can do.

In Celtic lore, the apple represented the Earth Mother and her abundance – when cut across the middle it reveals a five-pointed star, an ancient symbol of the five elements. The Ancient Greeks told of the Golden Apples of the Hesperides that bestowed immortality on those that consumed them, whilst to the Norse the apples of perpetual youth grew in Asgard. Both the Church and those of more Libertarian persuasions can reasonably claim the parable of the forbidden fruit as their own, the former as a dire warning of what happens to those who succumb to the sins of temptation, bodily pleasures and free will; for the latter, it's at the core of the oldest story of disobedience. I like Dennis Gould's postcard poem 'Scrumpin' which reframes the story of Adam and Eve as a bawdy ballad of earthly pleasures. Certainly it would upset the apple cart of those whose idea of paradise involves bland tastes and always doing as you are told ... Sometimes it can feel as though we are at the end of History – that corporate culture and its plastic values have won. But what these stories tell me is that the apple has always had a special place in our culture, and with its sacred and magical importance, it always will. Whether in community orchards, forest gardens, permaculture plots, cider-brandy distilleries or at the guerrilla-gardened wild edges, the apple's story goes on.

Graham Burnett www.transitionculture.org/2008/09/23/transition-glastonburys-submission-to-mendip-district-councils-future-planning-document/
Ron Bates – 'A Background and History of St Laurence Orchard'
www.scrumpin.org.uk/orchard.html
www.slowfood.org.uk
Ron Bates interviewed in *Breathing Spaces*, a film by Paul Bates.
www.scrumpin.org.uk/film.html
www.powerof8.org.uk
www.tinyurl.com/yg47cdd
www.vahakn.co.uk/projects/fruit-city
Tamzin Pinkerton & Rob Hopkins. *Local Food: How To Make It Happen In Your Community*. Green Books, 2009.

A DEFENCE OF THE DACHA

Gavin Knight

THE RUSSIANS HAVE LONG SUBSCRIBED TO THE DREAM of escaping the city for the pastoral idyll of their country dachas. If you have been to Moscow recently you will see why. Witness the nightmare of streets so vast that you can only cross them via urine-stinking underpasses. It is associated with notorious traffic jams as much as with the Kremlin and Red Square. Muscovites, squashed into tiny Stalinist tower blocks, cannot wait to wave goodbye to the fumes of the USSR's military-industrial complex and disappear into the mythic vastness of the Russian countryside.

The Russian dacha system is common across the whole of the former Soviet empire and is one we could try to implement in the UK. Typically these small cottages are used as holiday homes by the city-dwelling owners and rented out the rest of the time to anyone wanting to escape the smog and wheels of industry, and to return to ancient roots of Russian folklore and live near woods and fields. In my travels in the former Soviet Union, I have stayed at many dachas, of different shapes and sizes. For the average, poorly paid Russian, the dacha is no bigger than an English summer house, with a few deckchairs on the porch where you can enjoy traditional Russian food and wine outside. Someone plays a few folk songs on the guitar and everyone sings along. A dacha can also include a small plot of land for vegetables or a vine for home-made wine. This potent *rosé* would be kept in large recycled Fanta bottles. The cottage itself could be made out of corrugated iron and wood. Having had many centuries of living off the land, the Russians are very skilled in building these small houses. Israel is home to 1 million former Soviet citizens so, in theory, many Russian-speaking settlers will be building their own 'dachas' there.

Sveta, a Russian who lives in London, explains: 'The dacha is a real tradition, the family goes to the dacha for the weekend or for holidays. In most cases the dacha has also a *banya*, which is a steam bath, a Russian typical sauna. People spend good time eating and drinking vodka. They would grow onions, herbs, marrows, potatoes and beans and lots of flowers ... oh and gooseberries, raspberries, strawberries, black and redcurrants.' She explains that the seasonal pilgrimage to the countryside does not require loading up the car. Some Russians do not even own a car and travel to their dachas on the slow, sleepy electric trains. 'Dachas have existed for a long time, before communism. Normally you take with you all you need. Sometimes dachas are in or near small village and in the village you have some *gastonomes* [food shops] where you can buy things you want.'

Russian dachas have their origins in medieval times. They were a gift, given to the serfs for their service. Since the dachas were also a means of escaping the dirt and grime of the modern city, it is no coincidence that the rise of dachas coincides with the creation of Russia's first modern city, St. Petersburg, in the seventeenth century. During the reign of the Tsar, Peter the Great, members of his entourage were given cottages near St Petersburg. The word 'dacha' means cottage, and comes from the Russian verb *'davat'*, which means 'to give'. Peter the Great gave out vast areas of land from the Gulf of Finland, near St Petersburg, to his own royal dacha of Peterhof. Academic Steve Lovell explains the roots of the Russian dacha in his book *Summerfolk: The History of the Russian Dacha*. As urban life expanded in the 1830s, the need to escape the city grew. This led to the dacha habit increasing. Tens of thousands of people lived in apartments in St Petersburg and had no ancestral estate or other property in which to spend the summer months. The city was hot, sticky and humid, heaving with people – much like it is today as commuters swelter into work on overcrowded commuter trains. Tenants therefore looked to rent dachas so they could escape from horrendous epidemics and save money. They were far cheaper than the tiny city apartments they rented. This led to the growth of the 'dachniki', people from the *beau monde* of St Petersburg society. Today dacha settlements are located at every stop of the train out of St Petersburg.

By 1900 all classes of people, from merchants to shopkeepers, had joined the 'dachniki'. For a time the modest pastoral idyll of the 'dacha' became confused with the rising Russian-middle-class aspiration for a second home. It became prey to the same snobbery that today is associated with the Hamptons in New York or the stockbrokers' clifftop second homes in Cornwall, which lie empty most of the year. By the nineteenth century 'dacha' came to mean 'country residence', an accessory for a comfortable lifestyle for rich second-homers with pads in town. It encompassed the huge Potemkin-style palaces in holiday resorts on the Black Sea such as Sochi and Yalta.

The Russian Revolution unleashed Marx's ferocious attack on property rights and the dacha reverted back to its former position as a gift from the state. During the Soviet time many of the cottages were expropriated by members of the proletariat and the size and type of dachas were restricted by planning laws. However, communism was as corrupt as the next ideology and climbing the greasy pole of the Communist party meant you could acquire a large country residence. By the beginning of the Stalin era the sought-after St Petersburg dachas belonged only to the top Soviet leadership. Russian President Vladimir Putin was holidaying in his dacha near Crimea when the nuclear submarine *Kursk* went down with all hands. Similarly, President Mikhail Gorbachev was imprisoned in his own dacha as a coup was staged in Moscow.

Well-known scientists, writers and composers were given fine dachas. Ivan Turgenev was the first to introduce the idea of the Russian dacha into literature, in his novels about country life. Chekhov sets *The Cherry Orchard* and *The Three Sisters* in country dachas, with the three sisters fanning themselves and looking out the window at ducks heading for Moscow.

After the collapse of the USSR, people were able to earn money as capitalism arrived in Russia. With it came the new bourgeois class, the so-called 'new Russian'. Free from narrow Soviet standards, self-made businessmen began to build gaudy palaces and fortresses to show off their new-found wealth. These were also labelled as 'dachas', but often boasted a mini-zoo or swimming pool, complete with crocodiles. Opulent dacha communities for millionaires and former Communist party officials appeared: Podmoscowie, Zhukovka, Nikolina Gora, Barvikha. All of them are situated along Rublevo-Uspensky highway around Moscow and they take the common name of Rublyovka or 'villages'. However, these gated oligarch communities have little connection with the traditional Russian village, as the local village shop sells Chanel, Gucci and even Bentley cars.

The dacha system as a modest home for serfs has remained a durable tradition that has survived the Russian Revolution, Stalin's terror and the last two decades of voracious capitalism which has seen Russia produce more billionaires than any other country except the US. It's roots lie firmly in Russian's cultural attachment to rural life. As Steven Lovell says: 'The Russian dacha has been invested with positive features of the Russian self-image: easygoing sociability, open-ended and vodka-soaked hospitality, rejection or ignorance of superficial niceties, appetites for physical toil, intuitive feeling for the natural world, and emotional freedom. In the post-war era they came to be highly valued for the connection they created to a rural way of life that many Soviet urbanites or their parents had only recently relinquished.' As the Soviet Union collapsed and Russians faced terrifying anxieties about their future, they all flocked to their dachas for the reassurance of the ancient traditions of rural life. Lovell states that in the early nineties, 90 per cent of the inhabitants of major cities had access to dachas or plots where they grew their own vegetables. As one Russian told me: 'When the country had problems with food, the dacha became the only means by which people could afford something more than the green tomatoes in the Soviet department store.' In the late eighties shiny red tomatoes appeared in Moscow, sold outside Kievskaya station, but the rumour went round that they had come from radioactive ground by the exploded nuclear power station Chernobyl.

One Russian, Stanislav, tells me: 'For the majority of Russians, the cottage remains a simple and convenient option for leisure, just as it was in the late nineteenth century.' Sveta remembers childhood holidays: 'We used to spend most of the summer at our dacha growing vegetables and flowers, going to the lake with friends and playing bingo in the evenings. Dacha is like cottage in England or a *maison de campagne* in France, it can exist everywhere. Maybe in the real dacha you have more family atmosphere. I have some friends in Belarus who are not very rich and they have their own family dacha. It is a bit like the current UK system of allotments. Also there is some sense of community around the dacha.' A typical dacha is Boris Pasternak's one in Peredelkino, which is where the romance takes place in *Dr Zhivago*.

Stanislav explains that integral to the dacha system is the idea of shared duties and responsibilities: 'You are entitled to enter a co-operative. After you became a member you would have paid for all the infrastructure like cutting down trees, dealing with drainage of the land, setting up electricity and water mains from scratch. Not many people could afford it or physically do it themselves even then.' Stanislav reiterates the importance of escaping the grime and smog of the city: 'Dacha is the place where you retreat from the city life. Where you find pleasure in gathering wild berries, mushrooms, fruits, vegetables, or whatever your dacha allows you to gather. Where you might go hunting for meat, again, if your land permits you to do it. On the wall you can have icons and family photos.' Sveta backs up this view: 'There is a cultural aspect to it too, because the majority of Russians still love outdoor activities like mushroom picking. Although these crafts are dying out.'

I remember staying with a wealthy married couple, both academics, at their dacha in the country in Ukraine. They had two Borzoi hunting dogs, and the host, Yuri, served me cognac out of a wooden barrel with a tap just behind his shoulder. I was fed on 'shashliki', marinated kebabs cooked on a home-made barbecue, with large boiled crayfish and fish. When I had eaten and drank so much I couldn't get up from my deckchair, I was suddenly bundled down a jetty into the nearby river, where I was expected to water-ski. On another occasion I sat in a dacha that was no more than a wood and corrugated-iron hut. The owner, a toothless character whose sister I was dating, plied me with homemade wine and pickled gherkins. Then for entertainment he fired an ageing shotgun into the night sky.

So why can't this wonderful rural tradition of the Russian dacha take off in the UK? It demands an enlightened planning policy. In Spain and Germany you can buy some land cheaply and put a shed on it and enjoy it. In Germany, there is an emerging trend amongst young families for a version of the 'dacha' called *Schrebergärten*. They have become extremely popular over the last five years. Nina describes them: 'They're normally close to the city. We live in downtown Hamburg and ours is ten minutes away. We have apples, plums, berries, et cetera. There's a little wooden house on it with 50 square metres of land. We sleep there in summer. The ones in Eastern Germany are even called dachas.'

The German *Schrebergärten* cannot be bought, but can be rented for 99 years from half-public, half-private institutions. Nina paid €5,500 for hers, which she considers to be very expensive. The rent for the land is around €180 a year, with electricity and water bills at only €100 a year. Her cottage was built in the late forties. 'All cottages in these gardens built before 1987 are protected; that means, you can keep up the original size. If you build a new cottage, you're only allowed to have 24 square metres including terrace.' There are 1 million *Schrebergärten* in Germany, most of them close to the big towns. You join a group (*Verein*) with 50 to 150 dachas, put your name on a waiting list and when a tenant leaves their garden, it is offered up on a first come, first served basis.

Nina says that Germans love planning laws and even have a 'Federal small garden law' (*Bundeskleingartengesetz*) which ordains how high the bushes are allowed to grow and that one third of the land must be used for growing produce. 'You're not allowed to have a permanent residence at the garden but the rules always depends on what kind of people are in your group,' she says. 'Our group is pretty punk. Half of the people there live there in summer, no one cares about the height of fences *et cetera*. So it's a bit up to the individual *Verein* on how strict to be with all those laws.'

Historically, these German 'dachas' served poor families as a source of fresh, home-grown vegetables and space and fresh air for people living in the smallest apartments. Young families tend to have a relaxed attitude, barbecuing and swigging beer, while next door a *petit bourgeois* might be obsessing about the height of their pallisade. There is also a German aversion to the power of supermarkets. 'Germans are very conscious about food,' Nina says. 'I want my kid to know that strawberries don't come in plastic boxes out of the supermarket. I want him to know an apple used to be a blossom and that kind of stuff.'

As you head out of a German city, rather than seeing the eyesore of an Asda warehouse or dreary suburban Barratt homes, tiny German 'dachas' with their carefully designed gardens stretch for miles. Dr Daniel Gottlieb Moritz Schreber, a nineteenth-century naturopath, wanted to create more athletics fields for the children in his home city of Leipzig. His son-in-law carried his work on in 1864 so that children could be taught the basics of gardening. German *Schreber* gardens differ from the English allotment system as they are more ornamental. The fruit and vegetables grow side by side with displays of flowers. The pursuit of a well-designed flower bed can even become competitive. Austria and Switzerland have also followed this system of cultivating plots of land. In Vienna they are so popular that there is a five-year waiting list. In Denmark and Scandinavian countries the allotment system is not only equated with gardening but also with socializing and having a beer with the family.

The English allotment system means that many people can enjoy healthy exercise, fruit and vegetables free of pesticides. They are rented to individuals to grow crops. The most common plot is 10 rods, an ancient measurement equivalent to 302 square yards or 253 square metres. However the amount of land available has been in steady decline for some time. From its peak of 1,400,000 in 1943 there was a sharp decline in allotment provision to around 500,000 in the seventies. Richard Briers and Felicity Kendal in *The Good Life* boosted interest. Local authorities sold off allotment land for high prices to housing developers, so by 1996 there were around 297,000 plots available. A 2006 London Assembly inquiry found that demand was at an all-time high but land was limited due to development of high-density building.

English allotments often include a wooden shed for tools. If we pursued the Russian dacha system then these sheds would become places you would sit or sleep in and enjoy home-made wine, folk songs and the company of family and neighbours. Insulation and a wood-burning stove would need to be installed if they were occupied in the autumn and winter months. Many people already have sheds that they use as 'garden offices' in their city gardens, so it would be possible to develop them for recreational rather than work purposes. Blue-collar city workers would head out of overcrowded tower blocks with their families to the fields of the country. Since rural life can be hard, they would form co-operatives to support each other, and divide up the costs of electricity and water. Rather than stabbing each other and playing the footage on YouTube, urban teenagers could forage in woods, cultivate the land and learn the peacefulness of rural life. Small barbecues would be arranged amongst English 'dacha' owners. The desolate inner cities encourage bored kids to inhale glue and write violent rap songs about inter-gang warfare. With regular trips to their dacha, they might start strumming the guitar around a wood fire and drink home-made wine. Ancient crafts would be kept alive.

Many revolutionary ideas have come out of Russia. Prince Peter Kropotkin, author of one of the *Idler*'s favourite books, *Mutual Aid: A Factor of Evolution*, was one of Russia's foremost anarchists. Now the dacha must come to the UK.

COMMON PEOPLE

(An Arbitrary History of Commoning; concerning Outlaws, Levellers,
Diggers and Charters of Liberty – with some piracy, witchery
and anarchy thrown in for good measure)

Warren Draper

What are kingdoms but great robberies? Indeed, that was an apt
and true reply which was given to Alexander the Great by a pirate
who had been seized. For when that king had asked the man what
he meant by keeping hostile possession of the sea, he answered
with bold pride, 'What thou meanest by seizing the whole earth?
Because I do it with a petty ship, I am called a robber, whilst thou
who dost it with a great fleet art styled an emperor.'
– Augustine of Hippo, *The City of God,* 410 CE

There was a big high wall there that tried to stop me;
Sign was painted, it said PRIVATE PROPERTY;
But on the back side it didn't say nothing;
That side was made for you and me.
– Woody Guthrie. *This Land is Your Land* (suppressed verse) 1944

I LIVE IN BANDIT COUNTRY. TO THE WEST IS THE VILLAGE
of Hampole; it lies at the very heart of what was once the vast
and ancient Barnsdale Forest. During the early medieval period
these woods, rich with game and deer, stretched from Wakefield to
Sheffield, covering much of what is now South Yorkshire. The impos-
ing forest may be long gone, but there are still small patches of woodland that were seeded from trees which once knew the impenetrable
shadow of the wildwood.

To the north, where Yorkshire's internal borders huddle together like newborn cats, lies Wentbridge; the only village to be named in *A Lytell Gest of Robyn Hode*. Dating from the fifteenth century, the *Gest* is one of the earliest known ballads of Robin Hood and it reveals that it was Barnsdale Forest, rather than Sherwood Forest, which originally provided home and sanctuary for the kind-hearted bandit and his bold outlaw kinsmen. After proving himself in various adventures, Robin was invited to live with the king in Nottingham Castle, but he soon grew tired of courtly life and longed to return to his beloved Barnsdale.

> 'Alas!' then sayd good Robyn,
> 'Alas and well a woo!
> Yf I dwele lenger with the kynge,
> Sorowe wyll me sloo.'

> Forth then went Robyn Hode
> Tyll he came to our kynge:
> 'My lorde the kynge of Englonde,
> Graunte me myn askynge.

> 'I made a chapell in Bernysdale,
> That semely is to se,
> It is of Mary Magdaleyne,
> And there to wolde I be.'

A few miles south of Wentbridge lies the village of Campsall; home to one of the oldest churches in the region. The church is dedicated to St Mary Magdalene. Local legend says that Robin and his beloved Maid Marion were married in this church, but Marion does not appear in the *Gest*. She is a much later creation, whose presence may allude to Robin's 'Marianism'; an attribute which was prevalent in the fifteenth-century ballads, but less so in later tales (Christianity, particularly Puritanism, would come to be less tolerant of these worshippers of St Mary Magdalene, who held women in such high regard).

The introduction of new characters such as Marion and Friar Tuck was just one of the ways that the Robin Hood story changed over time:

Robin was originally a yeoman, but he came to be portrayed as a noble who had lost his 'rightful' lands through duplicity; his woodland hide-away moved 50 miles south to Sherwood Forest in Nottinghamshire; his rallying against the clerics, the law and the aristocracy (hardly something to be expected of a nobleman, not to mention a friar's friend) became ever more sanitized as the story became more childlike; and his partisanship of the poor came to look more like charity than class war.

The modern, Errol Flynnesque, image of a cheerful, aristocratic, patriotic, tight-wearing Robin was largely the product of Sir Walter Scott, whose 1819 heroic adventure novel, *Ivanhoe*, was inspired by the same landscape that had played muse to the writer of the *Gest* some 400 years earlier. South of Doncaster, overlooking the Dearne Valley, lies Conisbrough Castle. Scott mistakenly believed that the castle's non-typical architecture meant that it was pre-Norman in date, and he used it as a reference for the book's 'Saxon' castle. It is in *Ivanhoe* that Robin is first named 'Robin of Locksley' and Scott is the first writer to have Robin split his competitor's arrow in two during an archery contest.

Geographical displacement is a matter for the tourist industry, but gentrification saw the very essence of the story change. When asked about Robin Hood, most people today would talk about 'robbing the rich and giving to the poor'; no doubt this is a noble endeav-our – one which I heartily recommend – but it is not a feature of the original stories. Money and possessions meant much less to the people of pre-capitalist England than they do to today's more consumer-minded brood, and the Robin of the *Gest* was more than happy to keep his (not so ...) ill-gotten gains to himself. But in feudal England acts of solidarity, support and kindness – offering shelter, protection, food and clothing – could mean the difference between life and death. The modern Robin Hood story fails to convey the full insurrectionary nature of the original ballads; for this was a tale of land, liberty and mutual aid rather than bravado, honour and tights.

In her 1998 article, 'Robin Hood: Earl, Outlaw or Rebel', Judy Cox writes:

In one of the earliest ballads, 'Robin Hood and the Monk', there is a sense that the solidarity of the outlaws and the freedom of the forests provide security against the alien, corrupting forces of organized religion and the legal system. Another early ballad, 'Robin and the Potter', reveals the monetary edge to the restrictions of the town, which one historian has interpreted as expressing artisans' dislike of producing artefacts for the market, 'an early vision of alienated labour'. Historian Stephen Knight provides an insight into the early popularity of the Robin Hood ballads: 'The semi-mythical sense of resistance and opposition to the "statutory" forces of state, church and emergent mercantilism seems deeply embedded in these tales and references ... *The Gest*, after all, advocates massive theft from the church, civic insurrection against and murder of a properly appointed Sheriff, breach of legitimate agreement with a King.' It is 'a story with much potency among people who experience institutionalized oppression and therefore require the relief of fictional forms of dissent'.[1] The Robin Hood ballads were a major focus for the idea that oppressive authorities can be resisted, even if this usually remained an aspiration rather than an active opposition.[2]

... which, in turn, suggests that Robin and his merry men, in aspiration at least, were among the first organized anti-capitalists.

The ballads would have been performed by minstrels to an audience of the so-called 'Third Class' – yeomen, apprentices, merchants, journeymen, labourers and small proprietors – resentment would run highest among these people as it was they who bore the full weight of the 'Norman Yoke'. John Taylor writes, 'The targets of Robin Hood's criticism are the justices of the forest and the common law';[3] these justices represented laws which had been drafted by the powerful largely to protect the interests of the landowning classes, but the commoners knew of a much older (some might say 'higher'...) law.

The English can be rightfully proud of Magna Carta. In contrast to the exploitation, suffering and death which the eternal sunshine of the British Empire brought to the planet like a melanoma, the Great Charter of Freedoms, drafted by the barons for King John in 1215, helped to create a much more humane legacy for the people of our Sceptred Isle. Magna Carta enshrines the rights of *habeas corpus*, trial by jury, innocence until proven guilty, due process of law, prohibition of torture and the right to silence (each of which we are in danger of losing thanks to 9/11 and the 3000+ new 'crimes' which the Labour government has created since 1997). These medieval rights have provided a foundation for judicial systems around the world and have inspired more than their fair share of revolutions. But the Great Charter is only half the story.

The document which most people recognize as Magna Carta – the one which is proudly displayed in places such as Westminster, Lincoln Castle, the Bodleian Library, Australia's Parliament House and the US Capitol Rotunda in Washington DC – is actually one of a series of charters issued between 1215 and 1225 which together form Magna Carta proper. The Great Charter of Freedoms gets all the glory, but on its own it merely confirms provisions already voluntarily granted by Henry I many years earlier. It was a 1217 supplement to Magna Carta, the lesser known Charter of the Forest, that promised the commoners of England real and lasting freedoms. As the Great Charter reaffirmed legal securities against the arbitrary whims of the monarchy, the Charter of the Forest granted immediate and concrete rights, privileges and protections for the commoner against the abuses of the encroaching aristocracy. At a time when forests were an important source of food (for both humans and livestock), fuel (for heating and cooking), medicines (when folk remedies offered more hope than the king's physicians) and materials (for shelter and industry), the Charter of the Forest was unique in providing a degree of economic protection for the lower classes of society.

From 1217 until 1971 – when it was repealed by the then Lord Chancellor, Baron Quinten McGarel Hogg II QC; son of Douglas McGarel Hogg, the man who helped to reaffirm and fortify the rule of law following the 1926 General Strike (talk about 'like father, like son') – the Charter of the Forest created one of the longest running, and arguably one of the fairest, statutes in legal history. It guaranteed the rights to herbage (free grazing for cattle), assarts (clearing trees and grubbing stumps for gardening or growing grains), pannage (letting pigs graze woods for mast and nuts – especially important for cattle farmers, as acorns are poisonous to sheep and cows), chiminage (a ban on tolls for roads and paths), and estovers (the collection of wood for fuel, shelter and implements) on all common land. This effectively guaranteed that every man, woman and child in England had the basic right to subsistence from lands which were traditionally held in common for the mutual benefit of all. Small wonder then that this particular charter doesn't get its fair share of the limelight!

As with most concessions from the rich and powerful, the provisions guaranteed by the Charter of the Forest did not come out of the blue; in reality, it offered no more than that which was seen by the vast majority of people to be theirs already by right of birth. Birthrights are central to 'the commons', an idea which has developed independently in almost every human culture throughout history: that the land is a gift from nature – or Go – which should be treated as a common treasury for all living things; that everyone has the right to live off nature's bounty; and that no single man or class can claim sole possession of the land. This was a view elegantly espoused by priest turned pirate, Caraccioli, who observed:

> that every Man was born free, and had as much right to what would support him, as to the air he respired … that the vast difference betwixt man and man, the one wallowing in luxury, and the other in the most pinching necessity, was owing only to avarice and ambition on the one hand, and a pusillanimous subjection on the other … ambition creeping in by degrees, the stronger family set upon and enslaved the weaker; and this additional strength over-run a third, by every conquest gathering force to make others, and this was the first foundation of monarchy.[4]

It was Caraccioli who originally inspired the French pirate, Captain Misson, and together they would found Libertalia, a libertarian colony which stretched from Madagascar's Bay of Antongil to what is now the town of Mananjary. For 25 years Libertalia provided home and shelter for hundreds of emancipated slaves from all around the world. These free men and women (freed, that is, from the shackles of chattel, bonded and – in the case of the European sailors – wage slavery) called themselves 'the Liberi' and in their colony: 'no Hedge bounded any particular Man's Property,' and prizes and money taken at sea were 'carry'd into the common Treasury, Money being of no Use where every Thing was in common'.[5]

Access to the land (and therefore to natural resources) not only gave people the ability to provide for themselves in times of need, it meant that poorer people in rural areas, especially women, were not at the constant beck and call of farmers, proprietors and landowners. Common rights offered protection from exploitation and the country's commons, wastes and forests became, in the words of Christopher Hill, 'schools of economic democracy'.[6]

The freedoms granted by common rights were so empowering that commoning remained popular in the more rural areas of Barnsdale right up to the end of the twentieth century. Even when coal had become king in South Yorkshire and the Vale of York had been blighted by the giant power stations of Megawatt Alley, coppiced and pollarded woodlands still provided fuel for many a commoner (they also helped a lot of people get through the winter during the 1984–5 Miner's Strike). Over the last few decades many of these people found themselves priced out of their homes as rural work became ever more scarce. Unfortunately, the new, wealthier, inhabitants of Barnsdale's more pastoral villages seem to be more interested in 'aspect' than traditional lifestyles: central heating, uPVC double glazing, 4x4s, striped lawns and empty pubs are now the order of the day. But commoners were in trouble long before capitalism destroyed working rural communities. Widespread autonomy and self-reliance is damaging to authoritarian systems, and commoners have always been brutally condemned by society's more willing slaves.

During the Tudor period, the demonization and persecution of commoners grew ever more vicious as the demand for wood increased. Power in Europe (not to mention domination of the Americas ...) depended on a nation's control of the seas – and ships, of course, were made out of wood. Magna Carta was largely forgotten (which proved very convenient when Henry VIII decided to make one of the biggest land-grabs in English history), but common rights were still very highly prized. This caused major problems for those who wanted to clear-cut the forests in order to fuel a newly emerging empire. Then as now, the powerful chose to use fear as their primary weapon against liberty.

It was women who benefited the most from the freedoms offered by common rights, and the gathering of wood and forest foods was traditionally seen as 'women's work'; so it was women who were the main target of one of the most brutal forms of oppression in English history. The late sixteenth century saw a massive rise in witch trials (for 'trial', read 'persecution, torture and murder') as the 'supernatural law' of the Church was used to suppress the 'natural law' of the commons. Religion and morality may have been used to justify the callous actions of men, but it was crass economics that lay at the heart of this atrocity. It is no coincidence that evidence against witchcraft included association with the people's common rights to estovers, pannage and herbage. Hanging, drowning and burning would become *de facto* punishments for commoning.

The commoners of the seventeenth century fared no better. Under Charles Stuart common land was enclosed at an even greater rate and witch trials reached epidemic proportions; indeed it was restrictions to common rights and issues of forest law which helped to spark the English Revolution. As Peter Linebaugh says in his ground-breaking book, *The Magna Carta Manifesto* (from here on in I shall take a great deal from this great book, if only because it has a great deal to give):

> Cottagers, artisans, labourers, and poor farmers rioted to preserve their commons against attempts by Charles I to enclose them, for during bad harvests and stagnation in the cloth trade, they depended on income supplements from the forests – pannage, grazing, firewood, construction timber, game. Authorities complained that common right, and common pasture in particular, supported beggars and gave license to thieves, rogues, and 'naughty and idle persons'.[7]

Widespread suffering at the hands of a tyrannical monarch would guarantee revolution, but Magna Carta would also have its part to play. For the second time in its history, the Great Charter would be used to bring a king to heel.

It was the leading constitutionalist of Parliament, Edward Coke (1552–1634), who did most to revive the fortunes of Magna Carta. As Linebaugh shows:

> Coke helped to transform it, first by amalgamating *habeas corpus* with chapter 39, second by inserting it into the colonial charters of Atlantic colonies, third by affirming that Magna Carta's *nullus liber homo* (free man) equalled all the people, including women, and fourth by linking Magna Carta to Parliament.[8]

Coke's attempts to empower Parliament went much further than he could possibly imagine; he had given the *nullus liber homo* a powerful weapon to use against all tyrants – whether they be 'monarchs', 'dictators' or 'elected representatives'.

As the only man in English history to be tried for treason by both king and Parliament, 'Freeborn' John Lilburne (1614–57) knew a thing or two about tyranny; indeed he famously said, 'I neither love a slave, nor fear a tyrant' – which has obvious echoes of Caraccioli's 'avarice and ambition' vs. 'pusillanimous subjection'. A campaign to free Lilburne from the Tower of London in 1646 would spawn a movement known as the Levellers. Peter Linebaugh again:

> The goal of the Levellers was 'the right, freedome, safety, and well-being of every particular man, woman, and child in England'. Magna Carta became 'the Englishman's legal birthright and inheritance'. Lilburne said, 'the liberty of the whole English nation is in chapter 39. He addressed the soldiers, "we are at best but your hewers of wood and drawers of water. The ancient and famous magistracy of this nation, the Petition of Right, the Great Charter of England [...] which our ancestors at an extraordinary dear rate, as with abundance of their blood and treasure, purchased for the inheritance of us and of the generations after us"'.[9]

Lilburne recognized that Coke's interpretation of Magna Carta could pave the way for a previously unheard of level of social equality; a universal *levelling* of privilege and wealth. As the highest-ranking Leveller in the Cromwell's New Model Army, Colonel Thomas Rainsborough, stated during the Putney Debates of 1647:

> For really I think that the poorest he that is in England hath a life to live, as the greatest he; and therefore truly, sir, I think it's clear, that every man that is to live under a government ought first by his own consent to put himself under that government; and I do think that the poorest man in England is not at all bound in a strict sense to that government that he hath not had a voice to put himself under.
>
> As to the thing itself, property. I would fain know how it comes to be the property of some men and not of others. As for estates, and those kind of things, and other things that belong to men, it will be granted that they are property; but I deny that that is a property to a Lord, to a Gentleman, to any man more than another in the Kingdom of England.

Among other things, the Levellers called for the end of parliamentary and judicial corruption, toleration of religious differences, the translation of law into the common tongue and an elected judiciary (sadly these demands remain all too relevant today, but where is our Lilburne or Rainsborough?). To meet these goals the Levellers intended to wrestle power from the gentry and rich landowners as well as from the king. Cromwell however had other plans: Freeborn John would spend years in prison and exile before dying of fever in 1657, aged 42; in October 1648, much to Barnsdale's shame, Thomas Rainsborough would be murdered by Royalists in Doncaster during a bodged kidnap attempt (which was widely believed to have been orchestrated by Cromwell as a direct attack on the Levellers); and mutinies at Bishopsgate and Banbury in 1649 would see Levellers such as Robert Lockyer executed to discourage further dissent. By the end of 1649 the Leveller cause had effectively been crushed, but not before they had inspired an even more radical, land-based form of levelling.

Gerrard Winstanley (1609–1676) was a victim of the economic recession which followed the first Civil War. On becoming bankrupt in 1643, he said, 'I was beaten out both of estate and trade, and forced to accept the goodwill of friends crediting to me, to lead a country life'; but 'country life' would dramatically change Winstanley's view of the world. In January 1649 he published *The New Law of Righteousness*, in which he wrote:

> Everyone that gets an authority into his hands tyrannizes over others; as many husbands, parents, masters, magistrates, that live after the flesh do carry themselves like oppressing lords over such as are under them, not knowing that their wives, children, servants, subjects are their fellow creatures, and hath an equal privilege to share with them in the blessing of liberty ... so long as such are rulers that call the land theirs, upholding this particular property of mine and thine, the common people shall never have their liberty, nor the land be freed from troubles, oppressions and complainings.

This echoes the need for economic and social equality espoused by the Levellers, but realizing that this would be worthless without equal access to natural resources, Winstanley goes even further and suggests that in a state of liberty:

> Everyone shall put to their hands to till the earth and bring up cattle, and the blessing of the earth shall be common to all; when a man hath need of any corn or cattle [he may freely] take from the next store-house he meet with. There shall be no buying and selling, no fairs or markets, but the whole earth shall be a common treasury for every man ... There shall be none lords over others, but everyone shall be lord of himself, subject to the law of righteousness, reason and equity.

Winstanley saw that the commons could be extended to create a form of agrarian communism that would, if widely implemented, ensure socio-economic equality and negate the need for a ruling class. The movement Winstanley helped to create called themselves the True Levellers, because they sought to level 'real property' as well as titles and wealth.

By April 1649, just a few months after the publication of *The New Law of Righteousness*, food prices in England were at an all-time high. The True Levellers responded by planting vegetables on common land on St George's Hill near Cobham in Surrey. They invited 'all to come in and help them' and promised them 'meat, drink, and clothes' in return. This cultivation of common land, which earned the True Levellers the nickname 'Diggers', was meant to inspire similar actions among the poor. The Diggers believed that the poorer sections of society could become self-sufficient – and free themselves from both serfdom and wage slavery – by manuring, preparing and sowing commons, forests and wastelands; the Diggers hoped that this would neutralize the monopolies of the landowners and pave the way for Winstanley's agrarian revolution. Digger communes did appear throughout the country, but, recognizing them as a threat, local clergy and landowners were quick to organize violent opposition. Diggers were beaten by paid hooligans and extensively fined by magistrates; their cattle were driven away, their crops torn up and their makeshift homes burnt; General Fairfax even sent troops against them, but this tactic was soon abandoned when the troops started to take an interest in Digger ideas. Harsh conditions and even harsher treatment would lead to the downfall of the True Levellers.

Numerous seventeenth-century radical groups met with the same end and, without organized opposition, parliament – and the landowners it served – would come to enclose even more land than the monarchy before them. The mercantile classes that had been the focus of peasant ridicule and resistance in the *Gest* would finally come to dominate both the physical and political landscape of England. Capitalism would cover the commons in 'PRIVATE' signs and help turn a well-fed peasantry into a starving rural – then urban – proletariat.

Winstanley himself wasn't overly impressed with Magna Carta; he felt that 'the best Laws that England hath (*viz.* Magna Carta) … are yoaks and manicles, tying one sort of people to be slaves of another.'

He did however believe that pre-Norman, Anglo-Saxon England was a golden age for common rights. There can be little doubt that the English peasantry was better off before the Norman Invasion, but modern science suggests that the common rights enshrined by the Liberties of England are much more ancient than Winstanley could possibly have imagined; much older, in fact, than England itself...

The generally held – but largely romantic – view of British history is that the Scots, Irish and Welsh are descended from Celts who arrived in the area comparatively recently, while the ancestors of the English are for the most part the Anglo-Saxons who drove the others into the hills as the Roman Empire was collapsing. But modern science paints a very different story. Research by Stephen Oppenheimer of Oxford University shows that 70 per cent of Scottish men and 68 per cent of the English have DNA that suggests they are descended from people who arrived in Britain more than 7,500 years ago from the Basque region of Northern Spain.

> 75–95 per cent of British Isles [genetic] matches derive from Iberia ... Ireland, coastal Wales, and central and west-coast Scotland are almost entirely made up from Iberian founders, while the rest of the non-English parts of the British Isles have similarly high rates. England has rather lower rates of Iberian types with marked heterogeneity, but no English sample has less than 58 per cent of Iberian samples ... The ancestors of some 88 per cent of the Irish, 81 per cent of the Welsh, 79 per cent of the Cornish, 70 per cent of Scots and 68 per cent of the English arrived here during that period ... None of the later immigrations contributed anything more than 5 per cent to the gene pool.[11]

The Basque people themselves have always been been big on social equality and common rights. Linebaugh describes how, on paying a visit to the Basque region, the first vice-president of the United States, John Adams, was astonished to find that 'the Basque have "never known a landless class, either slave or villein". Well before the regicides of modern European revolutions, "one of the privileges they have most insisted on, is not to have a king."'[12]

Linebaugh also tells us that the Basque have their own Charters of Liberty:

> The liberties of the Basques were traditionally renewed at an oak standing on ground in Guernica. The liberties derive from the fueros or charters of the eleventh through the thirteenth centuries. They are similar to Magna Carta – providing jurisdiction, defining customs, delineating tenures, documenting pasturage rights. The Castilian king swore at Guernica that he and his successors would maintain the fueros, customs, franchises and liberties of the land. The charters began as an orally transmitted code of uses and customs. The details of commoning varied from valley to valley, village to village, but clearly indicated a precommodity regime.[13]

The comparisons between the Basque liberties and those of the Basque-descended English are striking. I am more dreamer than thinker and do not claim to be an authority on such matters; but is it too far-fetched to hypothesize that the 'liberties' which appeared in England and the Basque country during the medieval period might have an ancient common ancestor? That the idea of 'the commons' may even have been 'orally transmitted' by poorer people throughout history regardless of which regime happened to be in power? And that maybe these culturally inherited ideas were drawn upon whenever – and wherever – the people's common rights were threatened by newly emerging property rights? We cannot know; but the possibility warms my heart.

Guernica, of course, would witness a terrible – and highly symbolic – attack on liberty that would change the face of modern warfare.

Unlike most of Europe in the 1930s, Spain was still a largely rural, peasant-based society. Authoritarian, state-based ideologies such as capitalism, communism and fascism shunned the peasantry as anathema to their shared dream of 'technological progress'. Marxist dogma insisted that it was the urban worker, rather than the peasant, who was the prime agent of revolutionary change; but in Spain it was the peasantry who were instrumental in creating a truly revolutionary society.

As with the Basque peoples, Spanish peasants had little regard for tyrants, and during the nineteenth century the Andalusian countryside witnessed a surge of revolutionary agrarian movements. Eric Hobsbawm:

> In the late 1850s there is news of roaming peasant bands, and even of villages taking power ... [T]he first indigenous revolutionary movement which attracted specific attention was the revolt in Loja and Iznajar in 1861, several years before the irruption of the Bakunist apostles.'[14]

This deeply held 'peasant anarchism' would complement the teachings of radical educators such as Francisco Ferrer y Guardia and strengthen the work of the urban anarchist collectives in cities such as Barcelona and Zaragoza. Common cultivation of the land provided an unprecedented level of autonomy, and by 1936 much of Spain was in the thrall of a 'beautiful idea'; a beauty poignantly captured by George Orwell in his 1938 *Homage to Catalonia*:

> I had dropped more or less by chance into the only community of any size in Western Europe where political consciousness and disbelief in capitalism were more normal than their opposites. Up here in Aragon one was among tens of thousands of people, mainly though not entirely of working-class origin, all living at the same level and mingling on terms of equality. In theory it was perfect equality, and even in practice it was not far from it. There is a sense in which it would be true to say that one was experiencing a foretaste of Socialism, by which I mean that the prevailing mental atmosphere was that of Socialism. Many of the normal motives of civilized life – snobbishness, money-grubbing, fear of the boss, etc. – had simply ceased to exist. The ordinary class-division of society had disappeared to an extent that is almost unthinkable in the money-tainted air of England; there was no one there except the peasants and ourselves, and no one owned anyone else as his master.[15]

The anarchist experience during the Spanish Republic debunked many authoritarian myths. Far from needing a 'boss', anarchist farms and factories became more efficient than they had been under feudalism or capitalism. Some areas abandoned money altogether, but even where it was still in use, goods were available at a quarter of their previous price. Anarchist zones worked on entirely libertarian principles; decisions were made through councils of ordinary citizens without any sort of bureaucracy (this system was even honoured by the anarchist militias; they had no rank system, no hierarchy, no salutes, and 'leaders' were elected by the troops). But, as I mentioned earlier, widespread autonomy and self-reliance is damaging to authoritarian systems, and the anarchists would come under attack from fascists, capitalists *and* communists during the Spanish Civil War.

On April 26th 1937, in a horrifying precursor to the bombings of London, Dresden and Hiroshima, a German Luftwaffe squadron known as the Condor Legion attacked Guernica with bombs, incendiary devices and machine-gun fire. Noel Monks, a correspondent for the *London Daily Express*, reported:

We were about eighteen miles east of Guernica when Anton … started shouting. He pointed wildly ahead, and my heart shot into my mouth, when I looked. Over the top of some small hills appeared a flock of planes …

We were still a good ten miles away when I saw the reflection of Guernica's flames in the sky. As we drew nearer, on both sides of the road, men, women and children were sitting, dazed. I saw a priest … 'What happened, Father?' I asked … He just pointed to the flames [and] whispered: 'Aviones … bombas … mucho, mucho …'

I was the first correspondent to reach Guernica, and was immediately pressed into service by some Basque soldiers collecting charred bodies that the flames had passed over. Some of the soldiers were sobbing like children. There were flames and smoke and grit, and the smell of burning human flesh was nauseating. Houses were collapsing into the inferno.

… The only things left standing were a church [and] a sacred Tree, symbol of the Basque people.

The 'sacred Tree' was, of course, the oak where the Basque people traditionally renewed their liberties, but by 1939 all liberty in Spain would be crushed beneath the iron glove of fascism. Today nothing remains of the 'beautiful idea', but the massacre at Guernica did lead to the creation of one of the most important artworks in human history.

The Spanish Republic had already commissioned Pablo Picasso to create a mural-size painting for the 1937 Paris International Exhibition, but after hearing about the terrible events in the Basque country he deserted his original idea and on May 1st 1937 he began work on *Guernica*. The painting that he produced is so haunting that it has the power to put even latter-day tyrants to shame. On February 5th 2003 a large blue curtain was used to cover up the tapestry copy of *Guernica* which hangs in the entrance to the United Nation's Security Council room. This was done so that Picasso's famous image would not be visible to cameras when Colin Powell gave a press conference to try and justify the then forthcoming war with Iraq. Australian MP Laurie Brereton said in an interview after Powell's speech:

> There is a profound symbolism in pulling a shroud over this great work of art ... We may well live in the age of the so-called 'smart bomb', but the horror on the ground will be just the same as that visited upon the villagers of Guernica ... Innocent Iraqis – men, women and children – will pay a terrible price. And it won't be possible to pull a curtain over that.

Today our televisions bring us daily 'Guernicas' from around the world; a highly fascistic form of capitalism is attempting to make 'property' of every aspect of human life, including our 'common' genetic, cultural and intellectual heritage; and our ancient, hard-won liberties are being steadily rolled back in the name of 'security'. Freedom in the 'free world' has more to do with 'brand choice' than land rights, but that hasn't stopped more and more people trying to get 'back to the land'.

Piecemeal, largely individual, cultivation of gardens and allotments can make a real difference. During the Second World War these 'home-grown' initiatives supplied 10 per cent of the nation's food; this may not sound like a lot, but this 10 per cent provided the vitamins and minerals essential for health and allowed farmers to focus their efforts on producing carbohydrates and fats. But we can become even more resilient and further increase yields by reintroducing the notion of communal cultivation; in other words, by resurrecting the commons.

Our neglected parks, fields, wastelands, industrial sites, car parks, railway embankments, tow-paths, spoil heaps, quarries and landfills are all commons in waiting.

Winstanley was right; but so – until such time that the commons are once again protected by the statute books – was Robin Hood. It is a sad fact that today's commoner may have to chose between what is legal and what is right; in order to practise their ancient common rights, they may be forced to live outside the law.

At the time of writing, in the heart of Barnsdale, latter-day Diggers are planning a symbolic squat of Doncaster's 'Earth Centre'. Costing somewhere in the region of £50 million, the Earth Centre was originally conceived in the late eighties as a response to the World Commission on Environment and Development's call for 'vast campaigns of education, debate and public participation' concerning sustainable development. Sadly, as the money started to roll in, the project mutated from 'an exhibition of sustainable development practices and an international centre for related research and education' and became a rather crappy theme park. In 2004, following what the *Guardian* called 'a roller-coaster ride of false starts, wild hopes and dashed plans' (what we locals call 'cock-ups' and 'sell-outs'), the Earth Centre closed its doors for the last time. Let's hope that Barnsdale's latest band of 'merry men' (who happen to be mostly women – Robin the Marianist would be delighted) can save these facilities for future generations and open up a much-needed debate on common rights. And what of Robin himself – what would he make of modern Barnsdale? I have a feeling that Keats was not far wrong when he wrote:

> And if Robin should be cast
> Sudden from his turfed grave
> And if Marian should have

Once again her forest days,
She would weep and he would craze.
He would swear, for all his oaks
fallen beneath the dockyard strokes,
Have rotted on the briny seas.
She would weep that her wild bees
Sang not to her – strange that honey
Can't be got without hard money.

– John Keats, 'Robin Hood. To a Friend',
The Poetical Works of John Keats, 1884

1. S. Knight. *Robin Hood: A Complete Study of the English Outlaw*. Blackwell, 1994.

2. J. Cox. 'Robin Hood: Earl, Outlaw or Rebel?' *International Socialism*, issue 78, 1998.

3. J. Taylor & J. D. Strayner [eds.]. *Dictionary of the Middle Ages*. Charles Scribner's Sons, 1988.

4. Capt. C. Johnson. *Pirates*. Creation Books, 1999.

5. Anonymous. 'Pirate Utopias', *Do Or Die,* issue 8, 1999.

6. C. Hill. *The World Turned Upside Down: Radical Ideas During the English Revolution*. Maurice Temple Smith, 1972.

7. P. Linebaugh. *The Magna Carta Manifesto: Liberties and Commons For All*. University of California Press, 2008.

8. Ibid.

9. Ibid.

10. Ibid.

11. S. Oppenheimer. *The Origins of the British: A Genetic Detective Story*. Constable & Robinson, 2006.

12. Linebaugh, op. cit.

13. Ibid.

14. E. Bobsbawm. *Primitive Rebels*. WW Norton & Company, 1959.

15. G. Orwell. *Homage To Catalonia*. Secker and Warburg, 1938.

Alice Smith

FOOD AND FIBRE

Jean-Paul Flintoff

HETHER YOU RAISE SHEEP TO EAT THEM OR TO USE their wool, you need to supply them with earth, water, feed, antibiotics and much more. The same applies to crops, as I have discovered on my allotment – though I'm not going to tell you, just yet, which crops I have been growing to turn into clothes.

It's a sign of how far we have come from self-sufficiency that few people understand how closely food and clothing are related. But if you think about it for a moment you must see that it's crazy to boycott apples that have been flown in from New Zealand while happily buying clothes made of cotton that has been grown half-way round the world.

And if people are horrified that Britons throw away a third of the food we buy, why don't they worry that we spend, on average, £600 a year on clothes and throw away £400 worth? That's more than a million tons of clothing rubbish each year in the UK.

When I first became aware of all this, as a journalist, working on assignment, it set me on a path that led me back to the land – quite literally, to grow my own food and fibre, but also in a more metaphoric sense, hinted at by the ecologist and writer Alastair McIntosh when he conjures us to 'dig where we stand'. That is, I tried to remould my life so that it was shaped as much as possible by the land around me: the natural and manmade resources in it and the people who lived in it, rather than the people and things from far away, on whom the global economy depends, and whom we often hinder even when we are trying to help.

Consider, for instance, the havoc we create when we donate our unwanted clothing to people overseas.

Joe Turner of the Freedom Clothing Project points out that the sheer quantity of free clothing dumped on 'developing' countries destroys the market for local clothing. If you ever wondered why rioting Africans in far-flung villages all seem to be wearing Gap sweatshirts, it's because the local clothing industry has been destroyed. Over time, as people in Africa and elsewhere forget how to make clothes, they become dependent on cheap imports – just like us.

Gandhi recognized something like this effect in India, decades ago. Under British rule, Indians had become dependent on British mills to spin and weave Indian cotton.

Gandhi gave up wearing Western-style clothing and adopted the practice of weaving his own clothes from thread he'd spun himself. He even invented a portable spinning wheel that he took with him to political meetings.

Gandhi rightly predicted that if Indians made their own clothes, it would deal a devastating blow to the British establishment. Within a few years, the cotton mills in Lancashire – where many of my Flintoff forebears spun Indian cotton for export back to India – had closed. And when India achieved independence Gandhi's insight was acknowledged by the addition of the spinning wheel to the national flag.

Gandhi's idea was revolutionary because it showed that a whole country's destiny can be determined by individuals doing something very small indeed. This should hardly be a surprise, of course, since most of us are aware that our individual choices as consumers, multiplied many times over, have enormous impact.

A good example of this is our overwhelming obsession with price, which puts downward pressure on the quality of products we consume. After manufacturers have increased efficiency and economies of scale, the pressure of bargain hunters leads to the exploitation of producers – from sweatshop workers to battery chickens – and finally a decline in the quality of the goods.

Molly Scott Cato is an economist and the author of the brilliantly provocative book *Market, Schmarket*. She argues that the economic system elevates profit to the exclusion of all else, including quality:

There was a time when Marks & Spencer just made good knickers and you could always buy them there. They may have been a little more expensive but the extra was worth paying because the knickers were comfortable and lasted. In the underwear department these are important considerations. But I challenge you to find a decent pair of underwear in today's high street.

Jeremy Paxman, the notoriously severe TV interviewer, said much the same in an email to Sir Stuart Rose, chief executive at Marks & Spencer, which was subsequently leaked.

'I've noticed that something very troubling has happened,' Paxman wrote. '[M&S] pants no longer provide adequate support. The other thing is socks. Even among those of us who clip our toenails very rigorously they appear to be wearing out much more quickly on the big toe.'

There is a market opportunity for somebody to produce decent underwear, says Scott Cato:

I would certainly pay a premium price. But instead all suppliers of these items are competing on price, outsourcing production and using only the cheapest materials, so that knickers are see-through and fall apart within months. This is the way the best profits are made and the best knickers are no longer of any concern.

Is there an alternative? Well, we could make our own clothes – but can we afford to?

Ralph Borsodi, an economic theorist, decided to research the economics of home-made goods in the early twentieth century, with results that astonished him.

By his own account, the idea arose in 1920, when Mrs Borsodi set about canning and preserving fruits and vegetables for winter use.

'It's great,' he said, 'but does it really pay?'

'Of course it does,' was her reply.

Over a period of several days and nights, they set about calculating the costs involved and comparing them with commercial production. It wasn't easy, because quite naturally they'd kept no record of how many minutes they devoted to, say, their row of tomato plants.

'We did finally come to figures which I felt we might use,' he wrote later. 'The cost of the home-made product was between 20 per cent and 30 per cent lower than the price of factory-made merchandise.

How was it possible, I kept asking myself, for a woman working all alone to produce canned goods at a lower cost than could the Campbell Soup Company with its fine division of labour, its efficient management, its labour-saving machinery, its quantity buying, its mass-production economies? Unless there was a mistake in our calculations, this experiment knocked all the elaborate theories framed by economists … into a cocked hat.

What economists had overlooked – he eventually concluded – was that while production costs in factories had decreased, year after year, distribution costs had increased. Indeed, Borsodi came up with an economic law: distribution costs tend to move in inverse relationship to production costs.

By his calculations, more than two-thirds of the things the average family buys could be produced more economically at home than they could be bought factory-made. So he installed a loom at home, capable of handling fabrics up to 44 inches wide. 'With such a loom, even an average weaver can produce a yard of cloth an hour. A speedy weaver, willing to exert himself, can produce 30 yards per day. Since it takes only seven yards of 27-inch cloth to make a three-piece suit for a man, it is possible to weave the cloth for a suit in a single day on a small loom, and in less than a day on a loom able to handle 54-inch cloth.'

What particularly thrilled Borsodi, he said, was not the speed and economic value of domestic production – it was the outlet for sheer creativity.

By turning his hand to a craft, he realized that the Industrial Revolution had destroyed, or certainly reduced, people's capacity to be fulfilled by their work. You may be surprised to learn that Adam Smith had himself identified this danger in *The Wealth of Nations*, acknowledging that the fine division of labour leads to a 'mental mutilation' in workers.

Another economist, E. F. Schumacher, argued in his influential book

Small is Beautiful that to organize work in such a manner that it becomes meaningless, boring, stultifying or nerve-racking for the worker 'would indicate a greater concern with goods than with people'. And to justify it by saying that it makes time for leisure would be a complete misunderstanding of one of the basic truths of human existence:

> Work properly conducted in conditions of human dignity and freedom blesses those who do it and equally their products. If a man has no chance of obtaining work he is in a desperate position, not simply because he lacks an income but because he lacks this nourishing and enlivening factor of disciplined work, which nothing can replace.

In other words, enforced 'leisure' is not true idleness – it's a form of oppression, whereas choosing to make things in our own time is enriching.

Inspired by the arguments – and positive example – of Borsodi, Schumacher and Gandhi, I set about making my own clothes a year or so ago. I bought myself a treadle-powered sewing machine, knitting needles and crochet hooks, and began to make a whole outfit: fitted shirt, woolly jumper, hat, jeans, socks, even shoes (using a kit) and underpants. This last item might never have satisfied Paxman, but brought me a good measure of satisfaction.

But I was troubled by Borsodi's argument that home-made is cheaper than factory-produced goods. It simply didn't appear to be true: it was inconceivable that anybody working at home and knitting a jumper, for example, or weaving fabic even on the widest possible domestic loom, could produce garments as cheaply as the high-street chains.

I checked this with a member of the Guild of Spinners, Dyers and Weavers. She taught me to spin, and explained that producing a single skein of yarn would take an accomplished spinner like herself about eight hours.

Eight hours!

At the time of writing, the national minimum wage is £5.52 an hour. So a single ball of bamboo yarn, if you paid somebody to spin it, would cost at least £45, and that's assuming that the fibre cost nothing. To make a man's sweater you'd need several skeins, and if you wanted somebody to knit that for you, you'd pay for a similar amount of time. We're talking about something like £500 for a sweater.

The all-too obvious explanation gradually dawned on me: it's impossible to get something cheap without somebody, or something, being exploited.

But when I happened casually to expound my theory to somebody I know and respect, he rejected it.

'That's not true.'

The person in question has a degree from one of the world's leading business schools, which could mean either that he knows what he's talking about or else that he's been trained up in exactly the kind of half-baked, self-serving economic theories that Borsodi once mistakenly subscribed to.

I should have pointed out that by trading internationally in things, such as clothes, that we could have produced ourselves we are exploiting – wasting – natural resources, particularly fuel, which isn't going to last all that much longer. (Can you imagine somebody saying, before oil was discovered – or indeed after it has run out, whenever that may be – that it's a sensible idea to get British clothes made in India or China?)

Instead, I said that I thought the international clothes trade systematically exploited people: 'We export the work to India, or China, because we think it's OK to pay people there less than we would pay our neighbours, or our families, for the same work,' I offered rather earnestly.

He didn't miss a beat. 'There's nothing wrong with that. It's right to pay the market price for labour in those countries.'

I was stumped: this struck me as both heartless and correct. But afterwards, when I'd got home, I concluded that it was only heartless.

Why? Because the market price for labour in countries such as India is distorted, and unjust. I knew this because I'd recently read the memoirs of Wangari Maathai, the Kenyan woman who won the Nobel Peace Prize in 2004.

Before the British came to Kenya, Maathai wrote, Kenyans used animals, particularly goats, as currency. The British did not want to be paid in goats but cash, and also wanted to create a workforce. So they – we – introduced an income tax for men in most parts of the country that could only be paid in cash. This immediately created a cash-based economy, and the colonial government and British settlers were the only ones with money in their hands. So Kenyans were indirectly forced to work on settlers' farms or migrate to cities to work in offices, to earn money to pay taxes. And you can be sure that they weren't paid the same rates as English workers doing similar jobs in England.

By the time Kenya won independence, its economy had come to depend on international trade in currencies that Kenyans don't control – so Kenyan labour remains cheap.

People sometimes tell me that my fondness for local, seasonal food is misjudged: I should continue to buy Kenyan mangetouts, they tell me, because this provides Kenyans with a valuable source of income. I'm not convinced. I think Kenyans would be better off growing food and fibres for their own use. Furthermore, I'd argue that by trading with Kenyans, or Indians, for food or services at a low price I'm undercutting my neighbours. In the long run, I may be putting my neighbours out of work. Why would I do that? To ruin your neighbours is as crazy as depleting your soil. Or to put the point more positively: I shall continue to enrich my garden by composting kitchen waste, and I shall try to enrich my neighbours by giving them meaningful work to do at a fair price.

Some months ago, after joining the board of the care home on the other side of my garden fence, it dawned on me to try getting a spot of creative work into the lives of the sometimes rather bored-looking residents.

If the Quaker philanthropist Elizabeth Fry could improve life for prisoners by giving them fabric and sewing kits, and Gandhi could do something similar for Indians, perhaps I could help the aged? After all, I'd seen how my wife's 97-year-old great-aunt, Peggy, had been enlivened by the task of helping me to make my first fitted shirt.

But could I really get the residents knitting? I went to see the manager, and the woman who valiantly strives to entertain them, and then asked the residents themselves. Quite a few looked delighted. I started to dream about setting up some kind of market for their knitwear.

In effect, I had all but reinvented (though so far only in my imagination) the Victorian workhouse. And why not? After all, work is nourishing and enlivening, according to Schumacher. Conducted in conditions of human dignity and freedom, it blesses those who do it and, equally, their products.

Come to that, children might enjoy a spot of decent work too.

I went to see Camila Batmanghelidjh, whom I've known for years, since I first wrote about her extraordinary work with disturbed and often violent children living in south London. Many of these children are brought up, effectively, by their siblings or their peers, because their parents are all too often dead, addicted to mind-altering substances, or in jail. Quite a number never attend school and don't even exist, so far as officialdom is concerned. Many turn up at the premises of Camila's charity, Kids Company, determined to cause trouble – because that's the only behaviour they've learned.

It was lovely to see Camila again. She told me how some of the children I had met were now getting on. One small group of former child-soldiers, previously hardened to rape and cold-blooded slaughter, had recently been enrolled at higher-education establishments and took Camila out to celebrate over a pizza.

I told Camila that I had a plan to help her in bringing a sense of useful purpose into the children's lives. It was this: she should get somebody (me, if necessary) to teach them crochet. They'd love it. I could show them how to make "plarn" (plastic yarn) out of carrier bags, and they would never lack for raw materials. Who knows, perhaps they could sell what they made?

'We need to stop kids carrying knives,' I announced, 'and get them to carry crochet hooks instead.'

Camila didn't absolutely leap into the air, but she smiled and agreed that it was a nice idea.

And there's nothing wrong with spreading ideas. Soon after, Camila sent me an email.

'I'm going to bear in mind your gift in knitting. I wonder whether we should start a knitting marathon and fund-raise for it.'

I replied: 'I think a knitting marathon is a great idea. But don't forget crochet – the hooks (not as sharp as they sound!) are more portable than a pair of much longer knitting needles. I have visions of young people crocheting hoodies on street corners.'

So far as this went, it was great. But what about local materials? The crop failures associated with climate change, and resource shortages, may one day soon require us to produce our own fabrics. Can we do that? Recent research in *The Land* magazine has shown that Britain doesn't have enough land to feed itself – not organically, anyway, and at current rates of meat consumption – let alone also produce the fabric to clothe us.

Additionally, we suffer from ignorance: a paradoxical effect of being a colonial power is that people in Britain, having relied for so long on cheap cotton from overseas, have forgotten which local materials can be used for textiles. In our own way, we're victims of colonial history too.

So what materials are there? Well, there's wool, obviously – from 60 different sheep breeds. And linen, which some people may remember is derived from flax.

Another that is less well known is nettle.

In the early years of the twentieth century, Britain controlled 90 per cent of world cotton. For reasons that must be obvious, Austro-Hungary and Germany were keen to develop alternatives – acutely so, by the time of the First World War, in which they would have had to fight naked if cotton became unavailable.

The work of developing an alternative was overseen by a man legendary in the admittedly small nettle-fibre industry: Professor G. Bredeman of Hamburg University spent decades growing the finest varieties of nettle.

Nettle fibres are long: anything above 1⅜ inch is equal to the best Egyptian cotton. Nettle can be dyed and bleached in the same way as cotton, and when mercerized (bashed) nettle is only slightly inferior to silk. It has been considered much superior to cotton for velvet and plush.

At night, after watching gloomy stories on the evening news about climate change or failing energy supplies, I cheer myself up by imagining that the future won't be all bad if we can only get our act together and start cultivating more nettles.

And hemp. I must confess that when I first heard about hemp for clothing I thought immediately that this was bound to be second-rate, suitable only for shabby dope-fiends and beardy-weirdies. I was mistaken. Check out this fulsome plaudit, which I found online, from an American clothes-maker:

> Of all the fabrics that I have known and loved, my favorite is Romanian hemp. When I opened my first packet of Romanian hemp fabric swatches I felt a tingling sensation like I was discovering an ancient treasure … What more beautiful plant is there than this hempen plant for naturally treading lightly on the planet?

Quite so. Like nettle, hemp is resistant to pests so requires no chemical pesticides or fungicides. It's fast-growing, so it chokes out weeds, so no herbicides are needed. The long fibres are broken free from the stalk with nothing but water, before being spun into yarn and woven into fabric.

Under Henry VIII, hemp was considered so useful that it was illegal not to grow a bit of it. Now we've gone the other way, because the plant is related to cannabis and, though entirely free of narcotic effect, it cannot be grown legally except with a Home Office licence, and even then only if it's locked away from public access.

Well, I don't have a licence, but I do have a garden that's inaccessible to passers-by. So last summer I illegally sowed a handful of hemp seeds I'd bought in a health-food shop. At the same time, I transplanted some wild nettles on to my allotment.

It was late in the year, and the plants had only a short time to grow, and by autumn they were still very short. But as I'd been advised, I cut them down and left them on the ground to rot, and did the same with my nettles. After a few days, I peeled strands of hair-thin fibre from the stems and twisted them into short but incredibly strong thread.

It sat on my desk for several weeks, a much prized trophy – until it was swept away by persons unknown and, presumably, put out with the rubbish.

CHARLIE CAKE PARK

Boff Whalley

CHARLIE CAKE PARK IS IN ARMLEY, LEEDS. SOME PEOPLE might say Armley itself is a shithole, a white-trash mish-mash shithole of redbrick and high-rises and boarded-up pubs feeding off a shopping centre full of betting shops and Cash Converters and pound shops and pizza takeaways. Armley's landmark is a carpet warehouse called Mike's Carpets. Mike's Carpets is a shithole, I won't argue with that.

Three famous people came from Armley: Barbara Taylor-Bradford, Alan Bennett and Zodiac Mindwarp – three corners of a literary triangle united only by the fact that they all got out of here as soon as they could; and never came back. Working-class writers have a habit of (and let me generalize wildly here) leaving a place early doors and then milking their experiences there, in writing, for the rest of their lives. In the case of these three, aside from the odd bit of Alan Bennett, Armley's been left unmilked.

The reason some might call Armley a shithole is because there are red-haired feral kids hanging round the newsagent's waiting to sell you drugs and steal your purse; there are YouTube films of local lads robbing the local school: there's a purple-painted Health Centre and a sign outside the taxi rank saying: 'Distinguish Your Cigs Here.'

But it's not a shithole at all, don't listen to them. Armley is a mish-mash all right but some of this jumble of a community, lately livened up by an influx of Russians, Poles and Lithuanians, is working out how to look after itself and create something for itself, and the main focus of this creativity is Charlie Cake Park.

Charlie Cake Park is a bit like Central Park, except it's smaller and doesn't have an ice-skating rink or a zoo, or a place for visiting rock bands to have their photographs taken. But it does have an underground toilet that's been filled in, and three benches and a tree swing. Charlie Cake Park belongs to Armley Common Rights Trust, and is one of the dwindling parcels of common land donated to the people of Armley in 1793 under the Enclosure Acts. It's named after a man with a baking business and a horse. Charlie hawked his cakes and breads up and down West Leeds 160 years ago, and the hill at the top of Armley Town Street – formerly a tram stop, before trams were ousted by the almighty god auto – became a hill worth resting upon. People would gather and buy his cakes there, at this small triangular piece of grass. They say his cakes were eaten by the Queen on a visit to Leeds in 1853, but we don't care about that. What we care about is this piece of triangular grass named after a bloke with a horse and some cakes.

Charlie Cake Park spent those last 160 years evolving into a place to hang out with your carrier bag of Special Brew, a place for your dog to shit, a place to gather in young packs, a place to rip the branches off trees and shout at the young lasses who'd got off the bus, a place to piss and a place to mess up. The council didn't do anything about its upkeep because they couldn't profit from it. It didn't belong to them; it belonged to the people.

Then at some point a handful of years ago something changed. People became aware that in newly wealthy Leeds, spare land was being gobbled up and developed; school playing fields were being sold off for seventies suburban dreamhome clusters, the old recreation grounds ('recs') were being turned into supersized Asdas and the vast grey car-park sprawls that cling on to their hem. And so Charlie Cake Park became something to treasure and protect.

The Armley Common Rights Trust was inspired in part by other local people carving out fresh ideas among the tired old terraces – the West Leeds Festival was one woman's idea, which quickly became an annual month-long collection of arts events from the motley to the magnificent. Music, dance, theatre, all of it a million miles from those tepid Council community 'fun' events peopled by volunteers in bright yellow T-shirts on double-decker buses.

A local theatre group, Interplay, became the hub for festival-inspired events that continued throughout the year. And into the mix came Charlie Cake Park; a focal point. A place to gather. From out of nowhere came the Charlie Cake Baking Competition, the first of many – the park was cleaned up, marquees erected, and upwards of a hundred cakes piled up along trestle tables. And the crowds! Suddenly the whole of human life was there, wrestling to champion this triangular patch of grass as ours, the people's, a place we could all use.

Volunteer groups got involved – landscaping, re-planting, tidying. The Trust worked their arses off, opened the park to all-comers, and the dogshit slowly disappeared as the picnickers and tree-swings appeared. Money came from grants and donations, money for lawnmowers and compost bins and plants and signs for the gates and tarmac for the paths.

The Common Rights Trust took on not only this small park over the road from the off-licence but all the accumulated baggage which came with it: the bureaucracy, planning, form-filling, meetings, meetings, meetings, meetings. The Trust learned to side-step the council's long-tongued loopholery and learned to suss out the shady landsniffing infiltrators, people who wanted to buy up the people's land and use it for more flats and betting shops and Cash Converters. The Common Rights Trust were clearing the shit out of the park in more ways than one.

And now Charlie Cake Park isn't a shithole at all. It's a place known for its urban picnics, Easter jamborees and winter carol singing. There's an annual calendar produced by Leeds art students celebrating the park and its 'Make, bake & grow' ethos. According to the Trustees, the hardest part of creating and sustaining the park isn't the digging and litter-picking but maintaining a committed volunteer group. Nevertheless, they've done just that: they've managed to pull off something quite remarkable with this little park in the middle of Armley's hubbub of cultures, ideas and lifestyles.

Up across the river in wealthier, trendier Leeds, they're gathering on the campuses to discuss 'the environment' as if it's a set of theories and abstractions. Changing the world by changing lightbulbs and by protesting at airports. Over here in Charlie Cake Park, squashed between the car-jammed no-ball-games streets, three or four generations of Armley people are meeting up to enjoy a hard-won patch of green named after a baker called Charlie.

That's the way to change the world: Charlie Cake Park was a shithole, and now it's not.

Joe Wilson

GWASHATA

THE HUNTER-GATHERER
ROAD TO HAPPINESS

Stuart Watkins

T O BE AN IDLER IS TO VALUE CERTAIN ACTIVITIES ABOVE
others: useful work above meaningless toil, peace and contemplation above thoughtless striving, artistic creation and crafts-
manship above alienated production, loving relationships with friends
and families above power and subordination and exploitation, individual happiness above false claims of duty, festivals for collective joy
above lonely survival. Unfortunately, as soon as we even begin to talk
about these values, let alone put them into practice, we find that
society as a whole has other priorities, higher values. The most fundamentally important of these is the work ethic, which we all imbibe
along with our mother's milk, and according to which work is good
for you and good for society. Family life, looking after the health of
ourselves and our loved ones, education, democratic deliberation and
action, the free development of talents and interests, indulging in
pleasures ... these things can be tolerated in Western culture as long as
they can be fitted around the working week.

For those of us who value these things above work, this state of
affairs raises a vital question. Might society be organized along different lines, in which these currently neglected values become priorities?
In search of an answer, let us go back to the first form of human social
organization that ever existed – the kind of society in which human
nature was forged.

★

191

In 1954, the anthropologist Colin Turnbull felt he'd found something to do with his life that was really worthwhile. Reading his classic book, *The Forest People* (1961), it's hard not to conclude that what he had found was a lost Eden. Deep in the Ituri rainforest in the northern Congo in Africa, living in simple huts made from the leaves and branches of trees, were the Mbuti pygmies, hunter-gatherers who made their living foraging for roots, nuts, berries and other foods growing wild in the forest, and hunting game animals with bows and arrows and nets.

Having no crops nor livestock to care for, nor technology to attend to, no bosses or chiefs or state machine to tell them what to do, and living in an earthly paradise with an abundance of food readily to hand, the Mbuti dedicated themselves to a life of songs, rituals and dances. What is important for our purposes is that this lifestyle seemed to produce free and happy human beings. The Mbuti were, says Turnbull, 'infinitely wise' and lived the lives they did not because they didn't know any better or were ignorant of alternatives, but because they had an intense love for the forest and believed it to be a better and kinder place than the outside world that threatened to destroy it. In the forest, the pygmies had 'found something ... that made their life more than just worth living, something that made it, with its full complement of hardships and problems and tragedies, a wonderful thing full of joy and happiness and free of care'. In short, they were idlers.

So how did this idling life work out in practice? Turnbull returned to the forest in 1956 to find out – to live with the pygmies, do everything they did, share their food, join in with their rituals. But living with idlers is not without its frustrations, especially if you arrive with chores for them to do. To carry out their research, anthropologists necessarily rely on the support of other people, such as informers and translators, so one of Turnbull's first tasks on arrival was to re-establish contact with his pygmy guide, a young boy called Kenge. Turnbull was obviously very fond of the youth, but he tells us that he still had to fire him regularly – 'every two or three weeks'. Why? Well, because Kenge was a typical pygmy, a typical hunter-gatherer, which meant he was 'disinclined to do anything he did not want to do'. For example, soon after taking him on, Turnbull gave Kenge some money to go and get supper. Kenge took the money gladly, then promptly disappeared for the night to the beer-house. He returned much later, drunk, and gradually sneaked the blanket off Turnbull's back before falling fast asleep. When fired, Kenge would shrug and take it as an opportunity for a three-day holiday, before returning as if nothing had happened and cooking breakfast for Turnbull. Turnbull would tuck in, only to have the plate snatched off him again by Kenge before he'd finished. The remains of Turnbull's breakfast would then be handed around for others to share. From Kenge's point of view, this was the only correct and moral course of action. After all, it was obvious Turnbull was relatively rich and well fed – why should he eat his fill while children standing nearby went hungry?

This lackadaisical attitude to work and intransigent demand for a fair share was a constant source of anger and irritation to the Africans who lived a settled life in the villages. The pygmies would occasionally descend on these villages to exchange game for plantation products and do the odd spell of work for money. One minute the pygmies would take a job and start work; the next, they would shrug off the job like a heavy coat in a heat wave, up sticks, and, like a rustle of wind in the grass, disappear back into the forest, carrying whatever they could steal from the plantations with them. The forest was like a dark, impenetrable wall around the plantations, and the villagers feared what was on the other side of this wall, believing it to be the home of evil spirits. The pygmies, naturally, encouraged them in this belief. It meant they were unlikely to be pursued when they fled their jobs.

*

So you can see where the idea that the pygmies are lazy, lawless savages – shared by the African villagers no less than Victorian bigots and colonialists – comes from. But once we follow the pygmies back into their forest, any idea that their indifference to wage work must be due to inherent indolence must be abandoned. Carrying everything they own on their backs, the pygmies move at such a pace that Turnbull had to run to keep up. They walked swiftly, moving with grace and ease while singing songs; Turnbull lagged behind, slipping and tripping over roots, getting whipped by springing branches, sometimes having to crawl through areas the pygmies sprinted through with no trouble. After travelling for half a day, they arrived at Eden – the camp they had settled on as home for the near future.

But there was no time yet for idling – the camp became a hive of activity. Men set off to hunt and cut down the necessary wood and leaves to make huts; women fought over the best places to set up home. The pace did not let up for three or four days, as more families arrived. Cooking and sleeping arrangements were settled upon, adjustments made to the huts, and hunting and gathering carried on. Eventually, the pace of life settled down. The huge abundance of food and game was shared around, and the celebrations began – a festival of singing and dancing that would go on for weeks. And it was this that was the really important – the most sacred – activity. Occasional work was obviously necessary, but the forest, thought of as a loving mother, would provide, and hence the really serious thing to do was give thanks to the mother by singing and dancing and living well.

The point is that when it comes to really living – self-directed activity for their own benefit rather than work for the enrichment of others – hunter-gatherers, like good idlers everywhere, can be as energetic and industrious as anyone else. Colin Turnbull's pygmies seemed to understand instinctively and without effort something we in the West have forgotten – that self-directed activity is life, but wage work is slavery, and the two are not at all the same thing.

★

Interestingly, you'll find the story is much the same around the world. Wherever free people are introduced to wage labour, they see it for what it is and resist it bitterly – fleeing it if they can, fighting against it or minimizing its impact if not. It takes a few centuries of capitalist development before capitalists can enjoy the luxury of a population that meekly accepts its position in the labour market as natural and inevitable. This point is never made more strongly than when the people studied are hunter-gatherers, or have only in recent times moved away from hunting and gathering. And nowhere is this clearer than in Peter Gow's *An Amazonian Myth and Its History* (2001).

Gow, an anthropologist at the University of St Andrews, lived for
many years with the Piro on the Urubamba river in Peruvian
Amazonia. One of the most interesting points for the purposes of this
essay is that the Piro, despite their undoubted admiration for the technological wonders and wealth and power of the whites, nevertheless
believe that we in the West live inferior lives to their own. The Piro
would often ask Gow about 'the land of the gringos', and want to
know: 'Is there forest in your country, are there any trees?' Gow tried
to reply that there were some, but, on continued questioning, had to
admit that, compared with where the Piro lived, there were, really, no
trees and no forests in the land of the gringos. As Piro experience of
the gringos was tied up with working for them as lumberers, cutting
down trees and watching as they were shipped off downriver, it was
logical to wonder why the gringos had no trees of their own. Gow's
answer never failed to fill the Piro with dismay. Living without forest
seemed unimaginable. They would ask, 'So, how do you make gardens, what do you eat?' Added another, 'How might it be, then, do
they live just from machines?'

   To the Piro, our world appears 'deeply unattractive', says Gow,
because making villages in the forest is not just about shelter. It's about
what Gow says is a 'key local value' for the Piro: *gwashata*, 'to live well,
to live quietly'. 'Living well' is the ideal of everyday life for the Piro. It
means living without malicious gossip, without fighting, in a peaceful
village surrounded by generous and helpful kinspeople, in good
health, eating abundant quantities of 'real' food (for the Piro, 'real'
food, as opposed to the food they sometimes bought from the gringos,
was freely available in the forest, or in the gardens they made in the
forest). It means organizing good rituals to celebrate birth and marriage, and so on, some of which would go on for over a month – or
until the beer ran out. *Gwashata* means literally to reside continuously,
to reside and do nothing else. *Gwashata* means living life slowly. The
Piro, says Gow, live in 'villages filled with people much like themselves, constantly sharing food with each other, visiting and being visited, and talking over all the minor events of the day'. For a Westerner,
the Piro pace of life can initially seem very boring:

'Nothing much ever happens and, used to a more rapid pace of life and with the short attention span of my … society, I was initially often very bored living there. As the new pace of life grew on me, I began to notice its virtues, in the easy companionship, the minute attention to shifting moods that are subtly expressed, and all the time and space needed to attend to a natural world of such beauty and variety, where the river, the forest and the sky are ceaselessly changing.'

Gow himself came to 'live well' in the village, but it was clear to the Piro that, as a rule, 'white people are not very thoughtful about social life.' The missionaries and the bosses always seemed to be away from their kin and without children: how, then, did they reproduce? Perhaps, like snakes changing their skin, whites live for ever: an idea only confirmed for the Piro when they heard of plastic surgery. And what of our social values? The Piro despised and feared them, says Gow: the whites seemed to them to love social inequalities and took 'pridefulness in world transformational action' – let's call this pridefulness 'the work ethic'. The Piro themselves eagerly embraced change, but they saw it as something to be managed within the context of 'living well', not something to be pursued as an end in itself.

That the Piro had their own ideas about the capitalist West and some important lessons for Gow was ironic as he'd imagined that he was the one with something to teach. Like the long line of Christian missionaries who came before him, Gow came with a message. As a Marxist and left-wing activist, he had gone to the Urubamba on a 'consciousness-raising' mission to explain to the Piro how they had been systematically robbed, dominated and exploited, in the hope that this would better inform their struggle against the capitalist and colonialist invaders who now lived among them. Gow's mission was brought to an abrupt end by a Piro leader, who said sternly, 'We are happy for you to live here among us learning how we live. That is fine. But we don't want you to tell us what we should do.' As Gow had been brought up on punk, this was a demand he could hardly object to. Instead, he did what anthropology does best, which is listen and learn. And what he learned most of all was how it might be possible to 'live well'.

★

In the West, we're not so much 'living well' as the living dead, says
Jerome Lewis, an anthropologist at University College London. Lewis
is our very own, modern-day Colin Turnbull: he has lived and worked
with the Mbendjele pygmies of Congo-Brazzaville, not so very far
from where Turnbull was. I remember when I first heard Lewis speak,
at a small anthropology evening class run from a ramshackle community centre in Camden, London. I was struck by his infectious enthusi-
asm, how he came alive and puffed up with pride whenever he talked
about the hunter-gatherers he had lived with. In comparison with the
Mbendjele, says Lewis, we in the West are only running at about 20 per
cent of our capacity as human beings. When he talks about the
Mbendjele, it's as if, inspired by his memories of their life, he wakes up
the other 80 per cent in himself. As David Edwardes puts it in *Free to be
Human* (2000), 'human beings can only be sane, healthy, happy and
fully alive when they are strong, independent, critically aware, self-
confident, self-directed and self-moved.' As a hunter-gatherer, you are
'free to be human'. In the West, such human characteristics are likely to
cause you some trouble, especially if you have to work for a living –
the average capitalist workplace does not welcome independence and
self-confidence, rather the opposite: obedience, willingness to do
whatever is demanded by the bosses. The Mbendjele, like all hunter-
gatherers, not having any bosses, demand a full share in life – in every
decision that affects the community, and in the wealth that is socially
produced. They have a healthy disrespect for social inequalities and
hierarchies and attempts by some individuals to dominate others.

   This might puzzle those evolutionists who argue that humans are
essentially chimps with shoes. In the chimp world, social organization
is based exactly on 'dominance' – the ability to use or threaten violence
to win key social positions or gain privileged access to valued
resources. Life for a chimp is typically hierarchical and full of political
intrigue, with alliances between individuals opportunistic and vulner-
able to cheating and defection. Modern anthropology, on the other
hand, as we have seen, understands hunter-gatherer life to be quite
unlike this – in fact, almost the exact opposite. Status and competition
certainly exist in hunter-gatherer societies – but the spoils go not to
the most dominant or assertive individual, but to those best at joining

with others in transcending internal conflict, displaying generosity and suppressing attempts at dominance. The anthropologist who has taken all these insights furthest, and turned them into an impressive grand theory, is Chris Knight. First expounded in detail in his book *Blood Relations* (1991), Knight takes insights from sociobiology, archaeology and social anthropology to explain this radical gap between chimp and human life. His theory, bonkers as it may sound on first acquaintance, is that our hunter-gatherer ancestors, the first humans on the planet, were the first 'revolutionary communists' or, if you like, militant trade unionists, who established culture by overthrowing primate aggression and selfishness and putting in its place a system of solidarity and mutual aid – that is, a distinctively human way of life. The social problems we now face, in Knight's view, are due to the fact that we have, in a sense, regressed to the primate system (call it capitalism). Our task now is simply to repeat the revolution that made us human; for humanity as a whole to throw off primate-style hierarchies and acquisitiveness and return to truly human, hunter-gatherer-type social organization.

★

So, let us attempt to draw a few tentative conclusions. Is all this supposed to mean that we must literally go 'back to the land', return to a hunting and gathering way of life? Well, there are certainly some who think so. It is the position, for example, of 'primitivist' thinkers such as John Zerzan. His ideas may be 'good to think with' – engaging with the most extreme side in any debate forces us to challenge all our preconceptions, as the anarchist anthropologist David Graeber argues in his *Fragments of an Anarchist Anthropology* (2004). But personally, I can't see any way of taking Zerzan's proposition too seriously. We needn't leave our armchair to understand that a small society of hunter-gatherers would be highly unlikely to survive the year in the British Isles. If the whole population followed suit, mass starvation would be the certain result. It's a complete non-starter.

I therefore doubt that a sustainable human future will involve going 'back to the land' in the literal sense of returning to hunting and gathering, or to some mode of peasant production. But we *will* certainly need to grapple with the idea of how we might live in a relationship with nature that doesn't put unbearable pressure on the Earth's ability to sustain life. That means that the pursuit of endless economic growth and mass consumerism must go if we are to survive as a species – a truth that is as much a matter of simple mathematics as of politics. For more on what hunter-gatherers might have to teach us about environmental management, see Jerome Lewis's article on the Mbendjele system of forest conservation in issue 2 and Sian Sullivan's critique of 'green' capitalism in issue 3 of the *Radical Anthropology* journal.[1] Here, I will simply note, with Marshall Sahlins in his classic *Stone-Age Economics* (1972), that there are 'two possible courses to affluence'. One is the way we are familiar with; the market system and mass consumerism, the one that has brought the planet's life-support systems to the brink of disaster. The second is what Sahlins calls 'the Zen road to affluence'. Taking this road means recognizing 'that human material wants are finite and few, and technical means unchanging but on the whole adequate. Adopting the Zen strategy, a people can enjoy an unparalleled material plenty... free from market obsessions of scarcity.' In other words, we must exchange our Western values based on work and capital accumulation for something like the Piro's *gwashata*. As we've seen, that means learning to live well, live quietly, make peaceful villages – perhaps in the heart of our cities – surround ourselves with generous and helpful people, and organize parties that go on for months, or until the beer runs out. As individuals, we can make a start whenever we choose. As a society, it will mean eventually dismantling the whole wages-for-work system.

Unfortunately, for Western industrial societies, there is no map for this Zen road to affluence and idleness. It is true, as critics will be quick to point out, that there are no absolutely solid, certain grounds for believing that hunter-gatherer-style, stateless, anarcho-communist, egalitarian democracy is possible in Western industrial societies. But then, science has always proceeded perfectly well without the need for certainty, and it is equally true that there are no absolutely solid, certain grounds for believing that these things are not possible either.

1. See www.radicalanthropologygroup.org

And there is plenty of anthropological and historical evidence that they might be. There is what Graeber calls anthropology's vast archive of social and political experiments – experiments most of us have never heard of. There is the long and ongoing history of the everyday struggles of ordinary people, fed up with meaningless toil, bravely attempting, in their own small ways, to storm heaven.

So, to conclude, although there is as yet no definitive map of the road to an affluent and idle society, there are many signposts. All we have to do is walk the road, keeping our minds open to the full range of human possibilities. As Noam Chomsky puts it:

> There are no magic answers, no miraculous methods to overcome the problems we face, just the familiar ones: honest search for understanding, education, organization [...] – and the kind of commitment that will persist despite the temptations of disillusionment, despite many failures and only limited successes, inspired by the hope of a brighter future.

HOW HEDGEHOGS
CAN SAVE THE WORLD

Hugh Warwick

WE NEED TO LOVE, YET WE HAVE SLIPPED AWAY FROM one of the most important relationships we can ever form: the love of the land, the wild and the natural world.

Hedgehogs helped me to understand our relationship with, for want of a better word, the natural world. In his cogitations on the 'The Hedgehog's Dilemma', Schopenhauer was pondering the ways people relate to each other and hit upon a very pleasing analogy. He argued that when two hedgehogs want to get close to each other they always end up hurting each other, so back off, and become lonely and bereft. So they try again, to solve the dilemma of getting as close to the one you love without hurting them. He saw this repeated in relationships between people.

But I believe it is an idea with wider implications. The most important relationship we have is with the world around us. It informs everything about us, from our health to our happiness. And we are in a hedgehog's dilemma with the natural world. When we try to get close to it – if, for example, we all decided we wanted to live like Henry Thoreau did at Walden – we would destroy what we came to love. But now, we have gone too far in the other direction. We have become a majority urban species, many of us leaving any hint of the natural world behind. We are becoming as bereft as lonely hedgehogs. This is making us ill, and it undermines our ability to fight for our lives.

So where are we going to find a solution to the dilemma? How are we going to get close enough to the land without destroying it? How are we going to find a way of falling in love again?

What really did it for me was a night out with Nigel. Up to that point my interest in hedgehogs had been fairly pragmatic. Lots of people had been looking at the inner workings of the animal, for example, the hormonal fluctuations of hibernating hedgehogs, but very few at what hedgehogs get up to in the wild. That is not say the inner workings of hibernating hedgehogs are not fascinating. Indeed I would go so far as to say they are preposterous. This is an animal that, for the coldest months of the year, shuts down almost completely. Its heartbeat is imperceptible, ticking over at one or two beats per second, and as for the breathing; if you are so minded, you can seal a hibernating hedgehog up in a box containing nothing but nitrogen, come back a couple of hours later, prod it awake and find that it is just fine.

You can see why I prefer studying animals in the wild.

I was looking at how well young hedgehogs survive in the wild after a period of time being cared for by people and being released far from where they were found. This was not just academic: there are over a thousand people in the UK alone who take in sick and injured hedgehogs, look after them and release them. But there had been no work done to find out whether this was worthwhile. If all the hedgehogs died on release, then there was little point caring for them in the first place.

To do the work, I had attached small radio-transmitters on to the hedgehogs' spines. All I had to do was find each of the twelve animals throughout the night, record where they were, weigh them, and note any behaviour. Actually, what I had to do was just get to know my hedgehogs. This is something that many scientists tend to avoid. There are sound reasons why it is better to assign numbers to the study animals; there are probably monographs published on the sins of giving animals names.

But I was living alone in a caravan and rarely meeting another person, apart from to beg a shower from the farmhouse, or to ask for access to a neighbour's barn when Freya took up residence. She had a habit of disappearing, until a badger ate her; spookily on the same day that Freya Stark, the person after whom she was named, died.

So they got names. And Nigel became my favourite. The reason was that he had a tendency to carry on hedgehogging when I came snoop-

ing. All of the other animals either did what hedgehogs are supposed
to do, i.e. roll into a ball; or, because they had become so used to me,
just ran. Which they can do with surprising speed; they hitch up the
skirt of muscle that hangs around them. This muscle is what makes
hedgehogs look so like clockwork toys when they walk; it hides the
legs.

But Nigel, well, he just continued doing whatever he was doing.

Though at four one morning, he was just watching. That is how I
found him as I climbed out of the caravan to go and clean my teeth. I
had finished my last round of hedgehog checks and was ready for bed.
But this was the first night without rain for almost a month and the air
was positively balmy. So, unhindered by electronics, I decided to go
and see what Nigel was up to.

Because he would let me follow so closely, I was able to see the
immense gamble he took. And this helped explain why so many
hedgehogs end up squashed by cars. The grassy verge was covered in
heavy dew. If Nigel had chosen to forage on the more natural surface,
he would have quickly become very wet. But the tarmac of the small
lane was warm and dry. So he chose the same option I would have
done. The tarmac also lured other animals: hedgehog food. So Nigel
got a double advantage: he kept dry, and a smorgasbord of inverte-
brates made themselves available to his ravenous jaws.

Over the next hour I got closer and closer until there came a point
where I was lying on my stomach and we were nose-to-nose. And then
he looked at me. Up until then, I had been observing, he had been
snuffling and getting on with the business of being a hedgehog. But at
that moment, he stopped and looked up at me. The importance of this
came slowly (I can be quite hedgehog-like myself), but eventually I
realized that there is no other wild animal that we can do this with.
Throwing bread at ducks in the park hardly counts as the foundation
of a meaningful relationship. And while you can get nose-to-nose with
your pets, they had the wildness bred out of them many generations
ago.

All of the other wild animals I have had contact with simply do not
allow this sort of intimacy. I have been very close to mice, voles and
shrews, but even if you can get a good close look without them taking

a bite – how can I put this nicely – once you have met one bank vole, you have really met them all. These are not animals oozing personality. But hedgehogs do have distinct characters.

The result of that night out with Nigel was a shift in my appreciation of hedgehogs, and a shift in my appreciation of the entire system that keeps both the hedgehogs and me alive.

But more importantly, it left me euphoric. It is a sensation that I recognize now in two very different environments, when I am out in the wild and when I have become wild. Whether it is letting my eyes stretch out to sea, or my hands embrace the ribbed strength of a tree, I feel happy; my heart sings. And the feeling I am left with after the dance is one of a similar warm contentment, for a while I have become close to the wild again, but the internal wildness.

The intensity of emotion that wildness elicits is hardly surprising. As a species we have spent 99 per cent of the time as hunter-gathers, part of nature. It is only in the last 10,000 years that there has been a slow move away from nature, so we have the coding of a wild animal deep in our DNA. Is it any wonder that the rapid race to urbanization is accompanied by a deterioration of well-being? We are being ripped away from our roots

Zoologist E. O. Wilson neatly explains how we humans manage as well as we do:

> People can grow up with the outward appearance of normality in an environment largely stripped of plants and animals, in the same way that passable-looking monkeys can be raised in laboratory cages and cattle fattened in feeding bins. Asked if they were happy, these people would probably say yes. Yet something vitally important would be missing, not merely the knowledge and pleasure that can be imagined and might have been, but a wide array of experiences that the human brain is peculiarly equipped to receive.

Wilson created a word to describe his idea: biophilia. He argued that we all have an innate need for contact with the natural world. This has been developed by many other people, perhaps most brilliantly in

Richard Louv's book, *Last Child in the Woods: Saving our Children from Nature-deficit Disorder.* As soon as I saw the phrase 'nature-deficit disorder' I instinctively appreciated the idea.

If good humour is in short supply at home, invariably it will be replenished in the woods. Climbing trees and splashing in mud are crucial to contentment. And research has gone further, even to the point of discovering that flats in a tower with a view that includes just one tree have a lower rate of domestic violence than flats with a view purely of concrete.

But does this all mean we are genetically predisposed to love the planet? It is a lovely idea, but is it just romantic tosh?

It is obvious that preferentially selecting environments that are safer and more productive would confer an evolutionary advantage. And given that this is something that will have played a very large part in our survival chances for the vast majority of our time as a species, it is not beyond belief that somewhere within our inheritable characteristics there would be preferences for habitats that were good for us.

Do not be fooled by those who love city life. Biophilia has competition from what has been described as topophilia – a love of place. But this is acquired, not innate. It is born from learning to love what is familiar. However, take us a little deeper and all is revealed. Each time habitat preferences are monitored, it is found that people gravitate to a savannah-like environment. Which is not a surprise as that is where most of our time as a species has been spent.

But why all this talk of love? Can't we just knuckle down and sort out the mess we are making for ourselves?

Stephen Jay Gould gave a compelling argument for love: 'We cannot win this battle to save species and environments without forging an emotional bond between ourselves and nature as well – for we will not fight to save what we do not love.'

And here is where we come back to the hedgehogs, and Nigel.

Conservation and wildlife organizations tend to use the charismatic mega-fauna to seduce us into a love of the natural world. Up to a point, this is fine. As a child I used to sleep under a large poster of a tiger. I was surrounded by images of the unattainable beauty of whales, elephants, lions and hunting dogs. Over the years I have seen all of them, and each time it was great … but … seeing the tail of a grey whale sink into the sea off the impossibly beautiful Clayoquot Sound, or hearing the constipated roar of a lion while wandering through a game reserve in South Africa at night are distant, one-way events: me as observer.

I was left with feelings of awe and reverence, certainly (as well as nausea and terror in those two examples). But love?

There is a risk of the relationship being promoted for us becoming superficial or even sentimental. I once ran a workshop with the title: 'Sentimentality is the enemy of ecology.' The idea came from the Buddhist principle of near and far enemies: the far enemy of love is hate, the near enemy of love is sentimentality.

We are often stuck in the mire of sentimentality and we need to move on through. But it can be difficult when the images of the natural world are of unobtainable beauty.

I believe this is very like one of the obstacles to more nurturing and sustainable human relationships. We are surrounded by and bombarded with images of unattainable beauty and excitement. At every turn there is another example of the charismatic mega-fauna from the world of celebrity. I am as likely to get nose-to-nose with a humpbacked whale as I am with Angelina Jolie. And even if I managed such an encounter, would there be a bond, a spark of connection? I doubt it.

We are all much more likely to fall in love with the girl or the boy next door. That is where we are going to find sustainable and nurturing love. We are not going to find it by gazing at images of implausibly beautiful actors and musicians (though I seem to remember spending a considerable amount of my youth imagining it might).

So this brings me back to, eventually, the hedgehogs. Hedgehogs are the animal equivalent of the boy or girl next door. They are truly attainable, it is possible to get close to hedgehogs, it is possible to get nose-to-nose with hedgehogs and it is possible to fall in love with them. Or at the very least allow them to act as a gateway to the whole unimaginable enormousness of all the wild we need to be in touch with.

Once we have that contact with the wild, just from the glint of untamedness in a hedgehog's eye, we are already moving into a deeper appreciation of the world. We can begin to fall in love. Remember, we will not fight to save what we do not love.

We can and do find love in the wild – the wild within and the wild without. That is where the dance comes into its own; it releases the wild within and allows us to fall in love with the world and, perhaps just as importantly, allows us to fall in love with ourselves. We are not fighting to save the planet because of the polar bears. No, we are fighting to save ourselves.

First find your hedgehog

The hedgehog, rather than the snail, is perhaps the ideal idler companion. While I recognize the slowness of the snail as a good indicator of a contemplative nature, there is simply less interest in a snail. The hedgehog, however, is perfect. To start with, there is the capacity to snooze for up to six months of the year. That presents the perfect cogitation space to develop radical new ideas. There is the ease with which we can enter into the hedgehog world. We need to slow down and change our perspective. We need to lie on the land and get nose-to-nose with this most accessible and charismatic of beasts. Even the task of finding a hedgehog is one that encourages pleasantness. The best method is to find a garden, sling a hammock, get a duvet, a small table and a large gin and tonic. Then let the hammock take the strain as you lie back and wait for the tell-tale snuffle of an approaching hedgehog. And while you do that, consider the poor fools sweltering in the back of a Land Rover as they charge across the plains of Africa in search of lions and elephants. The hedgehog wins every time.

Alice Smith

THE MERRY CAMPERS:
A HISTORY OF THE KIBBO KIFT

Matthew De Abaitua

'JERKIN AND HOOD. TENTS IN A HALF-CIRCLE. PITCHED AT sundown, gone in the morning. Outlaws ... ?' The hooded figures marched up the Long Man of Wilmington. The men wore knee-length braided shorts, brown leather belts, jerkins and pointed green cowls in imitation of the forest outlaws of Robin and his Merry Men. The women wore Arabian keffiyeh-styled headdresses to protect against the sun and one-piece knee-length dresses tied with leather belts. On the flap of their gray Bergen rucksacks, a mark was painted, a large letter K beside the curling smoke of a campfire and a single green fir tree. The men and women greeted one another with the Native American salute of the open palm, right hand raised high. All the hikers bore rough ash hiking staves, which pushed against the earth as they ascended the Long Man, singing a song of their own devising: 'The Kindred is Coming'.

Carved into the north-facing scarp slope of Windover Hill, the Long Man stands 200 feet tall. In each hand he clutches what appear to be two staves. The provenance of the Long Man of Wilmington is uncertain: we cannot be sure if it is a sixteenth-century tribute or a symbol of pagan antiquity. Today, the outline is defined with concrete, and the Long Man is visible to the traffic passing on the A27. But in the year of the hike, August 1929, the figure outlined in the long grass was a mystical watermark on the hillside.

Windover Hill and the surrounding area are rich with remnants from England's ancient past: Neolithic flint mines, Bronze Age burial barrows and a Roman terrace way. The hikers marched up the steep hill in their variant of the classical wedge formation and, at the heart of the Long Man, performed a brief ritual of dedication. Their voices echoed around the distinctive acoustics of the concave slope. Thus they reached back, far, far back into the void-faced hood of prehistory. Mankind's evolution has been a progressive degeneration, with alienation at every stage. First Man was alienated from oneness with his god, then cast out from the harmony of Nature. The process of separation was remorseless, each severance placing another partition between Man and the Golden Age. He lost his link to his ancestors. He grew apart from others, from his community and fellow man, until even his wife and his own children were alien to him. Each cut was made by the instruments of knowledge and industry, two scissor blades cutting in unison. The final divorce, the ultimate *decree nisi*, was issued by Freud: man was alienated from his own self. The hikers reached through the void and into the hood, searching for the rough hand of Neolithic man, their ancient guide to living in harmony with the subtle, undulating forms of the Downs.

Ritual completed, the hikers continued up over the featureless head of the Long Man to the brow of the hill. There, they looked down over the South Downs, a cumuliform landscape of 'whale-backed' hills and verdant valleys founded on a bank of chalk. Cloud shadows pass over ploughed wheatfields. In the distance, the coastal bays and the glittering English Channel and the seven peaks of the chalk cliffs. Known as the Seven Sisters, each Sister is the measure of a terrifying eternity: trillions of coccolithophores – nanoplankton – lived and died here in a deep warm sea, leaving behind their scales of calcium carbonate to build up over time into the gleaming white cliffs. On the beach, a stunning everywhere of light as the high sun is reflected by these geological mausoleums.

The Sussex Downs, their name derived from the Saxon word 'dun', meaning hill, were one of many sites in the English landscape stalked by these strange hikers. Their rituals summoned the ancient British pagan tradition, from back before the Romans, back to a Neolithic Albion of menhir, tor and cromlech, Silbury Hill and the White Horse of Ulmington. The ancient sites throbbed with dormant meaning. For a joke – in the Freudian sense that there is no such thing as a joke – one of their men stripped naked and squatted at the root of the enormous phallus of the Cerne Giant, as if drawing the sexual potency into himself. Sounds foolish now. In the twenty-first century, Stonehenge is a tourist attraction at which the passing traffic on the A303 slows to gawp, before speeding on to holidays in Dorset. But in 1929, the remains of English prehistory retained sufficient mystical charge to inspire this select group of hikers and campers as they sought to change the direction of Western civilization. They were the most intriguing and inspiring of English reform movements, an elite cell a few hundred strong, already nine years old: they were the Kindred of the Kibbo Kift.

*

On September 8th 1914, John Hargrave left the office of *The Scout* magazine to enlist in the Great War. A dark-haired twenty-year-old, slight in stature but very fit, Hargrave was one of the earliest members of the Scouts, joining in 1908, the year of its foundation. The fiercely independent son of the two artists, he had left school at the age of 15 to become an illustrator and author. His best-selling *Lonecraft* (1913) brought the idealism of the scout to the country boys who lived remote from organized scouting groups. The book was noticed by Baden-Powell,who invited him to become staff artist at *The Scout*. He was known as White Fox.

Beside the beechwoods of Buckinghamshire, on Mayhall Farm overlooking the River Chess, Hargrave said goodbye to his own troop of scouts. Then he went home to say farewell to his beloved father, who shared his passion for anthrolopology and the countryside. Gordon Hargrave was an artist and Quaker who had taken his family from his son's birthplace in Midhurst, on the Sussex Downs, an itinerant wandering around Westmorland and Cumberland, 'amid the purple heather and the sunset in peat-moss puddles'. A childhood spent in the birthplace of English Romanticism, the land of lakes and mountains where the boy Wordsworth slipped out, stole a boat and sailed by moonlight under the looming oppression of jagged night mountains. A land where boys ran free.

Lonecraft includes Hargrave's instructions on how to make a simple lightweight tent. Take a sheet of square canvas of 7 x 7 feet, insert four 1-inch curtain rings into the corners, add a triangular patch and rope that suspends the tent from a tree branch. Secure to the ground with three pegs. The tent sleeps one. *Lonecraft* was the work of a fierce individualist, a manual for self-reliance and self-control. Live pure, speak true, right wrong, follow the trail. Be like the Red Indian. Not a waster. Be silent and ready to act. Don't talk. Do something. In its precocious declamatory style, British heroes stand shoulder-to-shoulder with the stoic, wise Native Americans of Ernest Thompson Seton's Woodcraft movement: Saint George, King Arthur, Captain Cook, Robinson Crusoe. Paradoxically, this manual for solitude attracted followers. The young King George VI and his brother Prince Henry, Duke of Gloucester, were taken to one of the Lonecraft camps by their tutor. If Hargrave was sufficiently charismatic for the future king, you can appreciate the influence he wielded over the young scouts who followed him.

After enlisting, Hargrave served with the 32nd Field Ambulance 10th Division of the Mediterranean Expeditionary Force and was part of the disastrous landing at Suvla Bay, intended to break the deadlock of the Battle of Gallipoli. In his account of the experience, *At Suvla Bay, Being the Notes and Sketches of Scenes, Characters and Adventures of the Dardanelles Campaign* (1916), he does not spare the reader the gruesome details:

> I've seen men, healthy, strong, hard-faced Irishmen, blown to shreds. I've helped to clear up the mess. I've trod on dead men's chests in the sand, and the ribs have bent in and the putrid gases of decay have burst through with a whhh-h-ff-f.

The battle dragged on. The horror was unending. Men stumbled into his camp suffering from 'sniper madness', shivering and mumbling, emaciated, black with sunburn and filth from being pinned down by sniper fire for a week on the mountainside without food or water.

But there was no water waiting for them at the camp. Every injured man asked for it, but there was none to give. The memory of this thirst would have great impact upon Hargrave's intellectual development, ensuring that the economics of supply and demand were never far from his thinking. Into this parched atmosphere stepped a chap holding a glass of water that he had poured for himself back on the ship, keeping it safe and unspilt until he landed on the beach. Immediately the chap was surrounded by thirsty fellows. He was offered half a sovereign if he would give up his glass of water. That offer was upped to a whole sovereign. But he refused to take their money.

'You could have a gold sovereign, but you don't want it?' asked the men, incredulously.

'Of course I don't want it. I want the water,' replied the man. And he drank it down. Hargrave would retell this anecdote with some relish throughout his life, seeing in it a parable that elucidated the arbitrary value of money and the economic system it supported.

Under shellfire throughout August and September, his Lonecraft ensured his survival. He tracked along dried water courses and took cover behind thorn bushes, all the time sought out by the sniper's bullet. The Turkish soldiers were 'born scouts' and only those soldiers who had been trained in the cunning and craft of the savage scout came out top in the Great Failure of the Great War. Officers unable to find the North Star could not make their way at night, as they could neither strike a light nor read maps drawn on too small a scale to be of practical use. Entire companies of men were cut up because they lost their way, unable to read the signs of the land.

When his division was evacuated from Suvla Bay on 30th September 1915, John Hargrave was the only surviving non-commissioned officer from his section. Of the 25,000 men who had landed, 6,000 survived. Although his survival proved the value of scouting, the war itself indicted the leadership of Baden-Powell's movement, ageing examples of the same contemptible officer class who had failed the men of Suvla Bay: veterans of the Anglo-Boer War (1899–1902), 'a war marked by set-backs, stalemates and stasis', men who had made their names at the frontiers of the British Empire in small wars to secure colonies or protect the business interests of chartered companies.

The Great War was the end of the Age of Empires. Something new had to follow. Had to. This need for urgent renewal drives John Hargrave's polemic *The Great War Brings It Home*, published in 1919.

Here he argues that the Great War demonstrated the failure of our 'disorganized civilization' and could only be cured by outdoor education and open air training camps.

What the Great War brought home, he wrote, was the end of the legitimacy of the aristocracy: 'The upper classes have realized that the "masses" really are human beings after all – And the "masses" have realised that the "upper ten" are really just the same as they are.' The Representation of the People Act of 1918 enfranchised women and the poor, transforming an electorate of 7.5 million voters into more than 20 million people. Hargrave was not a natural democrat. He would not be ruled by a committee. He envisaged a new elite for this new electorate, one not determined by birth but by fitness, art and camping, with himself as unquestioned leader.

★

In spring 1919, John Hargrave holed up in his Caravan Camp, at Mayhall Farm. Every Moon, his patrol of Scouts (all 17 years old or older) met around the council fire, and practised their woodcraft at weekends, or as often as work in London permitted. In a green-and-orange showman caravan, Hargrave wrote and painted, then bedded down in his A-type Canadian tent, handmade for him by his friend 'Wander Wolf'. Weighing about 10lbs, the tent was fashioned from Egyptian cotton and bamboo poles with a fly sheet that came down to the ground. This camp attracted followers, as his camps always did. In late March, the *Punch* review of Hargrave's book *The Great War Brings It Home* admitted his ideas for renewal were sound 'but not for those of us who, even in a case of great national urgency, cannot get away from the tyranny of convention'. The positive critical response to his polemic further inflated his sense of manifest destiny as a leader of unconventional men. He continued in print to rail against the direction of the scouting movement, demanding stiffer tests and fewer badges, real outdoor scouting rather than indoor games and lectures, less drill and more tribal tradition, more scouting and less shouting. His lobbying for a training ground for Scouts came to fruition with the establishment of Gillwell Park camp in June of 1919. As

Commissioner of Woodcraft, Hargrave was the natural choice to lead the training ground but Baden-Powell passed over him and appointed Francis 'Skipper' Gidney as Gilwell Camp Chief instead: Gidney was described by Baden-Powell as 'the perfect Boy-Man', an epithet we must assume to be a compliment.

Being passed over in this way contributed to Hargrave's alienation from the scouting movement. That August, he was visited at the Caravan Camp by 'Little Wolf', C.J. Mumford. They talked all night and formed Lodge Ndembo, consisting of seven men, whose purpose was to 'precipitate' the Woodcraft element out of the Scout movement.

The practices of the real Ndembo are detailed in J.G. Frazer's *The Golden Bough*, published in 1890, and again in an expanded 12-volume edition between 1906 and 1915. Frazer describes how, in a region of the Lower Congo, a simulation of death and resurrection was an initiation rite into an African secret society. 'Dying Ndembo' involved a boy or girl falling down in a pretended fit and then being carried to an enclosed place outside of town (perhaps to a camp?). 'They are supposed to have died. But the parents and friends supply food, and after a period varying, according to custom, from three months to three years, it is arranged that the doctor shall bring them back to life again ... When the doctor's fee has been paid, and money (goods) saved for a feast, the Ndembo people are brought to life.' Upon their revival, the Ndembo people pretended not to be able to eat and were known to commit acts of violence, for which they were forgiven, on the presumption that their social conscience had not survived the resurrection. They talked gibberish and behaved as if still under the influence of the spirit world. They were given a new name, completing the transformation. Hargrave was fascinated by the rites of the Ndembo. Here was a rigid organization that gave direction to a primitive society, that maintained tribal traditions and beliefs through initiation rites. Control came through magic and taboo. The role of a camp set apart from the people, to which the boys and girls were taken to be transformed, did not escape his notice. Nor did the importance of taking a new name.

In the same month as forming Lodge Ndembo, he travelled to the newly formed Scout training camp of Gilwell Park and was appalled by what he saw, setting down his wrath in an article for *The Trail*. Under the pseudonym of 'Our Red Hot Bolshevik' Hargrave lambasted the behaviour of the Scouts, who ran around blowing bugles when they were meant to be stalking rare birds. The emphasis on parade over the survival skills of woodcraft demonstrated that the Scouts had learned nothing from the Great War.

By October, he was even challenging the role of Christianity in the Scouts. 'The Woodcrafter takes the trouble to study the comparative religions of the world,' he wrote, presumably with the volumes of *The Golden Bough* open upon his desk, 'in order that he may acquire wisdom from all the Great Teachers. This Woodcrafter considers "compulsory religious worship" (such as forced Church Parades and closed troops) not good.'

As Hargrave's confrontation with the movement entered its final phase, he was busy recruiting sympathetic scouts. Throughout that October, a Scalphunters club met every Wednesday, to which new members were brought. In November, Hargrave married his long-term love, Ruth Clark, the leader of a group of Woodcraft girls called the Merrie Campers and author of *Camp Fire Training for Girls*. Her woodcraft name was Minobi, meaning Glad Heart, and she brought her own followers to the nascent movement. By the end of 1919, the name of the Kibbo Kift was yet to be coined but the ideas and will for the movement were gestating, as was John Hargrave's first and only child.

★

After sunset on August 18th 1920, the Kindred of the Kibbo Kift was formed at Denison Hall on Vauxhall Bridge Road.

The Kin covenant, drawn up by John Hargrave and witnessed by his wife Minobi and Little Wolf, Cecil Mumford, attracted disaffected Scouts, left-wing politicos, former suffragettes, theosophists, vegetarians and artists. The seven-point covenant was as follows:

1 Open Air Education for the Children
  Camp Training and Nature Craft

2 Health of Body, Mind and Spirit

3 Craft Training Groups and Craft Guilds

4 The Woodcraft Family, or Roof Tree

5 Local Folk Roots and Cultural Development

6 Disarmament of Nations – Brotherhood of Man

7 International Education based on these points. Freedom of Trade between Nations. Stabilization of the Purchasing Power of Money (in all countries) Open Negotiations instead of secret treaties and diplomacy. A World Council.

The covenant proceeds swiftly from education to a reorganization of capitalism and the founding of a new global political authority. You cannot fault them for lack of ambition. Combined with the promise of mixed-sex, co-educational camps, the Kin covenant convinced ex-suffragettes such as Emmeline Pethick-Lawrence to join. Like Hargrave, she was raised a Quaker and had spent the Great War campaigning for the Women's International League for Peace. Denison Hall had been used as a Scout meeting place before and was known for its radical gatherings. Two years earlier, Emmelline Pethick-Lawrence attended a discussion on the Problem of Population at the hall, inspiring consideration of the new woman in the creation of the future race.

'In the eyes of the new morality,' wrote Pethick Lawrence in 1918, 'the ideal woman is no longer the meek drudge but the free instructed woman, trained in a sense of responsibility to herself and to the race, determined to have no children but the best.' Emmelline Pethick-Lawrence's experience of working with youth groups went back to the nineteenth century. She lent her standing to the Kibbo Kift. Her activist partner, Mary Neal, also joined. Mary Neal was a tall, lean woman with striking blue eyes. A pragmatist with a cutting wit, 'she brought into the atmosphere the sparkle of a clear frosty day.' In 1892, the two women took the girls of the Mission's Working Girls' Club away for a week together, pioneering seaside holidays for the working class. In 1901 Mary Neal joined Cecil Sharp in reviving the folk dances and Old English folk songs, which they would teach to the poor young people in their charge at a dressmaking co-operative in Somerstown, Kings Cross. She was a pioneer in the radical potential of art to transform the lives of the young and the poor.

Amongst Mary Neal's contacts in progressive London was the future prime minister Clement Attlee. Then mayor of Stepney, Attlee chaired a committee called the Camelot Club in Poplar dedicated to building up a youth wing for the Labour movement. Mary Neal secured Hargrave membership of this committee, giving him access to mainstream activists. Youth workers from the south London co-operative movement were drawn in by this stamp of political legitimacy, and so the ranks of the Kindred grew.

By the second Great Whitsun camping meeting Althing – of the Kibbo Kift, held at the large house of Emmelline and Frederick Pethick-Lawrence in October 1921, there were 200 individual members of the movement, drawn mainly from London and the Home Counties. In his essential sociological study of the Kibbo Kift, *Social Movements and Their Supporters* (1997), Mark Drakeford provides a sophisticated and insightful analysis of how the shared ideals of the various groups forming the Kindred provided sufficient centrifugal force to bind them together in their early years. The Kindred encompassed such diverse figures as the formidable May Billinghurst – a paraplegic former suffragette who fought back ferociously against the doctors who tried to force-feed her during her hunger strike, and whose wheelchair is visible in photographs of the Kindred's camps – to Baron Von Pallandt, a Dutch aristocrat with a deep interest in theosophy. Such a gathering of radicals and oddballs soon attracted the interest of the Home Office and Special Branch, who watched the Kibbo Kift very closely in these early days. They detected a faint communist influence but concluded that 'the leaders can, however ... be fairly described as cranks.'

Special Branch may have declared the Kibbo Kift to be mostly harmless, but the scouting movement disagreed. John Hargrave continued his attacks on their hierachy, writing in a left-wing journal *Foreign Affairs*, that 'They have earned their bread by war, got promotion and higher pay from war – and they are war.' In January 1921, a resolution was passed at the annual general meeting of the London Scout Council to prohibit White Fox from addressing any Scout meeting or contributing any further articles to *The Trail*. A letter from John S. R. Pankhurst, ex-sub-editor of the Patrol Leaders Page, in *Headquarters*

Gazette, protested the resolution, describing it as reactionary. But the running battle between Hargrave and Baden-Powell had reached the point of irreconcilable break. The Scout movement would continue to belittle and attack the Kibbo Kift in its formative phases, painting it as communistic and therefore entirely unsuitable for young people. White Fox may have imagined he held sway over hundred of thousands of young minds but there was no hope of overcoming such an immense power as the Scouts. The Kibbo Kift would not become a mass movement to rival Baden-Powell's. Nor would it become a Labour youth movement, as the Camelot Committee hoped. Its destiny was far stranger than that.

★

The Kindred camped four times a year, in tune with the seasons. They gathered at Crystal Palace and at Bradenham Common in High Wycombe. They met in Matlock in Derbyshire and Missenden in Shropshire, always in search of new camping grounds. At Whitsun, the Althing of all the Kindred took place. It was a group camp of 60 to 70 men and women and their children in over a hundred tents, arranged in a semi-circle on a large flat common bordered by a wood. At the Althing, there were wrestling contests and the performance of mummers plays. Here the Kindred held their council meetings, at which disputes were aired and resolutions made. Whole sheep were roasted and giant loaves baked with a symbolic K marked in the dough. Activity was divided between art and war, between the writing of songs and poetry, the playing of music, the embroidery of banners, the fashioning of puppets and masks, and trials to harden the spirit and stiffen the sinews, such as night hikes and fleet-foot races. Some of the Kindred survived solely on rations prepared the previous winter, to test out their preparedness for a state of emergency. Their formidable company of archers honed their skills.

What do the words 'Kibbo Kift' mean? John Hargrave explained the etymology: 'The words Kibbo Kift are Old English (Cheshire) meaning "Strength" or "any proof of great strength". They are connected with the old dialect words "kebbie", a cudgel, club or rough hook-headed stick or staff, and "kifty" meaning sound, good, genuine, OK, correct, proper, "good form" or in the tradition.' The triple K of their name appears, to modern eyes, to be drawn directly from the Klu Klux Klan, whose resurgence also took place across the twenties. If the Kindred were aware of this connection, they made no mention of it.

Language and art were crucial to the Kindred. The name Althing was derived from the Old Norse name for the gathering of the Viking council. 'Al' is also the Anglo-Saxon word for 'fire' and this ancient language gave the Kindred their 'gleemote', meaning concert. The Woodcraft movement drew upon the customs of the Native American Indian. Hence the Kin council was made up of six elected chiefs, while Hargrave was the uncontested Head Man. The men and women exercised in a costume based upon the garb of the Native American, with loincloths and G-strings for the men and short skirts for the women.

The art of the Kibbo Kift was a similar synthesis: Egyptian hieroglyphs upon monkish illuminated manuscripts. The Eastern dyad of yin and yang underlies the shape of their Great Crest. The costumes and artifacts of the Kindred of the Kibbo Kift are held at the Museum of London and include the ceremonial dress of the Kindred. While pointed hoods and staffs were used for hiking, more striking and secret outfits were used for ritual. These include the tabard of Kin Herald, Will Scarlet, which combine outsized straight shoulders with a potent central symbol. The appliquéd felt imagery is bold, simple and symbolic; an upturned tomahawk, pine trees under night and day, wavy lines denoting water. The colours are decisive and energetic: 'the vital man uses vital colour – red, yellow, blue and gold. Heraldic, primitive, full-blooded, vigorous.' A photograph shows Will Scarlet, a strikingly handsome man, with dark hair and an appealingly amused glint in his eye, calling the group to attention with a twist of his ceremonial noise-maker. This was how the otherworldliness of the Althing was summoned.

The Kindred had jobs. Hargrave himself worked at an advertising agency, and he had a talent for striking imagery and propaganda. Each member was given a new name by their friends within the organization. The naming and costume severed the link with the class-bound life outside camp, allowing each member to create themselves within a new order. Of all his interviews with surviving members of the Kibbo Kift, it is Mark Drakeford's conversations with Vera Chapman that communicate the excitement of the transformative nature of the Althing. After her time with the Kindred, Vera Chapman would go on to found the Tolkien Society and become an author herself. Her description of the presence of John Hargrave is, accordingly, vivid. The first time she saw him, he was in evening dress at a party in Kings Langley in 1919: 'He looked like Mephistopheles somehow, and I was rather fascinated by him. He had a sort of Byronic air about him.' Vera Chapman attended the Althing at the invitation of May Billinghurst, who knew her from Oxford. She remembers the camp as 'full of exuberance and excitement. You were lifted right out of this world. There was the mystique of totems and so on. The meeting began with quite a little bit of mysticism, ritualism ... you made your camp fire and made your invocation and that definitely set up a feeling of belonging to the other world. It was a magical and religious atmosphere. It was the religion of the spirit which you could not deny, out there under the sky.'

Being part of the Kibbo Kift was to live within a work of art, if only for a long weekend; an agrarian-futurist work of art, vigorous, disciplined, and ever-changing.

★

In 1924, the fifth Althing was held, at Bradenham Hill Farm in West Wycombe, Berkshire. Over the previous year, the ranks of the Kindred had expanded to nearly 500 members, with most of the growth coming from those groups who wanted to create a Labour youth movement. With his sense of manifest destiny, John Hargrave was too autocratic for these members. In modernist fashion, the centre could not hold and things began to fall apart.

Amongst the papers of the Kibbo Kift, there is a resolution critical of John Hargrave's leadership that was put forward at the 1924 Althing. The dissenting group sought some local autonomy from Hargrave in matters of recruitment, and saw his refusal to admit one of their nominees as being dictatorial. 'Trial in the absence and without the knowledge of the accused is a betrayal of elementary civil liberty.

We do not believe that a decent man or woman can tolerate it or remain associated with an organization which tolerates it, for a single moment.' Furthermore, Hargrave's pronouncements embarrassed them, particularly his continued needling of the scouting movement, calling them 'Scout boys' and insisting they were bad campers. Their censure of Hargrave is not extended to the rest of the Kindred. The resolution makes it clear that 'We regard Kibbo Kift as a free association of individuals, tribes, lodges, rooftrees and things, bound only by virtue of their signature of a common covenant. To this covenant we continue to give the fullest possible assent.'

One of the signatories to this resolution was Leslie Paul, founder of the Woodcraft Folk, the movement the splinter group went on to found, the leftist youth movement Attlee and the Camelot Committee had signed up for years earlier. The Woodcraft Folk continue to this day. In his autobiography, *Angry Young Man*, Leslie Paul regretted that this feud meant that more experienced and brilliant recruits within the Kindred moved on, leaving him and Hargrave to their 'impassioned puerilities'.

Vera Chapman was there when the resolution was put forward. The weather was bad. A cold and wet Whitsun. Once the motion of censure was on the table, Emmelline Pethick-Lawrence insisted that it be debated before discussion of any other items. The weather forced the debate into a nearby deserted barn. Twenty-two members took part in this tremendous argument, as the wind raged through the loose and rotting timbers, and rats scampered and squeaked away from the candlelight. The censure vote was defeated by 88 votes to 55, and with typical Kindred theatre, Leslie Paul and other dissenters marched directly out of the camp.

From the hindsight of his autobiography, Leslie Paul was less critical of John Hargrave: 'Having in my turn failed just as dismally to build a Labour Scout Movement after years of effort just as intense, I cannot blame him for deciding in advance that it was not worth trying.' Yet the man's manner still irked. 'I recall him in those days as tall, with sharp, almost Romany features, an aquiline nose, and a mass of wavy black hair ... Hargrave always spoke as though possessed of an absolute and even insolent certainty of where he was going and what he was doing.' For Leslie Paul and the Woodcraft movement, the story of the Kibbo Kift ends there. However, for those who were left behind, the schism of the 1924 Althing bonded them together all the more.

★

A prehistoric track stretches across 250 miles from the Dorset coast to the Norfolk Wash. For over 5,000 years, people have walked or ridden the trail. The first section we know as the Ridgeway, a chalk ridge beginning in the uplands of Wessex and bisected by the River Thames at Goring Gap, rising above the low ground and valleys that once would have been treacherous with woods and marshes, wolf and boar. At Ivinghoe Beacon in the Chiltern Hills, the second part of the track commences, the Icknield Way, a narrow corridor and ancient line of communication between south-west England and the east coast, a path worn steadily by traders, travellers and invaders as far back as the Bronze Age.

On a night hike returning to his encampment in Latimer overlooking the River Chess, John Hargrave crossed the Icknield Way, inspiring the closing address of *The Confession of the Kibbo Kift*, published in 1927, John Hargrave's public manifesto for a secret movement that was already seven years old.

Titled 'The Spirit', this song of the land draws upon William Blake's capitalized allegorical forces ('Dimly they felt the threat of Just Men') and James Joyce's compound neologisms ('They hew out heaven-timber from the quickbeam of their own body-wit by the stave that runs in the blood.') Add a heady pull on the Native American peace pipe, chased with a draught of the occult imaginings of theosophy, and you approach the style of 'The Spirit'. As an evocation of English mysticism, a seeking of wordless wisdom on an ancient trail, it is the closest Hargrave's writing came to the achievements of his modernist peers. Rolf Gardiner, an acolyte of D. H. Lawrence, briefly a member of the Kindred, was a critic of Hargrave but recognized the genius in 'The Spirit', describing it as 'a truly magnificent exhortation, the authentic voice of the seer crying in the wilderness of stupid wayward men; it is the voice of the gods in the soil of Britain'.

'The Spirit' is a shamanic call to enter a state of wordless wisdom and silent communion with the undersong of the British soil. Hargrave knew yoga and meditation through his association with theosophy. He synthesized Eastern ideas – the clarity of unbeing – with the sensual being of D.H. Lawrence, that knowledge in the blood, 'when the mind and the known world is drowned in darkness everything must go.' The night hike was a way into the deep knowledge buried beneath civilization. The charged sensation of being alone with nature, every sense alive to predators – this was being! This was life! No wonder scholar David Bradshaw has seen something of John Hargrave filling the red trousers of Mellors, Lady Chatterley's Lover himself.

'The Spirit' closes with a call for the great men to go into isolation and prepare themselves for the work to come:

I shall go where the great trees stand, deep into the half-light of the woods whelming upon the giant bodies of the beech. I know the place where the afterglow shines like a pale halo upon the hill, and there the ash and the elm take hold upon the earth, flinging their strength into the sky. And over the summit of the hill on slanting ground a crab tree and a crooked thorn crouch and clutch each other.

I shall come around them uneasily and pass under the ash and the elm with an intaking of breath, and so down the valley to the track that runs into the pine wood where the darkness closes in, and the feet tread noiselessly, and the lungs are filled with the scent of the hanging curtains, the needled carpet and the cones ...

Tread softly over the grass that springs out of the blood and bodies of old heroes of the Icknield Way long since gone to dust.

Back to the place of dwelling, to the encampment.

The land was where the Kindred overcame the servitude of their modern industrialized lives. The Kindred sought to tap into a strata in the cultural soil containing remnants of 'Anglo-Saxon, Viking, Celt, and the Neolithic builders of barrow, dolmen, and the old straight track,' a 'new and vital patriotism' aimed at overturning the capitalist and socialist alike. But the land was not an end in itself. Their educational policy, designed so that the child would recapitulate the primitive life outdoors, was 'no mere sentimental Thoreauism or imitation Tolstoyan attitude towards life'. Hargrave was in earnest in working towards social change. This was not just a series of interruptive gestures. Pragmatic, if possessed of a wildly contradictory philosophy, the Kibbo Kift was intended to lead. Technology would liberate man from work, and afford the leisure required to remake society. The prehistoric peoples of the land were just one of the sources this future could tap.

It is Hargrave's early concern with regenerating national stock and his mystical conflation of blood and land that has led some to describe him and his movement as fascistic. The Kindred were swimming in the same current of ideas as fascism. Blood and soil; regeneration of the race; the movement's later assault on the bankers and international finance: all hallmarks of the Nazis. James Webb argues in *The Occult Establishment* (1976) that not too much should be made about the crossover between fascism and the 'illuminated movements' (his description of groups such as the Kibbo Kift, driving for spiritual development in the psychic ruins of the Great War), in the twenties. While both the Woodcraft-inspired movements and the German *Wandervogel* shared a 'vicarious expectation of an idealistic revolution', and John Hargrave's books in translation were a leading influence on the *Bünde* (a precursor to the Hitler Youth), 'the only prominent member of the English illuminated group who joined a fascist party seems to have been the originator of the guild theory, A.J. Penty.' The Kindred was intended to be a movement that transcended party politics, beyond the Bolshevism of the Russian Revolution (1917) and Mussolini's fascism (Il Duce came to power in 1922). By 1922, Hargrave and his followers were being demonized by Nesta Webster, a prominent conspiracy theorist whose work built on the notorious forgery *The Protocols of the Elders of Zion*. She linked the Kibbo Kift with communists and socialists in a world-wide fraternity with the devil. Yet, despite the fact that their contemporary critics were fascists, the Kibbo Kift project shared some of its DNA with fascism, primarily its conviction that an elite cell of individuals could go amongst the people and guide them: this is syndicalist thinking that has no respect for democracy.

The futurist energy of the movement distinguished it from the gentler longings of the Edwardian era. In his essay on the generations of the twentieth century, Joshua Glenn characterizes those born between 1884 and 1893 (John Hargrave was born in 1894 but then he was precocious) as 'New Kids', a generation outraged with the world they inherited:

> The romantic anti-capitalism of their elders wasn't good enough for the New Kids, who dismissed 19th-century utopianism as a quietist longing for a mythical – often neo-medieval – golden age. Instead of looking backward nostalgically (i.e., retrogressively), utopian New Kids discovered and invented what Van Wyck Brooks called a 'usable past.'

Ancient Britain was Hargrave's 'usable past' which he employed in his syndicalist approach to democracy. Unlike his romantic elders, he expressed the agency of mankind in pseudo-scientific terms. 'The history of the human race is truly the history of ideas, and it would be possible to record the development of mankind as the work of a) individual idea-generators and b) group idea-carriers.' There is a biological metaphor at work here, in which the mass of men is infected by new ideas carried into their midst. More of a slow and evolutionary process than a revolution. (Revolutions smacked of Bolshevism.) Envisaging himself as an idea-generator and the Kindred as idea-carriers, he anticipates Richard Dawkins' theory of memes, in which ideas propagate like genes, using our minds as temporary hosts. There is science fiction within the Kibbo Kift project, from H. G. Wells' presence on the advisory board to their outlandish costumes. John Hargrave's followed *The Confessions of the Kibbo Kift* with a science-fiction novel, *The Imitation Man* (1931), about a scientist who transposes the alchemic formulas of Paracelsus (an abiding interest of Hargrave and described in the novel as 'the founder of the science of modern medicine, whose extraction of the "essential spirit" of the poppy resulted in the production of laudanum') into chemical formulas and succeeds in growing a homunculus in a glass jar. This is very *Brave New World*. Aldous Huxley's future dystopia also included children grown in jars, and was published the following year (his brother, Julian Huxley, was also on the advisory board of the Kibbo Kift, emphasizing the progressive futuristic promise of the movement, albeit one bulwarked with its 'usable past' of the collective unconscious seething under the English landscape).

There is undeniable similarity between the Kindred and the ethos of *Blut und Boden* – blood and soil – that arose in Germany after the First World War. Photographs from the Althings of the early twenties show the Kindred greeting one another with what – to our eyes – appear to be a Nazi salutes. Yet at that point the straight raised-arm salute did not belong to Hitler. As the Kindred developed and the nature of the fascist project became clearer, Hargrave was keen to distance himself from racially driven ideologies (a chapter in *The Confession of the Kibbo Kift* is entitled 'Racial Absurdities and Nordic Nonsense'). That same year, Richard Walther Darre wrote *New Nobility from Blood and Soil*, in which he set out his belief that peasantry was the life source of the Nordic Race. Darre, an advocate of small-scale organic farming, would go on to become the Third Reich's minister for agriculture – hence Anna Bramwell's description of the Nazis as 'the first radical environmentalists in charge of a state'.

Another contentious affinity lay between Hargrave and his sanctioning of the social credit ideas of Major C. H. Douglas, the author of *Economic Democracy*. Ever since he had watched that man refuse to sell a glass of water on Suvla Bay, Hargrave knew he needed a pragmatic core to his programme, one that addressed the fundamental condition of contemporary man as an individual whose fate was determined by the economic conditions in which he was placed – 'any attempt to ignore the basic necessities of earthly life and to soar towards the transcendental gleam must fall into paroxysmal ecstatics, Dionysian cults, and other inharmonic reactions.' The idea of Social Credit fulfilled this requirement. From 1924, study of social credit was compulsory for the Kindred. It was added to the third clause of the Kin covenant in 1927. Social Credit is a distributive model for wealth, the argument behind it being that consumers are made to work far too hard to earn their money, as the burden of all the waste in the system is passed on to them in the pricing of goods. The aim of Social Credit was to distribute the surplus created by the Machine Age in the form of a social dividend, paid directly to the people: the next stage in Hargrave's agrarian-futurism. The system is complex and would take a second essay to fully explain. Indeed, the cause of social credit led to the dissolution of the Kindred of the Kibbo Kift. The second phase of the movement began on January 3rd 1931, when John Hargrave inaugurated a reorganiza-tion of the remaining Kindred along paramilitary lines. The move-ment metamorphosed into the Green Shirts. Their numbers swelled by Legions of the Unemployed from the Midlands, the emphasis shifted from camping to marching, led by a troop of a hundred drummers. Hargrave split with his wife and threw himself into the street politics of the Great Depression. Green bricks would be thrown through the window of 11 Downing Street and an effigy of the governor of the Bank of England would be thrown down at the doors of the Old Lady. Social Credit's critique of the banking system echoes our current predicament – although, again, we must be wary of taking up the cudgels of history. As a letter from the British Union of Fascists to Ezra Pound attests, 'Sir Oswald Mosley has always welcomed the attack on orthodox finance made by the social creditors ... and he was glad to observe that a large body of intelligent people had at any rate seen through the old financial ramp.' Major C. H. Douglas turned out to be a raging anti-Semite, and on the eve of the Second World War, Hargrave and the Green Shirts disowned the originator of their creed. Even as the Allies fought the Nazis, Hargrave continued to lobby for Social Credit and saw the adoption of the rationing system, that is, the rational allocation of resources to the citzenry, as a partial victory for his cause.

★

John Hargrave died peacefully on November 21st 1982. He was 88 years old. His death is the final entry in the Kinlog, the official illumi-nated history of the movement. 'The Kindred of the Kibbo Kift is not dead,' notes this closing section. 'Its spirit lives on and will live as long as there are men and women with free hearts and minds, unafraid of the tyranny of the financial powers and their satellites.'

If John Hargrave was alive now, I imagine him sitting in a field beside a lightweight dome tent, the design inspired by the utopian vision of Buckminster Fuller, with a solar-charged laptop upon which he taps out his theories for economic reorganization in the wake of the banking collapse. If we lift the Kibbo Kift out of its historical moment, separate it from the era's current of dangerous ideas, and consider it for its true intent, then it is an inspiring, energizing force contrary to the forces of reaction. In *Plan of Action of the Kindred in the British Isles*, Hargrave writes, 'We have to dispel the overhanging feeling that "Britain is played out."' That 'played out' feeling is evoked in the pages of the reactionary press and in the resurgent Right. What is the narrative of Broken Britain if not a story of exhaustion, of a country tired of dealing with the complexities of the future and keen to cleave to the certainties of the past? Broken Britain is the moan of an old man. The Kindred existed at a similar moment in history to our own, a post-war malaise, an oppressive aging order, a time of political pessimism following a financial collapse and an embattled parliamentary system. It responded to contemporary ills with intellectual and physical courage, men and women alike, an energetic, creative community with ideas above their station. In the best tradtions of the *Idler*, they were anti-work and pro-play:

> The Kin repudiates the Legend of the Nobility of Work. It would prefer to see people doing less and less work and more and more Creative Play. The Legend of the Nobility of Work is based upon St. Paul: if any would not work neither should he eat.
>
> The Kin wishes to see man released from the Bugbear of Work … It wishes to see the whole of mankind more and more unemployed, less and less occupied with the toil of getting Food, Warmth and Shelter … Today, with all our machinery and applied science, most of our time is occupied in this toilsome business; even the capitalist is a slave.

BOLEX

PARTICULAR NONSENSE

IN CELEBRATION OF
THE ACT OVER AND ABOVE THE FACT

Penny Rimbaud

Convictions are more dangerous enemies of truth than lies.
Friedrich Nietzsche

PART ONE

ACTING OUT THE ALTOGETHER

U NCEREMONIOUSLY SNATCHED AS WE ARE FROM THE fluid matter of life itself, our birth is the first, but certainly not last, unsolicited incursion into what we later come to define as the 'self'. But that is to be blind to the fact that the self can only be aided into existence by other selves, not in its own image (for it has none), but in theirs. So what kind of self is it that is no more than a stage persona acting out whatever script it is that has been handed to it?

I THE EYE? CERTAINLY NOT.

The I of Descartes' 'I am' must first have been constructed by another I. Descartes' I is therefore not the I at all.

– WE THINK THEREFORE YOU ARE –

And thus we are created. Thus we are ascribed a role within the global pantomime. Thus, with the colourful exception of suicide (the only 'real' choice), we then quite simply have no option but to 'carry on'.*

~

Forgetting that, with the exception of *homo sapiens*, all living matter happily manages to exist outside the cognitive framework, there are those who, rather than trusting in life itself, prefer to engage in the self-serving construct of 'survival' (of the fittest). By abstracting the

---

* I am not here using the term 'carry on' in the negative sense, far from it. We are born of and carried by life, and I have no doubt that the unconditional nature of it will out against all the many human conceits (including my own) which might be thrown its way. This should, I believe, be cause for great celebration.

idea of survival from the totality of existence, this anthropocentric act of psychic enclosure deludes its advocates into imagining that they are somehow in control both of their own lives and of life itself (even whilst intuitively 'knowing' that, in fact, it's all completely out of their hands). It is this duality which is at the very root of all human suffering.

I commodify therefore I am,

at least I think so.

This endemic desire for physical and mental enclosure (imposed by others that we all might be other) has the effect of firmly placing the Descartes (the illusory 'I') well before the horse (the 'it'), in fact the horse never even gets a look in.

» RAUS, RAUS, KLEINES BIEST «

By overlaying human gravitas onto what otherwise is an entirely natural business, the authentic is contorted into the contrived, and the stage persona steps out into the footlights confident in his/her appointed role of self...

ONE **GIANT** STEP

Thus divorced from the primary I and, indeed, the intrinsic nature from which it stemmed, the stage persona of the secondary I is now obliged to shield itself from what it perceives to be the vagaries of life (these emanating from unresolved elements of the divorce from intrinsic nature). In finding itself, the stage persona becomes lost in a world where external confirmation is all.

– assurance through insurance –

– in fact, I think I don't have to think –

PHEW!

PASS ME THE PROZAC

Personally, whatever the circumstances, I've never found it particularly difficult to breathe, eat or sleep: they are such involuntary natural processes as to be autonomic.* The odd bath might pose a bit of a problem, but that's because I never actually 'need' one, and as for intelligent engagement, well, anything at all has meaning if:

    a) we want it to:
    b) we are able in the first place to snatch it from the whole to then identify it as a potential subject:
    c) we are prepared to engage in the Dadaesque multiple-bind of having given meaning to meaning that we might then give meaning to that which has no meaning beyond the meaning which we in the first place gave to meaning.

~

BEING AN END IN ITSELF,
MEANING CAN MEAN NOTHING BUT ITSELF.

As far as I am aware, and regardless of any survivalist construct, we live for however long we live. That's what life is about: it's all so gloriously random. There are those who rise and those who fall, and (for all our conceits) it's got nothing to do with us at all.

---

* yes, of course I acknowledge the hardship of deprivation, but that is an altogether different subject to the one which I am engaged with here. Suffice it to say, that those many who suffer deprivation through (primarily) the greed of global capitalism are far more likely to see the problem as one of communal (co)existence than that of the individualizing construct of Darwinian survivalism.

IN WHATEVER WAY THE TOUGH GET GOING, THE HAIR IN THEIR NOSES WILL JUST KEEP ON GROWING.

In the non-temporal, non-cognitive sense, life 'knows' because, logically, in its absolute state it contains all knowledge (past, present and future). It could be no other way. However, imagining that we might know better, we engage in the uniquely human conceit (if not heresy) of attempting to divest it of its totality through giving it (and thus ourselves) meaning. Birds don't do it, and neither do bees. They just get on with whatever it is they get on with ...

we're so very **small** >OUCH! minded.

Life has been around an awful lot longer than any one of us, so by my reckoning it gets the vote. Conversely, however, and dark as it may seem, I get the distinct impression that by being so completely removed from the primary I, most Westerners thoroughly resent the crude fact that life's just that little bit bigger than them. Like, who's in charge here?

THIS IS GROUND CONTROL...

Despite all our efforts to the contrary, life can neither help nor hinder itself; it just goes on regardless of our ruminations and, indeed, our fitness to enact them, but so, I would suggest, in the primary sense, do we, until such time ...

floating

I'm   **in a most peculiar way...**

...Kerrrash

but that's another story.

* * *

PART TWO

DON'T PUT YOUR DAUGHTER

OW OFTEN IT IS THAT WE SIT THROUGH, SAY, THE interminable boredom of a Wagnerian cacophony for no other reason than that we paid 'good money'* for the seat. Likewise, within the construct of mortality (the script), the primary I observes its stage persona from the stalls, unpleasantly aware that its boredom is, in fact, terminal: all form and no content.

Having stepped out onto the boards, and regardless of Mr Coward's protestations, we all play our parts with consummate ease: I the player, you the played. We're all interchangeable: I the played, you the player. Different personae, same script: clap one hand, turn a blind eye, exit stage left and watch dem boidies fly.

MY GOD, WE'RE ACTUALLY *DYING* OF

BOREDOM.

– in actually attempting to step out into the present,
what a profoundly presumptuous word 'actually' is –

~

---

* requiring a major essay to itself, the subject of 'good money' will, for the moment, not be discussed. Notwithstanding, let me simply say here that, effectively, there is no such thing …

and never mind the slashes

~

In lacking either the courage or conviction to actually 'just do it' (the Nike syndrome), I find it hard to imagine that I am the only one to have held their breath in the vain hope that if I did so for long enough I (and therefore it) might all just stop. Let's face it, if it was that easy there'd be no 'population problem' (that being the problem manifested in the traffic jam when, with an utterly self-interested and rare disregard for oneself, one asks 'who are all these people?'). Yes, the consensual world is everyone and everything but oneself:

NOT TO MENTION

DER ÜBERMENTION.

Invisible to itself and blinkered to anyone else, the stage persona prowls around in a state of nervous anticipation looking for another self to call 'itself': a six-shooting sheriff in the City of Oz: because, because, because...

...IT'S ALL SO DAMNED OUT   THERE.

Forever blaming the script (the state of mortality) for all its ills, the stage persona is forced to seek out whipping-posts for its compromised intellectual state and, thus, its moral* paucity.

★ ★ ★

---

* I refer here not to the theatrical prop of social morality, but to the Kantian 'categorical imperative' – 'act only according to that maxim whereby you can at the same time will that it should become a universal law.'

PART THREE

HOLIDAYS ON THE RUN

3 DIE IN CARAVAN FIRE.
Yeah? Well where's MY fucking dinner?

UT, THREE DEATHS OR NO, LIFE REMAINS A TENACIOUS bugger with no respect whatsoever for our sentimental whims and pompous conceits (or, clearly, our temporal nature). So here's the nub: we resent life because it carries on while we as entities within it are condemned (through constructs of our own making) to cease. Hence the many Armageddonist cults which, with complacent disregard for the irrepressible quality of life itself, inform us that life is going to be as short-lived as we, its self-appointed *dramatis personae*.

DROP MY BOMB – CRASH MY CAR. IT'S YOUR ONLY SALVATION.

This self-serving line in the self-confirming concept of 'mutually assured destruction' finds its *nadir* in any expression of imperialist intent from the Great British Empire through Nazi Germany to the New World Order or, conversely, in the confirmation given to those powers through the reformist opposition of the likes of CND through the ANL to the Climate Camps.

EVERY 'US' NEEDS A 'THEM'.

By so readily conforming to the strategies of 'divide and rule', reformist protest simply compounds status quo interests. Likewise, intimidation and fear can only work as a tactic if there are those who are seen to be affected by it.

EVERY 'THEM' NEEDS AN 'US'.

Like it or not, beneath the smokescreen of Climate Change, the nuclear industry has been able to proliferate tenfold, and the great sinner of the mid-twentieth century is now being promoted by many so-called radicals as the salvationist saint of the twenty-first. In short, they're all at it, mutually preparing, promoting or prophesying an assured end to whatever tragic drama it is that serves that end:

THE
END
IS
NIGH

but has anyone seen my fucking cheque book?

Having adopted the secure if contradictory role of harbingers of death and destruction ('the war that will last a lifetime', 'the end of life as we know it'), our preachy postulators quite understandably become insecure about their own future. Fearful that their predictions might indeed become a reality that could deprive them of their *raison d'être*, rather than looking for genuine philosophical solutions, they then engage in extensive recruitment campaigns so that others might be bullied into sharing their misery and suffering their fate: one for all and all for one.

YOUR COUNTRY NEEDS YOU

and bugger the deaths in its name.

But never mind, there's a thousand-and-one other causes to sacrifice yourself to. History is littered with madmen and martyrs.

JESUS SAVES
(everyone, it seems, but himself)

Crucifixion is, however, a pretty easy game to play if you're gunning on

resurrection,

but if you're not, then pass me the

ah, now you see me ...
ho, ho, ho.

* * *

PART FOUR

TOEING THE PARTICULAR LINE

D EMOCRACY IS NOT THE SUM TOTAL OF ALL ITS PARTS,
it is the contrivance of division exploited by the few and
reflected by the many. In this (non)sense there can be no such
thing as a political solution...

this is the writing on the wall:
— there is only the philosophicALL —

In complete contempt of Particle Physics, we continue to see ourselves
as particular, this being a mirror image of what we are not, but which
is, in fact, the only identity that our stage persona can ever hope for.

RALUCITRAP:
and what sort of sense does that make?

However, whereas Narcissus was confined to the pool and might possibly have had to take into account the 'ripple effect', we have the fixed
image of the mirror and the lens, fragile as the glass from which they
are made, yet cast as granite within our soul. This is the GREAT
burden, the GRAND delusion, the DIS-EASE of reason ...

WE LIVE NOT IN THE AUTHENTIC ACTUAL,
BUT IN THE CONTRIVED FACTUAL,
AND THEREIN THE CRUNCH.

We pursue knowledge believing that it leads to understanding, but to
do this we must ignore all the implications of post-Einstein physics and
confine our view to the duality of the Cartesian singular (unless, of
course, we take the existential short-cut).

A VIEW IS NOT A POINT

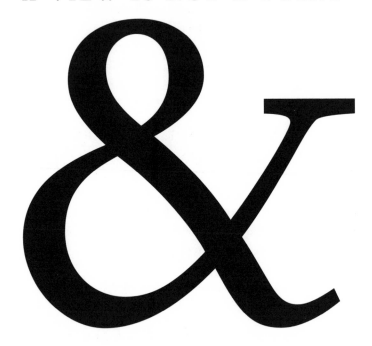

A POINT IS NOT A VIEW.

As 'I the thinker' we become considered in our opinions and circumspect in expression of them. We seek confirmation as proof from those wearing the same silly hats and suffering from the same silly conceits as ourselves (this being the battery-cage of academia, the assembly-line of Fascism and the tight-knit community of the Mafioso, these, incidentally, all being pretty much one and the same).

LIKE THE YELLOW STAR,
IT'S AN OFFER YOU CAN'T IGNORE

We employ common language to compound consensual ideas of common form. We pride ourselves in our demonstrations of integrity and consistency, these being best expressed through myopic linear thinking, the corrupted physicality of furrowed brow and affected stutter, and the tendency to say 'I th...th...think you'll find' whilst clearly being completely at sea in the vortex of human complexity and intrigue.

IT IS WITH SAVAGE INDIFFERENCE THAT THE CARTESIAN 'I' COUNTERS ITS OWN AUTHENTICITY.

Thus confined to the consensual cesspit, the stage persona slowly suffocates beneath the weight of convention and social order which in the first place had given it its name.

I the consumer am consumed
to be subsumed as the stifling voice of reason.

– THE POT CALLING ITSELF BLACK –

Each whimper another construct. Each groan another confirmatory bon mot. Each agonized screech another confirmation of status quo ideology: no pain, no gain.

What UTTER twaddle.

★ ★ ★

PART FIVE

CLIMBING OUT OF THE CARTESIAN WELL

N O MAN IS AN ISLAND, BUT EACH AND EVERY ONE OF us is irredeemably alone or, as Jean-Paul put it (conveniently forgetting that he was one of them), 'hell is other people'...

ceci n'est pas...

which is as good a start as any.

Like it or not, whatever our conflicts, whatever our joys, at this very moment everything is precisely as it is: set in stone. It could be no other way. However, we can't KNOW this because, just as much as today is yesterday's tomorrow, the 'this very moment' referred to only a moment ago has already slipped away and entered the field of memory (which at best, if not selective, will be inventive)...

ah, *oui*, I remember *eet* well...

But for all that, you are still here, the breeze is still coming in through the window, the tides are still turning, and the Earth is still spinning. Everything has arrived at this precise moment in the only manner that it could. But no matter, it has already avalanched into the past which is itself.

IT HASN'T SURVIVED.
IT'S JUST BEEN.

~ arbeit macht frei ~

The Birmingham train is bound for Birmingham, but, as Mr Porter knows, it could very well take you on to Crewe if to Crewe it is also bound. Paris is altogether another story. Nonetheless, at this moment, there can be no mistake: you are where (if not who) you are, and that's that. If you want to call it a mistake, tough. You just try to change it.

Ooh, but was it good for you too?

At the very moment of the impact of the motorway crash, you are having an orgasm three hundred miles away. They are inseparable. One could not have happened without the other. They are, indeed, one and the same; the solid matter of existence. Symbiotic? I should say so.

WELL, FUCK ME!
YOU?

* * *

PART SIX

SHIFTING THE SHADOWS

W E EXIST IN TENSION BETWEEN WHAT IS PERCEIVED
and generally accepted as material (matter) and the process
of perceiving it (experience). Driven by the assumption
that that which is material is common ground, and that our percep-
tions of it exist in a framework of common agreement, we blunder
through life engaged in a series of half-truths. The first and dominant
half-truth is the Cartesian conceit that proof of our existence in
the material world can be established through thought, the other
half being that the material world has a substance which somehow
magically pre-empts that thought. Yes, it might already have been
there, but it is we and only we who give/gave it form and/or, indeed,
content.

NOTHING AT ALL MEANS
ANYTHING AT ALL.

Whatever the observed, the process of observation is identical.
It can only be we who see the seen.
The process is the message …

NOT FACT,
BUT ACT.

Surely, then, as matter and experience are so fundamentally irreconcilable, any belief in the linear and temporal conceits of reason must stand to be beggared?

Cast as shadow in an empire of shadows,
we seek substance and meaning by clothing the illusory emperor of self.

AND THUS SPAKE NARCISSUS

Of all human ugliness, vanity is the greatest: a self-consuming obsession with the dead flesh of reflection. In the dark attics of self-deceit, the truth is written, the warts exposed, the conflagrations able to pursue the terminal. While Alice at least climbed through the mirror to a place where a Cheshire cat could literally fade from sight, and vanity was devoured by the poetic power of imagination, Dorian Gray perfumed his perversity, powdered his profanity and worshipped in the kingdom of Hades. Like the mirror-image, self-reflection is reversed and, in confounding the left/right logics of the brain, counter-creative. Yearning a static view of ourselves within the flux of existence, we catch site of that illusory self and confirm it by giving it a name:

THAT'S ME!
Jesus in resurrection.
Narcissus in the pool.

But who is it who sees that self, and who is it that steps away from the mirror if not the one-dimensional postage-stamp version of self with whom we have just conferred? (And how come it's always there when we go back to it?) The idea that we have of ourselves lurks not in front of the mirror but within it: a morose, static entity silhouetted against Blake's 'eternity's sunrise'. In short, we're framed.

Now you see me, now you

It is this idea of self which we present to others, mirroring their own conceits in a shared delusion of parity: collectors' items on the table of the Mad Hatter's tea-party:

'More ME, Vicar?'

But, as Alice was astute enough to observe, how can one demand more of   ?

THEN, LET THE TABLES BE TUꓤИƎꓷ.

★ ★ ★

PART SEVEN

TEMPERS IN THE TEMPLE

'FORGIVE ME, FATHER,
FOR I KNOW NOT WHAT I DO.'

To have an existence, any object must by necessity be observed, thus rendering it a subjective verbal experience (verb) as opposed to an objective, material fact (noun). Likewise, forever once-removed from our primary self (which knows no separation), rather than experiencing our experience, we are reduced to observing it. Within this construct, no object and/or experience can exist until such time as it is rendered static (nouned by the verb), and even then it can only do so in the form of an abstract idea which will require constant reactivation (verbing) to ensure any hope of its continued existence.

*'Heard the one about the greasy tit?
No? Well I couldn't quite grasp it either.'*

But just as the material world can be verbed into existence, so, with consummate ease, it can be verbed out of it.

NO.N!

– the final solution to Camus's little conundrum –

The noun is the heresy which becomes truth,
the truth which becomes lie.

OH, THIS IS THE LIE!

Is it reasonable, then, to claim that anything can be truly an object or truly an experience when, clearly, either there is no such thing as either, or, more logically (as current physics suggests), they are both the same thing (i.e. of the same matter)?

SO, HOW CAN ANYTHING MATTER OUTSIDE OF THAT MATTER?

Just as your experience is not mine, so your object. Your stone and your sadness are both a result of your verbing, as are mine a result of mine. There is no agreement, only assumption wearing the duplicitous mask of understanding. There is no 'material world', only the immaterial matter of ideas. How then can we expect or even hope for any real parity? However loud we shout, we are silent as the wind: form but not content, force but not power. And don't menace me with delusions of empathy.

PALE PIERROT'S PALOUR IS EMPTY
and never mind the stardust.

Stemming from the vampiric construct (compounded by Freud and his travelling freak-show) that we can practice empathy (*n.* **the capacity for understanding and sharing another's feelings or ideas**) we are given licence to the unholy trinity of gross presumption, abusive incursion, and the wholesale dilution of authenticity.

'I climbed the Montaigne.'
'Yes, I remember it well. We have our moles.'

Memory and the past upon which it supposedly feeds are not static nouns, but a result of the ever-illusive fluid of verbing. Then why suppose that the present (which in any case is already past) is in any way different? All are as much projection as the future. All are emotive acts of imagination founded on highly selected supposed realities implemented for no other reason than the convenience of the moment (which, yes, you've got it ...).

TICK-TOCK-TICK

– it can't go wrong –

Like memory, the past is employed as a source of stabilization by those unable to embrace the implied responsibility of an existence extending beyond the frailties of entity (deeply compounded through the empathetic pretences mentioned above).

GET IT T o Get he R.

— THAT'S AN ORDER —

To see, we must be together enough to be able to see. If the boat is beyond the horizon, there is no boat to be seen. Likewise, forever fractionalised as stage personae, we inhabit the spaces left behind by the primary self we never saw: the phantasmagorical realm of imagination haunted by ciphers.

Jesus verbed for our nouns.

The books are burned, the statues felled.

This is the alchemic pact, the Faustian tryst.

-TOUGH SHIT-

WE ARE AS ONE NOT IN OUR SORROW,
BUT IN THE SOUL WHICH KNOWS NEITHER.

★ ★ ★

PART EIGHT

BY WAY OF A DISCLAIMER

Moooooooooooooooneeeeeeeee!
'Ooh, turn the other cheek, you cheeky rascal.'

THERE'S A NARROW LINE BETWEEN THE BUDDHISTS'
metaphysical 'middle way' and the apparently innocuous everyday responses of 'yes', 'no' or 'maybe'. Trapped between two
opposites which are essential to its existence, the 'middle way' is
exactly that, a no-man's land, a line between the trenches where the
flying shells do no more than further heat the already hot air (but may
Buddha bless the poor sods on either side of the great divide).

THANKYOU, MAAM.

Likewise, 'yes', 'no' and 'maybe' are each an acknowledgement and
therefore confirmation of whatever it is they pertain to be responses
to. It makes no difference whatsoever whether you believe it or not,
but to actively not believe in something requires an active belief in
whatever it is that one is choosing not to believe in. 'No' merely confirms the existence of 'yes', 'yes' of 'no', and 'maybe' of both 'yes' and
'no'. In which case, how are we to truly stand alone and apart from this
utter nonsense?

DISEN G A G   E
– reality is a linguistic foible –

Out of my complete contempt for the pantomime of the consensual world, and in an attempt to engage more fully with life itself, I have recently taken to employing the invented word 'nos'* as an alternative to the smugly disingenuous approaches of 'the middle way' and the flawed presumptions of 'yes', 'no' and 'maybe'. In effect, nos quite simply means 'I am not here to be engaged with.' It politely informs the incursor that I the informant am 'not in', whilst allowing me to continue unabashed with whatever it is that I'm up to. In reality, this is of course precisely what any one of us is doing anyway, but, enthralled as we are by the stage persona's delusions of human relationship, we prefer to imagine otherwise.

~

Notwithstanding, and certainly notwithsitting cross-legged in a state of self-righteous subjugation, the common thread of 'life lifeing life' remains constant regardless of whatever survivalist conceits we the dramatis personae might choose to impose upon it.

OM MANE PADME BUM

Call it 'The Absolute' if you like, call it 'soul', or call it 'fried fish-fingers', but for God's sake don't call it 'self', for, lost in the multi-layered conceits of human understanding and psycho-complicity, you know not who or what that self is.

SO THERE.

'The absurd is the fundamental idea and the first truth.'
Albert Camus

* * *

* the Japanese word 'mu' has a similar usage to 'nos' in that it informs the incursor that their given question or comment is being taken as meaningless. But this isn't enough in that it is judgemental and therefore counter to true disengagement.

Epilogue

FUN DE SIECLE

[1] Yet still we endure, and 'though our breath be gasped or our eyes blinkered by opportunism, still we see light and are cast by it. But is it only as shadow?

[2] Still we endure that each structure be pulled down, each love paralleled, each pulse metered to ensure the dawn and trick the cockerel into silence, or is it only as echo?

[3] Oh yes, I heard the carrion call across vacant valleys where I laid rested in the waiting, but I was not moved. And closer they came, so close that I could smell the blood on fur and gape. These were the pallbearers of fellowship come to claim me, to bind me in the consumptive thrall of the consensual. Still I did not move. But was this but imaginings that better I might shape entity? What was it that I sought in the seeking, and they in theirs?

[4] So captivated we are by self-ideation, so far from existential self-creation, we carry the dead matter of the past and portray it as ourselves. Bred on this corruption, whilst devouring light we exhale darkness. Thus encaged, we define the limited parameters of our understanding as 'principle' and become as demons in the tempest. But I am not to be taken so easily.

[5] There's a terrible emptiness to those arts which deny alchemic fortune. Only in the hands of fools does the philosopher's gold become that of fools. Then, if the fool chooses a descriptive desolation in which we are requested to celebrate theft, let him suffer for his folly that his is torn from our eyes, born of hidden depths: that his is light confined to gilded frame as if, perhaps, eternity might be commanded or immortality trapped by his inconsequence. Is this, then, a denial of existence or merely a disregard for it? Certainly it's an abstraction, even dislocation, that here we belong and may well last beyond entity.

[6] But how diminished we are through expression, and how diluted through protestations of content. I sat by the river and saw only the sparkle, while those who passed me by were mere silhouette known only as description. And of course there is great force in words, but are those utterances plucked flower denying the seed, or fallen petal laid out to feed it? There is, after all, a great deal said of wholeness and of self-containment, but in that expression of illusory-self I believe petal, fall and frame to be equally gilded. So poor in description, we pull away at our ethereal flesh in a constant state of bereavement.

Then might I internalize you,
draw you not against, but into my form
that everyday collision is no longer possible.

[7]Each cries out to be heard, each cries out to be seen, yet I have witnessed flesh roses bruised by winter's frost, quite unaware of observation and quite removed from any observation of their own. I see these beauties as sentinels of wisdom where tragic life has no tragedy nor even comedy whereby it might be dismissed. Where petals fall, I await the great denouncement.

[8]And when sight explodes to pure light, and the flux is re-established, where all is particle and nothing particular, then at last we are free to fly beyond the boundaries of self-regulation. Or when sound is divorced from time that nonsense at last might have meaning, or even becomes the description, then shall we rise beyond self-imposition and know beyond the deluded practices of identity; angels of light carried beyond form to the Great Temples of Proximity where intimacy is common-ground.

[9]So bonded we are by the glue of assumption, so connected by the abstractions of reason, this being (quite wrongly) named The Enlightenment. In this folly, dewdrops have been gathered that the rainbow might be pinned-down for analysis, or the flourish of blackbird bottled in indifference that lesser songs might be documented by that meter and presented as composition. This is the principle, the modus of dysfunction which we describe as 'life fulfilled'. But the formula is self-devouring, Each winging of eternity is grounded by this arrogance. The divine scriptures are carved in slate that too is mortal.

IS IT ANY WONDER,
THEN, THAT WE SUFFER THESE WOUNDS, STAGGERING BEFORE FALLEN CHRISTS THAT WE TOO MIGHT FEEL THE NAILS?

Abigail Rorer

FROM CLASS As TO CLEMATIS: REFLECTIONS ON GROWING UP

Harry Mount

I'VE JUST GOT AN INVITATION TO AN OLD UNIVERSITY friend's fortieth. It's taking place at somewhere called Blagclub 3 in Holland Park in west London. He says on the invitation that it promises 'to be a great night at a great little venue'.

I don't think I'm going to go. Not because I don't like him; I still do, which is more than I can say for a lot of old heritage friends – the friends you're bound to by the ancient bonds of youth and shared educational institutions, even though you've now pretty much run out of things to say to them.

No, the reason is that I know I won't enjoy the loud music – my friend, as well as being a barrister and businessman, is also a club DJ.

I don't hold this against him – it would be mad and inhuman to. But the accumulated experience of something like 500 parties along those lines over the last twenty years means that I just know I won't enjoy it.

There will be sympathetic friends there, and plenty of good wine and food. But these – and the healthy obligation to be polite to my friend – are not enough to make me put up with the familiarly dispiriting rituals of the traditional club experience: of shouting, and repeating, pleasantries at people; of killing off all the pleasures of quickfire, naturally developing conversation with the inability to hear properly.

Now you might just call this a symptom of my dreary, encroaching middle age – I am 38. And you'd be right – I would have almost certainly gone to a great little night at a great little venue for his twentieth, thirtieth and even his thirty-fifth birthdays.

But to say there's something wrong and fogeyish in my refusing to go is to treat middle age pejoratively – as a gradual shutting down of the senses, as the death of the ability to appreciate the finer things in life, an ability supposedly granted only to the young and open-minded.

I think there's a different, more flattering way of looking at my decision, and at middle age, too – and that's as an increasing understanding of what really matters, and what you really like doing. Instead of being a stripping away of your sensual side, middle age is really a stripping away of your naïve side.

Yes, I used to, if not quite enjoy nightclubs, then see them as a necessary part of my life. That was where my friends went. That was where legend dictated that you met girls, although I never did; unless you count the time in a nightclub in Duke Street about ten years ago, when a slightly Gothy-looking girl started dancing with me and said after five minutes, 'Let's go.' At the time, I thought there must be something dodgy going on, so I made my excuses and left. I now think I had a momentary glimpse of what it was like to be Tom Jones *c.*1974, and I kick myself.

Perhaps if the Duke Street experience had happened more often, I would have genuinely enjoyed nightclubs. But it didn't, and I didn't.

Instead, I have gradually realized that I prefer quiet bars, and friends I can talk to in the perfect conditions for the sort of conversation I like – a bit of question and answer, a few anecdotes, a bit of comic fantasy building on comic fantasy, some mutual teasing.

In stripping away my misguided tendency to find false pleasure in nightclubs and settling on this genuinely pleasurable alternative, I think I am returning to a basic, atavistic human activity.

I'm sure dancing does have ancient, deep-seated roots, too. But by that I mean dancing in the age before extreme amplification: a natural instinct of combining sexual display with sexual interaction, accompanied by physical skill, along with whispered, Fred and Ginger-style conversation on the dancefloor – an entirely different pursuit from the Blagclub 3 modern form of dancing.

(This ancient form of dancing has only died recently, by the way – there's an instructive scene in a sixties Beatles film, where the four lads are chatting away at normal-conversation decibel levels at a nightclub bar, while girls are twisting away on the dancefloor yards away from them.)

The ancient form of dancing could in theory happily continue at fortieth birthday parties, and beyond – as it does in a few British dance halls, or among Greek OAPs doing Zorba dances in Athenian tavernas, or the ancient New York Argentinians you see practising the tango in Central Park on Sunday afternoons.

The new form of dancing – jumping up and down on the spot on your own to an extremely amplified soundtrack – is barely possible after the age of 35, without the assistance of reality-suppressing drugs.

I'm only just beginning to realize that this pattern – of young blindness giving way to more mature wisdom – has been going on in my life continually for almost twenty years. And the pattern always involves turning back – not necessarily, though frequently, to the land, but always to nature, and to those atavistic, ancient human feelings.

Extremely amplified music has only been around for twenty years; so it's no surprise that it hasn't been bedded into our old, natural rhythms. But even much older human rituals are still relatively new in historical terms: the cities we mostly live in these days in the Western world have only been around in their recognizable current state for around 300 years.

Homo sapiens has been around for about 200,000 years; it was only 10,000 years ago that we stopped being hunter-gatherers. It would be odd if we had thrown off our long-standing, deeply seated thought patterns – closely bound up with nature – in the course of the last few centuries; the blink of an eye in evolutionary terms.

Man is still naturally a creature of nature. He just takes a bit of time – 38 years in my case – working it out under the onslaught of modern technology, which is particularly effective on young, spongey brains attached to young wide eyes that are easily diverted by anything new and shiny.

So, as a teenager, the thought of a week on the remote Pembrokeshire coast – where my parents have a holiday cottage – bored me, if not to tears, then to extreme yearning for the bright lights of central London and my three-deck Aiwa stereo system.

It was only in my twenties that I realized what I'd been missing all those years of backing out of teenage holidays in Pembrokeshire – exchanged for morose trips to Covent Garden pubs that turned a blind eye to underage drinkers.

I distinctly remember – in one of my few definitive, datable, precise rite-of-passage moments – lying on the lawn in Wales in the Easter holidays before my history finals, at the age of 21, in 1993. Despairing of my notes on the Irish Question under Gladstone, I closed my eyes, spread my arms and legs in a star shape, and let the late-spring sun warm my eyelids.

Suddenly, for the first time, I heard birdsong. Of course, I had been surrounded by the sound all my life, but I had zoned it out as background noise, like I do with the low drone of indistinguishable voices in the office or quiet music in a bar. (I couldn't have zoned out the really loud stuff at my friend's fortieth – that's the problem, really).

Since then, I have become a minor amateur birdwatcher and zone in on all sorts of little thrills in life: the return of the screeching swifts to my street in Kentish Town in April; the guillemots laying their eggs on the Pembrokeshire cliffs in May; a blackbird serenading the prostitutes on Market Road, a thriving red-light district in Islington, on a cold dawn, the first thrilling intimation that spring is coming.

I say 'zone in', as if listening to the birds is a willed, conscious process. In fact, it comes naturally now, without any concerted effort. I think I am returning to a natural state – taking out the invisible earplugs of my youth, rather than actively inserting the hearing aid of middle age.

The same process has continued, at different ages, for the last twenty years. On those adolescent Welsh trips, and in my childhood London home, my parents would talk in passing about gardening. And those invisible earplugs immediately started working overtime. Words like 'camellia' and 'clematis' did just about stick to the sides of my mind – and I knew that they were plants – but I had no knowledge or interest in what they looked like.

And now, in the last two years, I have actually planted a camellia and a clematis in my own garden. And an olive tree, some mint, four climbing roses and a three-foot stretch of box hedge.

It isn't much, but it is a reflection of the complete inversion of my priorities since the end of childhood. When my parents used to leave me and my brother and sister while they went to Wales for the weekend, my mother had to drum into us the need to water the indoor plants. I now water my rosemary and parsley in the kitchen as an utterly natural part of my routine, without thinking about it or writing down a reminder on a Post-it note – it's become an innate habit, like doing my teeth or setting my alarm clock.

Virgil was on the money in the *Georgics* – his poem about the joys of rural life, published in 29 BC:

> *Felix, qui potuit rerum cognoscere causas,*
> *Fortunatus et ille, deos qui novit agrestis,*
> *Panaque Silvanumque senem Nymphasque sorores*
> *Quos rami fructus, quos ipsa volentia rura*
> *Sponte tulere sua, carpsit, nec ferrea iura*
> *Insanumque forum aut populi tabularia vidit.*

> How happy is the man who can work out the real point of things.
> How lucky is the person who knows the rural gods,
> Pan, the Old Man of the Woods and the Nymph sisters.
> He rejoices in fruit tumbling freely from his branches,
> In the fertile earth sprouting at will.
> He's never bothered with iron laws,
> The insanity of political life or dreary public administration.

I'm with Virgil; with only a minor quibble. He says the true pleasure of nature is only to be found in the country. The natural pleasures I'm talking about don't have to be rural, although they are drawn from man's rural origins. The country gives you more of a chance to indulge in them but there are plenty of people in the country who don't bother indulging.

On those Pembrokeshire cliffs, you're much more likely to see a tourist, or a blow-in like me, than a local – you take for granted what you have on your doorstep.

I can get just as extreme consolation from these natural pleasures in an urban setting. I planted those climbing roses in just the right spot in my garden that, when I open my curtains in the morning, I get a glimpse of them. They are made even more beautiful by their urban backdrop – a sprawling Edwardian council block in red and white brick, fronted by the higgledy-piggledy extensions at the back of the Victorian terraced houses that abut on to mine. The last of my white rose survived through the Indian summer into the first week of November, when a squally patch of rain came marching down from Scotland to blow away the last few petals. As a teenager, I never used to notice the most enormous changes to the landscape brought by the seasons; now the disappearance of a petal moves me.

The triumphs of nature don't have to be on an enormous scale, as Virgil spotted, again in the *Georgics*:

> *Laudato ingentia rura*
> *Exiguum colito.*

> Praise a huge estate
> Cultivate a tiny one.

These pleasures have become so natural – so inbuilt– that they rarely take a concerted effort to arrange, with the odd exception, like my careful planting of those roses. Instead they just spark off an improvement in my mood without my thinking about the natural cause behind it.

So I immediately feel better the moment I put my bicycle on the boat that takes me from Blackfriars to my Canary Wharf office. I have slipped the surly bonds of the Embankment and Farringdon Road – of traffic lights, of downcast commuters, of being forced into a particular path by the streams of traffic – and I have found the freedom of water.

Going back to the river – like going back to the land – brings a whole set of pleasures that our ancestors must have taken for granted.

Open skies and sea room on either side, ever-changing light effects on the water, no possibility of congestion in a sparsely-populated seascape. (The Thames is staggeringly empty these days, probably emptier than it's been since before the Romans, with the collapse of waterborne traffic that came with the tube and the car.)

Now of course the Thames Clipper I take to Canary Wharf has an engine. I am not against modernity for its own sake and I am certainly not one of those people who live in a forties house with a Bakelite phone and antimacassars thick with Brylcreem.

But modernity is at its most pleasurable when it absorbs those atavistic human activities into technological advances. Where it becomes unbearable is when it forces man into situations he had rarely previously encountered in his first 200,000 years on earth. We were born to float along rivers since the year dot – it doesn't matter whether we're propelled by oars or internal combustion; the sensation is much the same.

We were not programmed, say, to live underground; nor were we conditioned to be squeezed up in close proximity to our strange fellow man, although strange fellow woman can be pleasurable. Thus the pain of being on a packed tube train; thus the pleasure of talking to an attractive stranger in a packed bar.

And so it goes on. Man was not built to hurtle at 70 miles an hour along a concrete track surrounded on all sides by other men hurtling along at the same speed. Cars and motorways remove you from the landscape and standardize it, while walking and bicycling reintroduce you to its unique and varied beauties. Travelling at 10 miles an hour is much more natural – the speed of a fast human on foot, or a cyclist, or the typical horse.

Trains, by this analysis, are, I suppose, unnatural, but they do offer the ancient inbuilt pleasure that comes from contemplation of the landscape; something you can't do on the tube. It's interesting to see who looks out of the window on trains; it's a pretty good benchmark of how much pleasure people take on their journey. Tourists always look out of the window; commuters never do.

Well, not on the train, anyway. On my boat to work, even the bankers heading to Credit Suisse in Canary Wharf put aside their

BlackBerries and newspapers and sit on the open rear deck, gazing towards the sun rising over Deptford, their overcoats speckled with Thames water, as the boat swings south into that huge bend in the river – the one that figures prominently in the opening credits of *EastEnders*.

It's striking, too, how the people who work on the river boats are jollier than the guards on the tube. Part of it is because their customers are happier, and so they are, too. Part of it is because the boats work so well – 98 per cent punctuality rate at the moment, which, admirable as it is, isn't so hard to achieve on an empty river. But the main reason for the pleasure is that it's a skilled, outdoors job depending on understanding nature. There's usually tremendous jokey competition between the two ship's mates as the boat approaches the Canary Wharf pier. From 15 foot out, one of them hurls the boat's looped rope at a mooring post. If he gets it right, both mates stay quiet, in tacit acknowledgement of the achievement of judging the boat's speed and the conflicting currents of the eddying Thames. If one misses, the other laughs out loud and teases him, in a friendly competitive spirit.

It's an achievement they both value; they both want to improve their skills. It's also an important achievement – get it badly wrong, as they very occasionally do, and the captain screams down from the bridge at them. Beneath the banter there's the constant low-level supply of adrenalin that comes from dealing with an unpredictable measure of mortal danger.

The technology of modern life has removed us further and further from that threat of mortal danger, and we are no happier. In fact, we're much sadder, if recent figures on the soaring amount of anti-depressants taken in the Western world are anything to go on.

One of the reasons for this is explained by the American psychiatrist Abraham Maslow (1908–70). He was the one who came up with the idea of the so-called hierarchy of needs. First, we need to satisfy physiological needs – for oxygen, food, water, sleep and sex. Once those are satisfied, we move on to safety needs – for security of body, employment, resources, morality, the family, health and property. Then comes the need for love, then esteem and so-called self-actualization – the need for creativity, spontaneity and to achieve your full potential.

As societies get richer and healthier, they fulfil more and more of the basic needs, except for the most elusive one of all – the need for happiness itself. This is not satisfied by rising gross domestic product, or by discovering how to make penicillin. It is of course an impossible aim to satisfy. But a certain form of basic happiness, if only in brief moments, comes from satisfying a need that Maslow never considered – the need for man's modern, technology-driven, recently manufactured world to chime with his ancient, more natural day-to-day existence.

Clifford Harper

EVERY GARDEN

Tim Richardson

EVERY GARDEN IS A POLITICAL ACT.

EVERY PLANT IS A POLITICAL PRISONER.

THAT STATEMENT IS NOT MEANT TO IMPLY THAT EVERY allotment owner is presiding over some kind of vegetable Guantanamo Bay. There are, however, cultural implications bound up with the apparently beneficent or at least harmless pastime of growing fruit and veg for the table. Whether the gardener feels political or not when feeling under the earth for the first potatoes or fending off slugs with grit and old beer, there can be no doubt that the decision to delve is, at this particular moment of ecological dismay, an act of powerful political piquancy. In fact, as this short essay aims to show, gardening for food is a pastime which has a considerable political pedigree. That is despite the cosy, 'Alan Titchmarsh' popular view of gardening as an even more banal cousin of DIY, something to do when one has grown old or failed in life. That patronizing stereotype should be a red rag to the bullish instincts of all those suspicious of the state-prescribed work ethic. For gardening is, to paraphrase Francis Bacon, the most purely idle of human pleasures; it is possible to be as amply rewarded for very little as for a great deal of work, and – gloriously – there is no sure connection between the amount of energy and effort expended while gardening, and what results from it. You can be a good gardener by doing very little, and a bad gardener by doing too much. The weather and other intangibles constantly undercut the 'virtues' of hard graft. And from a political point of view, the gardener as 'home-worker' is about as far removed from the developed capitalist system as it is possible to be, growing produce for home consumption in a kitchen just a few yards away ('food yards'…), and usually donating any surplus food to friends and neighbours for free.

But to get back to the current craze for grow-your-own. Allotments now boast lengthy waiting lists and, to judge from book sales at least, thousands of people from their twenties to forties (most of them women) have taken up horticulture. The influx of these novices has led to considerable bemusement on the part of the traditional, middle-aged, male, marrow-growing constituency out there in shed-land. The motivation among the newcomers is not a sudden urge to grow gigantic vegetables but instead stems from a desire to grow both for flavour and as a way of being quite sure of the provenance of the food on the kitchen table. There is a great deal of mistrust around the food industry as a whole, let alone retail outlets such as supermarkets or the ethics or otherwise of the meat industry. There are growing and sometimes well-founded suspicions, too, about large-scale commercial organic horticulture. As a result, the twenty-first-century grow-your-own movement has a slightly apocalyptic, post-industrial, millennarian savour to it, as if people are hunkering down in preparation for Armageddon. This time, however, it appears the apocalypse is expected to be ecological rather than nuclear in flavour. Better start bottling those plums, then.

In reality, it is only allotments in the most affluent and fashionable areas of cities that are experiencing a surge in interest – elsewhere, allotments are still being closed down for lack of interest. But it could well be the case that these elite (or bourgeois) early adopters of a low-tech sensibility in a high-tech age are in the vanguard of a wider movement. It would take a brave television chef or gardener to gainsay 'going organic' or cast doubt on the real ecological impact of domestic vegetable growing; that would be horticulturally and nutritionally incorrect. Perhaps mass public opinion will follow in their wake.

From the standpoint of garden history, we have been here before: the current high visibility of the grow-your-own phenomenon is reminiscent of the 'Dig for Victory' campaign of the Second World War, only the enemy now is climate change rather than the Nazis. In fact, there was a concerted campaign aimed at encouraging domestic veg production during the First World War, too, when allotments first appeared on railway land. But it is the forties incarnation of patriotic gardening which still looms large in the national consciousness and that is because 'Dig for Victory' achieved enduring success as a propaganda campaign. As such, it remains as much a part of folk memory of the war as the Battle of Britain.

The truth is, while a (small) proportion of the populace certainly did grow their own for some part of the Second World War, the effect it had on homegrown resources was negligible compared with less exciting innovations such as increased mechanization in agriculture (all those Land Girls driving shiny new tractors) and the reclamation of marshland or other unused hectares for large-scale crop-growing. Even so, despite these measures, during the first years of the war Britain remained dependent on ship-borne supplies of grain from Canada and the USA. Mrs Miggins's back-garden radishes were just not part of the equation from the Ministry of Food's point of view. Imagine if Britain had been invaded and London had become a second Stalingrad? In that context the Dig for Victory campaign would barely be recalled today. The real message of Dig for Victory, as sent from the government to the beleaguered populace, lay in the way it fostered a sense that British people of all classes were 'all in this together', with pictures of the lawns of stately homes being ploughed up next to images of cheery Cockneys brandishing bunches of carrots. It was good propaganda material for a nation under threat and bombed from the air, but not yet physically invaded. 'Potato Pete' was one of the manically smiling cartoon characters used on posters, bizarrely encouraging people to eat either himself or his tuberous confederates, and perhaps he did cheer people up by making them feel that everything would be all right in the end. One should never underestimate the morale-boosting power of the chip in British life.

The similarities with today's horticultural zeitgeist lie in the way vegetable gardening is effectively being marketed by the politicians and their civilian lackeys as a way of 'making a difference' to the environmental world order, even if the effect of this in a global context is virtually nil. The sense of eco-guilt which politicians seek to imbue in each of us, as if we are all individually culpable in some way for the conundrum of our deteriorating if not dying planet, needs assuaging somehow, and gardening does seem to salve consciences, just as recycling seemed to a decade ago. There is also a class element to this. A relatively high proportion of eco-commentators and activists are upper class or upper middle class. This particular cause appeals to a strong inbred patrician sensibility. Whether or not these activists would feel comfortable acknowledging it, the eco-movement re-emphasizes ancient links between land and agriculture and British political and social power; those who feel linked to the landed or gentry classes will often experience a sense of rightness about being involved with land custodianship in some way. On a deeper cultural level, horticulture itself has long been considered an inherently virtuous pastime – think back to that period in the Garden of Eden, before Man's first disobedience. Gardening does indeed tend to make people feel good about themselves, also healthier mentally, physically and perhaps even morally (though that last conflation is surely illusory).

Vegetable gardening can serve, too, as a form of political or cultural protest. The last time Britain experienced a surge in the popularity of self-sufficiency on this scale was in the years following the Middle East oil crisis of 1973, when for the first time there was genuine uncertainty as to whether there would be enough energy to go round. The answer today is clearly 'no', but it was not as obvious then. This was the period of the *Whole Earth Catalogue* and John Seymour's seminal guide to self-sufficiency, when the idea of alternative lifestyles first gained serious currency. The movement quickly became considered such a part of mainstream culture that it could be satirized in a television sit-com such as *The Good Life* (where I have to say I always identified more with Gerry – he of the checked trousers and G&Ts – than with the insufferably smug goody-goody Tom).

The equivocal relationship between food production and political power goes back to the beginnings of organized agriculture in Britain and is tied up with the facts of land ownership. Until relatively recently there was a direct link between land ownership and political power in that only those who owned a certain acreage could vote, let alone become eligible to become an MP. When the Tory party's traditional hegemony was first threatened by the nascent Whig party in the late seventeenth century, it became desirable for politicians of every stripe to re-emphasize their country credentials by pursuing the latest ideas in estate management. This was really a peculiarly British admixture of the vogue for emulating the Virgilian or Ciceronian concept of the civilized country retreat away from the noise of town, with a down-to-earth appreciation of the inherent virtue and utility of agriculture. It led to a new emphasis on the importance of horticulture and self-sufficiency at estates – increasingly, orchards and kitchen gardens were integrated into the designed landscape, which gradually became more naturalistic when compared with the formal decorative parterres and fountains of the Baroque tradition (associated with Catholic Europe). For a Whig grandee such as the Duke of Newcastle of Claremont in Surrey, who was prime minister twice, gifts of baskets of ripe peaches sent to his political friends and enemies in London served as a way of emphasizing how competent and relaxed he was at his country estate, undercutting Tory jibes that the Whigs were all nouveaux riches. At this point the humble apple could become the chief symbolic subject of a patriotic poem such as 'Cyder' (1708) by the Whig propagandic poet John Phillips, a sensuous evocation of English agriculture which paints a picture of the country in a kind of Edenic state of ripeness:

> …whilst English Plains
> Blush with pomaceous Harvests, breathing Sweets.
> O let me now, when the kind early Dew
> Unlocks th' embosom'd Odors, walk among
> The well rang'd Files of Trees, whose full-ag'd Store
> Diffuse Ambrosial Streams.

Fruit was venerated in British culture from the medieval period up to the mid-twentieth century, when it finally became commonplace. Exotic fruit, requiring expensive hothouse production or contact with plant collectors abroad, was a particularly potent status symbol, with the pineapple at the top of the tree – witness the celebrated painting of the king's gardener, John Rose, presenting Charles I with the first pineapple grown in England. Fruit for dessert, and not just exotic hot-house produce such as pineapples or melons, has for centuries been considered a delicacy at any English table. Those eighteenth- and nineteenth-century dessert services by Royal Worcester and other English potteries, with individual apple or pear varieties lovingly painted on to each plate and bowl, are a reflection of the esteem in which fresh-picked fruit was traditionally held. And it was often paired with cream, of course, another agricultural product which was frequently sentimentally venerated in literature. In some of England's most extravagant houses today it is still possible to enjoy fruit served as a dessert course in the traditional Victorian aristocratic manner, with fruit bushes or dwarf trees wheeled into the dining room on trolleys so that diners can snip off their own fruit and enjoy that fresh-plucked flavour.

All of that may seem a long way from growing carrots and spuds out back in the hope they might furnish a meal or two. But given that for most people today this is a lifestyle choice rather than an economic or nutritional necessity, the current grow-your-own movement has to be seen as part of the continuum of political gardening in this country.

All of the above is not a cynical attack on the idea of turning a garden over to vegetables. I have done it myself, and am much more content with my own plot as a result. For years I pursued the ideal of creating a kind of miniature Sissinghurst in a succession of London yard gardens, which were originally designed for hanging out washing and housing the lavatory. In a yard garden, a more utilitarian approach feels much more appropriate, though I do still have ornamental plants such as roses around the edges of my central plot. Gardening for food in the current 'climate', as it were, feels good because it is a way of asserting oneself in the face of apparently insurmountable ecological odds. So what if it makes little difference to the fate of the planet? There is a lot to be said for veg gardening as a powerful demonstration of personal autonomy and political expression. In that sense, it can be seen as a benign yet eminently useful form of direct action – and the so-called 'guerrilla gardeners', who go out at night and garden dismal public spaces, ought to mentioned in this context. This is going to sound pretentious to some, but perhaps the garden might be understood as the arena where we act out the drama of our relationship with nature on a personal, domestic level. It's a physical relationship, too, an authentic expression of 'being in the world', to stray into Heideggerian phenomenology for a moment.

Every garden is indeed a political act. Every plant is indeed a political prisoner. Which makes every gardener a tyrant. But each of us, in our own private realm, can at least rehearse the kind of tyranny over which we wish to preside.

Alice Smith

SENSE SUBLIME:
THE ROMANTICS VERSUS
THE ENLIGHTENMENT

Lee Rowland

ONTRARY TO POPULAR OPINION, THE ROMANTICS WERE not simply a bunch of wet poets who tediously harped on about the importance of nature. They weren't even particularly interested in nature herself as an independent phenomenon. To understand what they were trying to do, we first need to be aware of that which they were railing against. Indeed, it was nothing less than a battle over the very essence of the human mind and its place in the universe – and it is a fight that still smoulders today under the smothering blanket of materialist science.

The Enlightenment project was in large part built on those methods of science explicated by Sir Francis Bacon, and the findings of Sir Isaac Newton, whose astonishing work *Principia Mathematica* was the first to express natural phenomena in purely mathematical and mechanistic terms. Once these foundations had been laid, the next century witnessed a blossoming of ideas and approaches to man's place in the universe which have yet to subside. At its core, the new view posited that man was separate from the world, a lone consciousness looking out on to natural phenomena, and that by using rigorous and strict methods of investigation, the human mind could determine the essential properties of the objects in the world. Human consciousness is a separate entity under this guise, and it alone has the capability, through detached observation, to explain nature quantitatively and to derive

275

laws that specify cause-effect relationships between phenomena. In short, we can investigate the world using the methods of science and ultimately understand it mechanistically. Taken to its logical extension, the implication, and more often than not the assertion, is that phenomena can be *reduced* to a discrete number of rudimentary laws that operate on elementary material particles. That, in a sense, is it: all there is to the understanding of life, the universe and everything.

Although this is without doubt the dominant view among scientists today, and most other disciplines that adopt a scientistic perspective, it was by no means the order of the day in the times preceding the Industrial Revolution. Perhaps one of the most famous figures to challenge this view was the Romantic German polymath, Johann Wolfgang von Goethe. His monumental and profound study of the morphology of plants, *Metamorphosis of Plants*, was a systematic attempt to apply a method of science that had a very different flavour from the methods employed by those of a reductionist leaning. His approach was to bring human consciousness into the investigation, not simply as a tool for observation, but as an intrinsic part of the scientific process. For Goethe, it wasn't sufficient to measure objects as separate from the mind; one had to bring them into the imagination, and discover the essence of things as an extension of human consciousness. In other words, for the Romantic scientist, the mind and nature are in mutual participation, not distinct and eternally separate realities. The Enlightenment scientist extolled human rationality; the Romantic scientist, human creativity. (Astute readers will not see such a difference between the two faculties, yet the distinction is pertinent because of the chasm in sensibility that the two approaches create.) The reductionist view sees the natural world as a collection of independent physical objects that can be manipulated by the application of mechanical laws. In contrast, the Romantic apprehended the inextricable link between the imagination and the ineffable ideas that permeated the universe, and understood that consciousness and nature do not exist independently, but are in mutual caress. To them, nature was not there to be exploited: it was the creator of conscious perception.

This notion was upheld and illustrated by the great Romantic poets of the eighteenth and nineteenth centuries. Heed these words of Percy

Bysshe Shelley, which end his poem 'Mont Blanc':

> The secret strength of things
> Which governs thought, and to the infinite dome
> Of heaven is as a law, inhabits thee!
> And what were thou, and earth and stars, and sea,
> If to the human mind's imaginings
> Silence and solitude were vacancy?

In this poem, Shelley appears to be exploring his instinct that the beauty of the world and the human imagination are co-dependent. Throughout this piece, written whilst ensconced in the wilds surrounding the Vale of 'Chamouni' (our modern Chamonix), and therefore under the awe of Mont Blanc itself, he infuses intense observation of the 'awful scene' with the meditations of his consciousness to bring forth language that expresses a vision of his surroundings which is not merely observation, but seeing things anew. Consciousness is transforming the external world, and the external world is transforming the imagination.

In his 'Lines Written above Tintern Abbey', Wordsworth went further. Sensing that the human mind and nature were infused with the same 'thing', he explored the idea that the separateness of man and nature was one of perspective and not one of substance:

> For I have learned
> To look on nature, not as in the hour
> Of thoughtless youth, but hearing oftentimes
> The still, sad music of humanity,
> Not harsh nor grating, though of ample power
> To chasten and subdue. And I have felt
> A presence that disturbs me with the joy
> Of elevated thoughts; a sense sublime
> Of something far more deeply interfused,
> Whose dwelling is the light of setting suns,
> And the round ocean, and the living air,
> And the blue sky, and in the mind of man,

A motion and a spirit, that impels
All thinking things, all objects of all thought,
And rolls through all things.

This is deep stuff, and more often than not I prefer simpler poetry. Yet I love these lines, both Shelley's and Wordsworth's, because they get to the essence of our place in the universe; and really, what could be simpler than that? Science has been trying to establish the truth of this relationship for centuries, and becomes ever more complex, and still I can't help feeling that there is truth here in the poets' thoughts, without verification, without careful measurement, without the application of rigorous methodology, but in something far truer, and arguably more reliable: the inspiration of imagination.

If we accept what I have argued for thus far, it seems pitiful that this way of thinking is so massively out of favour in today's society. The Romantics campaigned vehemently for a respect for nature that went far beyond environmentalism. They were not simply suggesting that we treat nature kindly and try to preserve it. Writing about a daffodil was not intended to instil a detached appreciation of daffodils. The purpose of their work was to advance a challenge to the Enlightenment view by showing that nature was *part of us*, that we are part of nature, and that we ignore this axiom at our peril. They might have had a chance if the Industrial Revolution hadn't marched so efficiently across Europe and smashed all other credos into smithereens. The power and appeal of the Industrial Revolution, which was predicated on the methods and the vision of the Enlightenment, was quite simply that the proof was in the pudding. Loving nature, staring at nature, frolicking in nature, whilst good fun, didn't achieve anything. Nothing got done. Specifically, no progress. The Romantics had no overt plan or specification for how life's external conditions would be improved (they were principally concerned with psychological improvement), or how humans would be able to control their environment for the betterment of all people. Industrialization brandished plans and goals in tempting abundance. It was a potent nostrum then, and remains so for many today. With industrialization would come better material conditions, easier working lives, enhanced entertainment technologies and an abundance of food. As a forceful and persuasive story it has yet to be surpassed.

Shelley said that 'nought may endure but mutability,' and certainly – curiously – change is afoot in the world of science. Moreover, change is evident in nearly all aspects of modern life, most relevantly in our attitude towards the environment and, suddenly, in our sacrosanct belief in progress. It is becoming increasingly apparent that our blind faith in science and progress has exerted tremendously detrimental effects on the health of both planet Earth and the human mind. It is exciting as well as frightening to discover that developments in science are revealing it to be woefully inadequate as the sole basis for our understanding of the universe; and that technology is a woefully inadequate foundation for the perfection of civilization. In fact, science and human progress seem to have become starkly antithetical to their intrinsic goals. Goethe warned of the dangers of man's subjugation of nature for his own ends in his epic Promethean poem *Faust*:

> Yet all your labour's spent for us alone.
> With your fine dams and bulwarks vast,
> You're but preparing a superb repast
> For Neptune, the sea-fiend, to feast upon,
> You're trumped and done for every way,
> Into our hands the elements play,
> Destruction onwards is striding fast.

Accordingly, a paradigm shift has been gathering apace in modern science for at least the last 30 years. New discoveries are constantly rubbing up the wrong way against the prevailing views at an alarming rate. Alarming for the positivists, I should add. Refined understanding in physics, such as quantum mechanics and atomic physics, are revealing the universe to be far stranger than the rational intellect can comprehend and, collectively, these findings are beginning to yield conceptions of the phenomenal world that go way beyond the simplistic characterizations of an independent material world *out there,* separate from human intentionality, which obeys universal laws that the human mind appears to passively observe. Time, space, matter, reductionism, a Godless universe: all are under revision by contemporary physics. A new cosmology emerges in the wake, positing the existence of principles in the universe that do not comport with a blueprint which only allows a blind, non-intelligent and meaningless void that by a freak accident happened to create the anomaly that is our home.

Furthermore, the evolution of life on this planet is also under scrutiny. There have been major questions over the absolute dominance of Darwinian natural selection as an explanation of living things. Unsurprisingly, such challenges are met with contempt and ridicule at first, but ideas such as James Lovelock's Gaia hypothesis, and Rupert Sheldrake's notion of morphic resonance, are gradually gaining acceptance. Lovelock himself understood the problems inherent in the Enlightenment view:

> From a Gaian viewpoint, all attempts to rationalize a subjugated Earth with man in charge are as doomed to failure as the similar concept of benevolent colonialism. They all assume that man is the possessor of this planet; if not the owner, then the tenant … The Gaia hypothesis implies that the stable state of our planet includes man as a part of, or partner in, a very democratic entity.'

Note how he too, like the Romantic scientists before him, considers humans as participatory in nature, in contrast to the Enlightenment scientist, who consider us as somehow above, or in control of nature. For my money, the greatest confrontation that modern science shall have to deal with – and we are already up against it – will be the stubbornness of human consciousness to reveal its tantalizing secrets to a reductionist paradigm. It simply ain't going to happen. If it does, I'm off to live in a cave. Actually, I might do that regardless.

Opinions and beliefs aside, there are more pressing reasons to reconsider the Enlightenment project. It is well known that science and its attendant belief in material progress are destroying our planet. What is not as widely understood is that our divorce from nature and the harm we do to our environment, the very world that permits our existence, is causing untold neurosis and psychic trouble for an increasing number of individuals, at an unprecedented and worrying rate. This has only become undeniably apparent to psychologists over the last couple of decades. Admittedly, Freud and Jung both touched on these matters, and environmentalists and poets began screaming in the wilderness long ago, but it has taken a while for the scientific fraternity to catch up. This is not a scientific paper, so I'll spare readers the details, but in a nutshell, psychologists have compiled a considerable body of research that convincingly shows that being in touch with nature makes people feel better. A more interesting conclusion from this work is that a considerable degree of modern psychological ailments may well be due to our retreat from the wildness of nature and the joys it brings to the heart and soul, and the healing effect that it has over the stresses of our industrialized lifestyles. As Theodore Roszak has noted, in a book that coined the term 'eco-psychology' in 1992, *The Voice of the Earth*: 'As every Romantic poet once knew, viewed against the background of an Alpine landscape, a stormy sea, a lovely sunset, personal problems take on a distinctly lesser scale … [T]here is no tranquillizer more effective than standing under a starry sky at night and breathing in the wonder.'

However, Roszak goes much further in his analysis. The main thrust of his argument is that humankind, as individuals, will never know themselves without a close and fulfilling relationship with nature. He spends a good deal of the book exploring the recent developments in cosmology, and relates the broader picture of the universe to our modern troubled psyches. Ultimately, he states, the earth is our home, nature is life and we are not separate from it, and the quicker we realize this, and the quicker we do something to redress the balance, the quicker and better we can get on with doing the human thing.

Which, incidentally, is not at all what we have been doing for the last few hundred years. The title may put some readers off, yet a remarkable early eco-psychology book, *My Name is Chellis and I'm in Recovery from Western Civilization*, Chellis Glendinning studies in exquisite detail the abandonment of our close relationship with the wild, and demonstrates why it is that we have got things so wrong. We have been led up the garden path. We are on a wild goose chase. Collectively, we don't know what we are doing here, and yet the conclusion is so obvious. I'd like to say what it is, but I don't want to spoil it for those who may read Chellis's book. I reckon a lot of *Idler* readers will know in any case. Needless to say, one aim we should have while on this planet is to stop screwing it up, and screwing ourselves up in the process. It seems insane to run the world according to the needs of the stock market, rather than the needs of human beings, and the planet on which our very existence depends.

Hegel hit a nerve when he said that a civilization cannot become conscious of itself until it is so mature that it is approaching its own death. Is this us? Are we crashing headlong into that event? If so, what are we to do? Well, chill out a bit for a start. Have a love affair with the earth. Go and lie in the grass, romp in the fields, let your mind and the earth become one, stare at mountains if you must. Whatever we do, we must not continue to be beguiled by the Enlightenment view. Their ideas led to the despoilation of nature and the loss of dignity for the majority of human beings. But we can reclaim Romanticism, and get back to the land. It is, literally, vital.

A WWOOFER'S TALE

Leanne Cordingley & Andy Wright

I N THE SUMMER OF 2007, ANDY WRIGHT AND LEANNE
Cordingley escaped the nine to five and set off on a journey into
the unknown. Eighteen months down the line, armed with skills
picked up through several WWOOFing experiences, they have settled
in mid-Wales where they grow vegetables, bake bread and generally
live the good life. They are founders of the Loop Project, through
which they hope to spread some of the knowledge and skills they
picked up along the way.

WWOOF (World Wide Opportunities on Organic Farms) is a
scheme which provides people with the chance to learn the skills
required to go back to the land. Hosts offer accommodation and food
in exchange for a few hours of work a day. In the UK alone there are
now over 400 organic farms involved in the scheme which offer the
opportunity to learn anything from growing vegetables and animal
husbandry to willow weaving and pottery. There follows Andy and
Leanne's WWOOFer's diary.

Croft 13, Cleadale, Isle of Eigg – August 2007

This was my first Scottish journey north of Glasgow. Having taken
the stunning West Highland Railway up to Arisaig and camped
overnight, I boarded the early-morning ferry over to Eigg. Seals swam
alongside the boat as we pulled into the harbour. On arrival, what
seemed like the whole island had come to meet the boat, along with
my WWOOF hosts: Sue, Neil and their son Struan.

At the croft I was shown around the garden, which was in full
vegetable-production mode. The island benefits from the warmth of

the Gulf Stream rushing up the west coast of the UK and late summer is a great time to come, as you get all of the best of the vegetable patch. I put up my tent and acquainted myself with the compost toilet and cold-water tap. This isn't a place to come if you like your creature comforts, but how many other locations can provide such a breathtaking view of the other two Small Isles, Rhum and Muck, when you wake up in the morning?

My main task during my time on Eigg was digging up potatoes, which is not the most glamorous of jobs but is essential for the family to be self-sufficient. I did find myself alone at times but the work needed to be done and you get to eat what you have dug up for dinner. I also got to make bread and pick and prepare other vegetables. We feasted on fresh peas, broad beans, lots of salad leaves and, of course, potatoes. Working hours depend on the host; here it was six hours a day with two days off a week. You get food and accommodation for all the time you are there, so the life of a WWOOFer can be a cheap one if, perhaps a little solitary at times.

As I had to leave the host's house after dinner, some evenings I was stuck in my tent with only my wind-up radio for company. However, I did go and explore, and with only one road on the island and less than 150 residents, it wasn't too hard to find my way around and get to know a few people. Luckily, I ended up hanging out with some locals, and I spent a couple of evenings in the 'pub' (actually the island café). I also got invited to a rave on a beach, which was apparently the first time one had ever taken place on Eigg. That was pretty magical, dancing on the sand with the water lapping at my feet. Not the kind of thing you would find happening on a 'normal' holiday.

AW

Plan-it Earth, Sancreed, Cornwall – July 2008

We headed almost as far south-west as you could for our first WWOOFing adventure together, to a village called Sancreed, in Cornwall. Our hosts, Rachel and David, had set up an environmental education centre on their smallholding and needed help in the vegetable garden. We arrived just before the school holidays commenced and were lucky to spend the first two nights in a yurt, which was normally rented out. Unfortunately, after our luxurious Mongolian sleeping arrangements, we were moved to an eighties caravan without wheels and a window that wouldn't shut.

Our main tasks were to keep the vegetable patches and polytunnels weeded. We cleared raised beds, moved muck around and mowed down thousands of nettles. This had to be done before they set seed and took over the place. Again, the life of a WWOOFer is not a bed of roses, but the sun shone and we ate fabulous food, including the best summer pudding I have ever tasted.

On days when the weather was bad, we did some web and graphic-design tasks on the hosts' website. This was not strictly a WWOOFing job, but it kept us out of the rain as the stormclouds blew in from the Atlantic. Leanne helped out in the kitchen, cooking for us and the family. She spent one rain-soaked afternoon preparing artichokes, not something she would want to do again in a hurry, given all the war wounds she received from this evil vegetable.

One day we participated in the Sancreed Pig Run, a bizarre event which involved a procession around the village headed up by an enormous papier-mâché pig. In times gone by, Sancreed was famed for its well flavoured pork. All the other parishes bordered the coast and so fed their pigs on fish scraps. Those who didn't fancy fish-flavoured bacon would purchase their meat from Sancreed. In the procession, our role was limited to carrying a pink balloon emblazoned with the face of a pig.

AW

Canon Frome, Herefordshire – August 2008

This was our first visit to a community, and we really didn't know what to expect. I had visions of crazy hippies on acid dancing around naked in fields with flowers in their hair. We were starting to consider the idea of living in an intentional community. Canon Frome had been recommended to us as an example of a community that 'worked': things got done and people didn't constantly argue (although in the early days a lot of disputes apparently were settled with a traditional fist fight!).

Far from the crazy love fest I had imagined, everything seemed quite sensible, very well organized and highly productive. Each person has certain responsibilities: it is recognized that some people can do more than others so all produce is shared equally.

We mostly worked in the walled garden doing general weeding, harvesting and preparing beds. The walled garden had a very effective rotation system. It is split into four sections, the same group of people manage the same plot each year and the crops move around. This is a great idea. You keep your own patch of land, so it's in your interests to look after it well and improve the soil.

The polytunnels were amazing. One was overflowing with different varieties of tomatoes, the other had melons, early courgettes and crazy-looking, bumper-cropping, wriggly, spiky cucumbers, from which on one single day they harvested a crop of 42! The cucumbers had a beautiful flavour, surprisingly cucumbery – surely a fundamental trait in a cucumber, yet somewhat lacking in the typical supermarket offering. What a fantastic variety: they'll be going straight on my seeds wish list.

We mentioned we were interested in cheese-making and on the last day of our stay we got the opportunity to give it a go. Taking it right from the start, Andy and I milked the goats and used the fresh milk to make halloumi. It's a fairly straightforward process and, unlike the hard cheeses it is ready within the day, perfect for the idle cheese addict who demands instant gratification for little effort.

That evening we prepared ourselves a small feast made entirely from Canon Frome produce: grilled halloumi from the batch we'd made that day, a salad of nasturtium flowers and various spicy salad leaves, garlicky courgettes and tzatziki. I was particularly excited about the tzatziki – yoghurt made that morning, freshly harvested garlic, mint picked minutes before the meal and cucumber straight from the poly-tunnel. This is what it is all about.

LC

Ratcliffe Farm, Culcheth – September 2009

Beccy and Tony have lived on this 110-acre farm for around four years. They share the farm with a real menagerie of animals: two cows, three sheep, three pigs, twelve hens, a cockerel, five mallards, two muscovy ducks, two geese, a shire horse, a huge grey horse and a flock of very noisy guineafowl. Things could get pretty lively! We spent a lot of time chasing around the farm after various birds and escaped cows.

As well as farming 100 acres of wheat and barley for animal feed, they have divided off several acres, converted them to organic and hope to build up to self-sufficiency. They are following John Seymour's five-acre model and so far seem to be doing very well. A couple of acres are used to grow feed for the animals, which are kept for their eggs and meat. A polytunnel provides, amongst other things, a great selection of peppers, cucumbers and salad, and there's a young but productive vegetable garden from which we dug up several sackfuls of potatoes. There are plans to plant up several acres with trees, which ten years down the line should provide enough wood for heating and cooking. Altogether, it's a very impressive set-up.

We spent most of our first day helping to build a cow shelter, which would allow them to keep the cows out over winter. With no experience, no plan and a jumbled pile of salvaged materials, we set to work. By the end of the day a sturdy cowshed was all but built. Feeling pretty proud of ourselves, we downed tools for the day and went to relax by the fire with a bottle of real ale before dinner.

At dinner the usual question of the motives for our vegetarian ways came up. We discussed how the demand for cheap meat and pressures over pricing from supermarkets has driven down the amount paid to farmers. This has led to a situation where it is very difficult to be confident that the welfare of animals is at a standard we would be happy with. We mentioned, however, that since seeing well-reared animals on the farms we'd visited, we might again eat meat, if we knew the animals had been kept at the same standard.

'What about rabbits?' they asked. 'Someone has dropped off a couple for us that were shot on our land; we're having them for dinner tomorrow night. You're welcome to join us.' This was a tricky one. Rabbits are pests, and if you don't control them they multiply rapidly and ravage your crops. For six years and four years respectively, Andy and I have never even been tempted to eat meat. In this situation, however, it all seemed different. As wild animals, they have led the ultimate free-range life. I went to sleep that night with images of cute fluffy bunnies hopping around my mind.

The rabbit and orange casserole the next evening was delicious.

LC

Prospect Orchard, Llanidloes – October 2009

In early October, we took the train to deepest darkest mid-Wales, where we were met by Bill Bleasdale in his clapped-out van. Our mission was to produce lots of cider using a traditional press which had been handmade by Bill and a local carpenter. This was a monstrous piece of kit with huge cast-iron bolts and thick, solid oak beams. The apples would have no chance!

Bill's orchard was young and didn't produce enough apples for him to be self sufficient. However, he had a list of local contacts that had provided apples for his Welsh Mountain Cider last year. Unfortunately, there was a late frost this year, which killed the blossom and reduced the yield, so we had to look further afield for trees. Having hunted down some orchards in Herefordshire, we relieved them of their harvest by using a highly skilled apple-collection technique – we climbed the tree, shook it hard and dodged the apples as they fell.

Daily life on Prospect Orchard was laidback, to say the least, and it took us a few days to slow ourselves down. We were under strict instructions not to come for breakfast too early, so we would lie in or go for a walk across to distant hills. Our retro seventies green caravan contained a lovely wood-burning stove which kept us toasty-warm on those wet and windy mornings when we stayed in bed even longer. Once the fire had warmed the caravan, it was just about time to get up for a leisurely breakfast. Bill lived in an old showman's caravan, where we ate meals together and drank copious amounts of cider (even for breakfast sometimes). We got so used to the slow life that we ended up staying over three weeks rather than just the week we had originally planned.

Being autumn, it was time to prepare the beds for the winter. So we weeded, manured and mulched the raised beds, chopped firewood and drank lots of tea in between. The weather turned out to be dry on a couple of occasions, which gave me the opportunity to get my hands on a scythe. This was the perfect job for a warm late-autumn afternoon. I'd sit in the sunshine on a log with a glass of cider to hand whilst sharpening the blade and spend a few minutes admiring the view. Then I'd slash away at the field until my arms couldn't take it any more. This process was repeated until a patch of grass was cleared. Despite being tiring work, it was incredibly rewarding and, dare I say, healthy – well, if you ignore the cider consumption!

But the main job of course was pressing apples. This only happened a couple of times whilst we were on the farm, but those days were intensely hard work. The process lasted all day and involved moving tons of apples from the van, cleaning them in an old bathtub, transporting them into the barn, scratting them (basically mashing them up) and putting them into the press. Bill was assisted by his team of WWOOFers. My job was head 'scratter'. The old scratting machine looked like a medieval torture device – woe betide anyone who got their hands, hair or anything else trapped in it. The scrat was formed into layers and, once full, the press was turned. Juice would gush out from the press into the waiting barrels, where natural yeast would turn it into cider within the year. Nothing else needs to be added to produce proper farmhouse cider.

Once the sun had set, people would turn up unannounced with banjos and fiddles, and we would often spend the evening sat around the bonfire listening to traditional folk songs whilst another demijohn of cider was polished off. Being from the city, the backdrop of the pitch-black sky and the sight of the Milky Way, something I'd never seen before, was truly stunning.

AW

Return to Ratcliffe Farm, Culcheth – November 2009
Clearly impressed with our now highly developed super-WWOOFer skills, Beccy and Tony had asked us to look after their

farm when they went on holiday in January, so we went back to learn the daily animal routines.

When we arrived, we walked into the farm house kitchen to find Beccy salting some bacon. 'These are our pigs,' she said. I was quite taken aback. We'd not had a chance yet to have a walk around outside, so I hadn't noticed the empty pig pen and I definitely wasn't expecting to see the animals here on the kitchen table covered in salt. A shocked 'Oh' was about all I could muster. Well, at least it's three fewer animals for us to look after in January.

After our experience with the rabbit on our last visit, it was obvious we'd be offered pork for dinner. After some thought, we decided to go for it, strictly in the interests of research! How glad I am we did! The dead pigs proved to be everything I suspected. The meat was entirely different from the dry old supermarket pork I had left behind me years ago. It was so tasty! The chops were huge, juicy and a good half-inch rind of flavoursome fat ran around the edge. Apparently, the health-conscious pork buying public have turned against fat, yet this is where all the taste comes from.

Later in the week we were offered roast pork for dinner. Strictly in order to check that the results of our previous research were accurate, we took up the offer. Not since I was small have I had crackling like it! Bubbling and crunchy on the outside with a sweet melt-in-the-mouth soft inside, I have to say it was my highlight of the week. However, part of me was angry, as I'd always thought the chewy, inedible crackling I'd eaten in the past was a result of bad cooking, but now I suspect it was a result of bad meat. I wonder how many people buying a typical joint of pork realize that the quality and taste of the meat they are being sold is far below the standard it could and should be.

Most of the work on the veg patch at this time of year involves getting the ground ready for winter. With all the manure available from the animals and stables, it's an obvious choice – they have literally tons of it. We put a good layer on the cleared beds and topped it off with part-rotted straw. This keeps the heat in, some will rot down and any remaining can be easily raked off the following spring. We've seen several variations of mulching on the WWOOFs we've visited, and this seems a particularly good one. The beds do look cosy tucked in for the winter.

LC

Lower Esgair-rhiw, Rhayader – November 2009

How the weather has changed since the last time we were in Wales! At Bill's we'd been treated to the last few days of autumn sun, and we'd missed the two weeks of rain in between, but here it was obvious it had happened. The ground was waterlogged, the sky was grey, everything was muddy and the shortening days meant each day seemed almost to be over before it began. Luckily we were treated to a fairly relaxed working day, which went some way towards making up for the gloomy weather. Work began after a leisurely breakfast some time after 10 a.m. and by 3 p.m. each day we were finished. With an hour break for lunch in between, it was a definite idler's pace!

Most of the work here involved digging up young trees which had self-seeded from the well-established oak, hazel, ash and cherry trees that were dotted around the two-hectare farm. Jules runs a project called 'Free Tree', the aim of which is, as its name suggests, to give away free trees. She is also involved in Transition Town Rhayader: they want to encourage people to plant fruit and nut trees around the town.

Jules has a pottery studio and on the last day I got to try my hand on the wheel. I'd been interested in pottery for years so this was something I had really looked forward to and one of the main reasons we had chosen that particular place to WWOOF. At first all went well. A fine, if slightly wonky, bowl was produced. 'Brilliant!' I thought, 'This is easy! I must be a natural.' I had visions of my pots in kitchens across the land. The next attempt put me well and truly in my place. Jules had retreated to her evening's yoga practice and, without her expert guidance, the pot which had been looking to be in good shape suddenly began to behave more like blancmange than clay. It began to wobble erratically, then the slippery clay span out of control. I should have been slowing the speed down, but in the panic sped up. The pot eventually collapsed into a useless, sloppy heap. Luckily, subsequent attempts were much improved; I even managed to produce something I was quite happy with. Much enthused, I agreed to return soon to dig up more trees in exchange for time in the studio.

LC

Moving to Llanidloes – December 2009

During our stay at the cider farm Bill had taken us to a party in town. It was held at a beautiful 200-year-old manor house which had been bought by a co-operative in 1992 and converted into seven flats. The land, 14 acres in all, including 9 acres of woodland, is shared communally. There's a large allotment and plans to keep chickens and bees. We found out that one of the flats would soon be up for rent. Although not really planning to move anywhere at that time, we were intrigued and arranged to come back for a visit.

In the daylight, walking around the grounds, we quickly realized that our perfect home had presented itself to us when we weren't even looking for it. We felt that everything we had done, all the skills we had learned and all the people we had met had somehow led us to this point. The chance was too good to miss and by December we'd moved in. Armed with our newfound skills, we were ready for a more self-reliant life in mid-Wales. It was an unexpected, but very happy, end to our WWOOFing experience.

SKATE FEVER

(for Adrian Mitchell)

Jay Griffiths

I HAVE SKATE FEVER. IT'S A SEASONAL ILLNESS WHICH USED to be very common in Britain but is now rare. It affects the Dutch, though, in their thousands. It strikes me like delirium with the brilliance of dream, when the lakes nearby freeze over and the ice issues an imperative: *Carpe Diem! Get Your Skates On!*

Sometimes years pass without the waters freezing, but this year and last year were both skating winters; a few precious days of frost and rapture. If *joie de vivre* could be distilled to one image alone, it would be a skating party going out to wake the lake. Last year, on a clear, full-moon night, I skated with friends by moonlight and starlight, with lanterns scattered around the edge of the lake, and we wore full evening dress plundered from charity shops; feathers, fascinators and fake furs.

Wrapped up and amazed, the wrigglers and rugglers (small children and puppies) stay at the edge, near the soup and the woodfire on the lake shore. The ecstasy (in its root, 'standing apart') comes from skating on, out to the lake's centre and further, to its far and silent shores, skating across the Zuyder Zee of mid-Wales.

This kind of joy is superfluous and therefore absolutely necessary. It is the deep meaning of revelry and play, as the historian Johan Huizinga wrote in his masterpiece, *Homo Ludens: Mankind at Play*, culture itself 'arises in the form of play': 'Play cannot be denied. You can deny, if you like, nearly all abstractions: justice, beauty, truth, goodness, mind, God. You can deny seriousness, but not play.' In homage to *Homo Ludens*, we played, interludic in the intercalendrical between Christmas and New Year, honouring the play ethic rather than the work ethic, playing races and a form of ice hockey with a skinny rubber chicken which squeaked; a local farmer came on skis and someone else tried to fly a kite. The Dutch have carnivals on ice, and old Dutch paintings of ice-merriment portray lovers and children and horse-drawn sleighs.

They are twin arts, the art of conviviality and the art of solitude, and skating is an oscillation between them both: you can join up with the party for hot chocolate laced with brandy and then swing away on a trajectory of glorious solitude, a world apart, ('all, alone, together', wrote ee cummings in his poem 'skating'). One skating day, I was circling the centre of the lake and found my movement mirrored in the sky as a red kite, similarly alone, was curious and circling overhead.

Wild-skating (as opposed to rink skating) always seems to suggest a twofoldness: both the vivacity of a party and the exhilaration of solitude; the water which freezes and thaws; the breath in and the breath out; life above in air and death below the ice. The act of skating itself involves twofoldness, a long arc out to the left and a curve back to the centre; a long arc out to the right and a curve back to the centre, each skate leaving slender S's, cut into the ice like cold calligraphy. The twofoldness is an image of balance, the balance which, skaters know, comes best from movement.

Sometimes the ice is black, so you can see the water below, and sometimes the surface is frosted like frozen dew. Once, several years ago, one of the lakes froze with crystals all across the ice so it looked strewn with flowers. Around each lake, the hills and mountains rise white, the trees are sketched with charcoal and sunlight is iridescent as it glances the ice, dazzling and perfect.

The silence is simple, coming from the stillness of ice and an immense and quiet sky. The ice is literally simple – the root of the word means 'without crease' – and it uncreases your mind. In an unsimple world, the iced lakes give clarity, make thoughts glide easy as skate blades. It is a simplicity I envy: I wish I had the simplicity of ice. I wish I knew the cold serenity of snow by which no flake is ever twisted out of true. Here, close to the clear heart of things, ice is a good teacher.

Everything is sharp: sharp skate blades, sharp frost, sharp light in the sun, and the contrast between day and night is sharpened by cold. Summer has an incoherent lushness, everything warm and lolling, rolling over everything else, slurred, heady with cider. Winter has the coherence of cold, exact and electric, compact as skates laced tight and sharp to the clean ice. Sharp with alacrity too, skating is a fleet and fleeting pleasure, swift to do and swiftly gone.

In the Dutch painter Bruegel's *Winter Landscape with a Bird Trap* the sense of swift movement in the skaters is such that, 450 years later, they look as if they're moving, for the eye jumps from figure to figure, each caught in a slightly different pose. The effect is like the early animation 'flip books', as the thumb flips through pages and the eye's persistence of vision gives the impression of movement: 'thumb cinema', as they call it in Germany.

Skating, diving and dreaming are all forms of flying. 'When to his feet the skater binds his wings ...' wrote the aptly named poet Robert Snow (not to be confused with Robert Frost, who wrote, 'Style is the mind skating circles around itself as it moves,' or indeed with Coleridge, who wrote 'Frost at Midnight'). The god Mercury was, according to Coleridge, the first maker of skates, and every skater has wings at their feet. This flight is compelling to watch; there are huge numbers of spectators for ice races in Holland, and millions of people watch ice-skating championships. And the birds (accustomed to watching us trudge) hover and gaze at skaters as we humans become occasional flyers on the evanescent ice.

★ ★ ★

IN BRITAIN, THERE were once crazes for skating, but hardly anyone goes wild-skating any more, feeling frightened, unfamiliar and unconfident. It's a shame, because skating is a virtually free pleasure, which prompts me to offer a beginner's guide to skating.

First find some skates. You need stiff boots, and you want the blades sharp. Near me, the winter skates began when a local doctor collected a motley assortment of skates, including a dainty Victorian pair and one pair of army training boots with blades screwed (slightly askew, it has to be said) to the soles, which means these skates are great for doing the involuntary splits but rubbish for doing straight lines. There is another pair of tough farm boots, loads of children's skates from charity shops and car boot sales, and a pair of Dutch speed-skating skates. With this, the good doctor began a local epidemic of skate fever.

You need to find a place to skate. The Fens, in East Anglia, had their heyday of skating in the nineteenth century, but people do still skate there when they can, with races and competitions. Lakes are lovely for skating, and Coleridge skated in the Lake District with Wordsworth, who was a 'crack skater', according to his sister, Dorothy. (I don't think she meant it as a pun.) Rivers are a terrible idea, obviously, because ice freezes too unpredictably. Fields which have flooded and then frozen are great for skating, and there is no need to test the depth of the ice. How do you do that on lakes? Take a hammer and chisel, or a battery-operated drill or, if you'll be lighting a fire, take a poker to heat up and make a hole in the ice. When you've drilled a hole, stick your finger in, and the ice should be three or four inches deep, about a fingerlength. This means it should be skateable, but let me at this point introduce the first rule of skating: be both bold and reckful. If in doubt, skate close to the edge. Don't skate on snow unless you're sure of the ice underneath.

Take a safety rope so that if anyone goes through the ice there's a chance of hauling them out. Take other rope for playing with children, puppies or sledges, and don't let them use the safety rope. Take lanterns and candles. Tea lights tucked into white baker's paper bags are really pretty on ice. Take warm clothes and extra socks and take 'second skin' blister patches, not ordinary plasters. Take a broom, too: if there has been a light snowfall, you can brush snow away and, more importantly, a broom is good for novice skaters, who can lean on it for support and (unlike a stick or a friend) it will not slip on the ice. Take food and drink and musical instruments. Tell kids not to throw stones or snowballs on the ice; it's fun, but it trips up skaters. Tell puppies not to crap on the ice, for the same reasons.

HOW TO SKATE.

JUST SAY YES.

Skating, like most things in life, is best done open-hearted. Trust each foot in turn, let your attention and your weight glide long on each leg. Lean forward into it all. Trust your wings.

Trust the ice, too, but only up to a point. Be observant of its moves and cracks, try to listen to its stories of thawing and refreezing or buckling as it has frozen deeper. This is when skaters yearn for more precise language, for the distinct words for ice in Inuktitut, the Inuit language, because the words discriminate between how ice is formed, which in turn tells you how it will – or might – behave. And for Inuit hunters out on the ice, how the ice behaves is what your life depends on.

When I was in Igloolik, in the Canadian Arctic, I asked people about words for ice, and I stopped writing by the time I'd noted 33, with full descriptions. Mark Ijjangiaq describes moving ice being dislodged from land-fast ice, leaving some of it cemented to the land-fast ice. This new addition is *nipititaaq* and is usually rough with pressure ridges. This ice pan in turn will move out but separate from the main block, and the terminology gets more precise still, for if this separate pan is high with pressure ridges, it is called *ijukaqut*. *Uluangnait* is when snow has fallen on newly formed ice and that ice has not yet become strong so the ice underneath is warmed and pushed underwater by snow. Then that ice is doubly warmed, by snow above and by water below. This, of course, is highly dangerous. Meanwhile, there are at least eight terms for the stages of ice-melt.

When one Inuit elder of Igloolik, Michel Kopaaq Piugaattuk, is asked for different words for snow, he reels off fifteen, hardly pausing for breath. Fifteen entirely separate words. Asking various elders, lists have been compiled of scores of words, with their full meanings. Some Europeans have scorned the idea of there being a famously large number of words for snow in Inuktitut, calling it a 'vocabulary hoax', and claiming that there is but one word for snow used with a variety of prefixes and suffixes. This is simply untrue, and rather overweening for Europeans who do not speak Inuktitut to pretend they know it better than Inuit elders.

In Europe, it is the Dutch who have the longest history of skating, going back to medieval times or earlier. Ice skates were made from the ribs of cows, which were drilled so they could be tied on to boots. By 1600, the Dutch were using curled wooden skates with steel blades. Old ballads, describing the great frost and ice fair on the Thames in 1684, speak of:

> The Rotterdam Dutchman, with fleet-cutting scates
> To pleasure the crowd shows his tricks and his feats
> Who, like a rope dance (for his sharp steels),
> His brains and activity lies in his heels.

It is a playful history; written records speak of the Dutch winters when 'all the world is out on skates, on business or pleasure bent,' people pulling sleighs made from packing-cases with 'a freight of laughing babies'.

There are paintings of skating in the Lake District by James Baker Pyne in the mid-nineteenth century which combine a sense of skating delight with a winter melancholy. Other paintings, such as *Ice Skating at Twilight*, by the nineteenth-century artist Conrad Wise Chapman, are more festive, and probably the most famous skating painting in Britain is the enduring, endearing skating vicar by Henry Raeburn. But the Dutch are the real old masters of skating painting. In Rembrandt's *Winter Landscape*, a figure in the foreground puts on a pair of skates (which do look like cow's ribs) and all the figures are wrapped in the warmth of Rembrandt's kindness and so they look as if they will never be cold again.

For all the sheer fun in Bruegel's *Winter Landscape with a Bird Trap*, there is a deeper hint that the birds are perhaps painted to suggest the human soul, a traditional symbol, and that there is brevity in the revelry of ice and life. The first Dutch artist to specialize in depicting winter ice-revels was Hendrick Avercamp, working in the seventeenth century, and his paintings (with eel-angling, games and skaters falling on ice) hum with the playfulness which the Dutch, culturally, associate with ice. Huizinga was also Dutch.

The most festive of competitions is the Dutch skating race, the Elfstedentocht, the 'Eleven-Towns Race'. It was first held in January 1909, and has been held only intermittently in the century since, because the 200-kilometre track will only freeze in the severest winters. One in eight of the population turns out to cheer on the 16,000 skaters, and there are stalls selling hot chocolate and pea soup along the route. The evening before the race is an enormous street-party in Leeuwarden, where the race begins and ends.

Over-riding the competitive element is a camaraderie of ice. Something funny happened on the way to the finishing line in 1956. Five people skated in together ('all, alone, together') and the judges withheld the prize. Why so? Because in 1933 and 1940, there had been joint winners, when the leaders chose not to compete but rather to hold hands and sweep across the finishing line together. The race organizers formally forbade the practice but the 1956 winners gloriously flouted the ruling and were disqualified. There are photographs of the five at the finishing line – faces of exhilaration and jubilation – five who skated for skating's sake. This is the best advice from the masters of skating: skate generously, for mean-mindedness cuts no ice out here.

The year has two generosities, the generosity of harvest as August augments into autumn, ripening and swelling, and that is of white beginnings and open futures where all is possibility, wide as a frozen lake when you can no longer see the limit of it. A white sheet of paper or dawn or hope all speak of the same generosity where nothing is prescripted and anything can begin.

Last year, out skating, I saw moonlight which was pale and gold. I saw the evening star rise bright and clear. Under the lake ice, the water boomed an eerie hollow moan, creaking below, an oboe of ice. And Adrian Mitchell died, as the earth was cold as iron, a poet's midwinter.

It seemed so wrong that he of all people could die, could have the warmth wrung out of him. He was so warm and I associate him with warmth of all kinds: warm wine, warm jokes, warm hearth and warm-heartedness above all. He was always warm and heart-ice repelled him, the cold, the mean-minded. I could never associate him with any ice except this kind – this kind ice for puppies to slip on, for kids to slide over. I was skate-happy that winter, but always underneath I heard a long, sad song for him; under those two weeks the grief-water rang so my soul-ice sobbed.

He was not someone who let scar tissue form, shining like glass, too many scars to sing. He was the opposite, refusing scars and welcoming song. I last saw him singing train songs. Pissed, gloriously choo-chooful, rosy with wine and friendship. They were trains with big engines, huge furnaces of heat. Big-hearted trains, big songs.

Big man.

Big as a lake, big as all sunset, big – that good old Anglo-Saxon word – big as a champion, big as a balloon, big as Blake, big man, friend. I loved him. The 'big man', in many traditional societies, is the one who gives the most away. He did this, giving young poets the courage, giving children the chance, giving words the whistle, giving poems the extra breath of jazz. I wish I'd gone skating with him.

Skating is effervescent and evanescent. Vanishing at a point of joy, fleet as the sparrow which Bede described, flitting into the mead-hall for a brief, warm moment, then out again into the cold and dark, those birds which symbolize the life of the soul.

Skate while you can. Of all my friends who skate, the one who knows better than any that life is short and skating days are precious is the good doctor, now in his seventies, who knows that all things rare and lovely must be seized on the instant – that in a lifetime there are so few skating days and each must be caught with glee. Skate while you may. ◉

John Lawrence, from *Nothingmas Day* by Adrian Mitchell (Allison and Busby)

A GLIMPSE OF PERFECTION:
LIFE IN THE 13th CENTURY

N. M. Gwynne

WE INHABIT A WORLD WHERE WE ARE AT LEAST HALF-consciously aware that possible perfection exists in every human endeavour. We may not actually *believe* this if, as with so many of us nowadays, our personal philosophy denies that truth, goodness and beauty are objective and universal. Even so, we know it in practice. We cannot help seeing it proved by occasional glimpses of perfection and near-perfection having nothing to do with fashion, whether in one part of the world or another or in one era or another.

Examples are not difficult to come by. The words and actions of Jesus Christ recorded in the Gospels. The Great Pyramid of Gizeh. Homer's *Iliad* and *Odyssey* and Virgil's *Aeneid*. The sculptings of Phidias and Praxiteles. Euclid's geometry. Aristotle's logical system. Demosthenes' and Cicero's oratory. Magna Carta. The *Dies Irae* as both poetry and music. King Saint Louis IX's Sainte-Chapelle in Paris. Venice's Saint Mark's Square. The Taj Mahal. The nineteenth-century Houses of Parliament in Westminster. Even the more-than-occasional sentence written by P. G. Wodehouse. All these are recognized, by all but the perverse, as 'ultimate' by the standards of any part of the world at any time in history.

So far so far only minimally controversial. Let us move on to what is much more so. Far from alone, I maintain that, just once in human history, a standard as close as possible to overall perfection as any human society can hope to achieve *was* achieved by a vast community, stretching over an area as big as Europe, and for a century and more.

An area as big as Europe? No exaggeration: the area *was* Europe. The century? The one labelled *The Thirteenth: Greatest of Centuries* in the title of perhaps the best book on the subject, by the learned author Professor James J. Walsh.

But were not the Middle Ages an age of tyranny, of the powerful over the weak; an age of frequent wars over things that our far more enlightened generation would not think worth fighting about; an age in which the vast majority of lives ended prematurely through violence or disease; an age of ignorance and of error – in religion, in politics and in just about every branch of science; an age of religious intolerance and of superstition; an age in which even the most basic comfort-providing amenities of life did not exist, and the average person's life was, in Thomas Hobbes's famous phrase in a different context, 'nasty, brutish, and short'?

My firmly held position is not mine alone, though. Please consider the following, by the much-admired English philosopher-author Frederic March in his *A Survey of the Thirteenth Century* (Macmillan, 1908). (As with others of the quotations I give in these pages, I have made occasional editing changes, mainly in order to save space, but never with the effect of changing the meaning of the original.)

> The whole thirteenth century is crowded with creative forces in philosophy, art, poetry, and statesmanship as rich as those of the humanist Renaissance ... In creative genius Giotto is the peer, if not the superior of Raphael. Dante had all the qualities of his three chief successors and very much more besides. It is a tenable view that, in inventive fertility and in imaginative range, those vast composite creations – the Cathedrals of the thirteenth century, in all their wealth of architectural statuary, painted glass, enamels, embroideries, and inexhaustible decorative work – may be set beside the entire painting of the sixteenth century...
>
> Now this great century, the last of the true Middle Ages, has a special character of its own, a character that gives it an abiding and enchanting interest. We find in it a harmony of power, a universality of endowment, a glow, an aspiring ambition and

confidence such as we never find in later centuries, at least so generally and so permanently diffused.

The thirteenth century was an era of no special character. It was in nothing one-sided, in nothing discordant. It had great thinkers, great rulers, great teachers, great poets, great artists, great moralists, and great workmen. It could not be called the material age, the devotional age, the political age, or the poetic age in any special degree. It was equally poetic, political, industrial, artistic, practical, intellectual, and devotional. And these qualities acted in harmony on a uniform conception of life with a real symmetry of purpose.

There was one common creed, one ritual, one worship, one sacred language, one Church, a single code of manners, a uniform scheme of society, a common system of education, an accepted type of beauty, a universal art, something like a recognized standard of the Good, the Beautiful, and the True. One-half of the world was not occupied in ridiculing or combating what the other half was doing. Nor were men absorbed in ideals of their own, while treating the ideals of their neighbours as matters of indifference and waste of power. Men as utterly different from each other, as were Stephen Langton, St. Francis, Thomas Aquinas, Roger Bacon, Dante, Giotto, St Louis, Edward I – all profoundly accepted one common order of ideas, equally applying to things of the intellect, of moral duty, of action, and of the soul – to public and private life at once – and they could all feel that they were all together working out the same task. It may be doubted if that has happened in Europe ever since.

My second choice is one of the best-known English historians of all, Lord Macaulay:

It is in the thirteenth century that we must seek for the origin of our freedom, our prosperity, and our glory. Then it was that the great English people was formed … Then first appeared with distinctness that constitution which has ever since, through all changes, preserved its identity; that constitution of which all the other free constitutions in the world are copies, and which, despite some defects, deserves to be regarded as the best under which any great society has ever yet existed. Then it was that the House of Commons, the archetype of all the representative assemblies which now meet, either in the old or in the new world, held its first sittings. Then it was that the common law rose to the dignity of a science, and rapidly became a not unworthy rival of the imperial jurisprudence ... Then it was that the most ancient colleges which still exist at both the great national seats of learning, Oxford and Cambridge, were founded. Then was formed that language, less musical indeed than the languages of the south, but in force, in richness, in aptitude for all the highest purposes of the poet, the philosopher, and the orator, inferior to the tongue of Greece alone. Then too appeared the first faint dawn of that noble literature, the most splendid and the most durable of the many glories of England.

Truth is not decided by experts, though, however eminent. And after all, plenty of experts can be found to oppose the views that I have just quoted. Truth is decided by unquestionably valid logic that is backed up by unassailable evidence. Let us, therefore, look more closely at some of the medieval human activities of which evidence survives, and see what unassailable logical conclusions we can draw.

ARCHITECTURE

SURELY THE BEST PLACE TO START IS WITH EVIDENCE STILL very much in existence, indeed effortlessly visible to the naked eye: the many medieval cathedrals, most of them built in the space of a single century, which are some of the greatest works of art ever created.

Anyone can design a building which will stand up. One of the important skills in architecture lies in designing buildings which will only *just* stand up. This skill reaches the level of genius when buildings are designed which, to all appearances, ought not to stand up but somehow do, and are breathtakingly beautiful as well. That is the level which was reached in the Middle Ages in respect of cathedrals, abbeys, university college chapels and the like to be found all over England, and at least one of which is within easy reach for inspection and admiration, wherever you may happen to be in England.

And not only all over England. Dotted throughout Britain, France, Germany and the Low Countries, the great cathedrals stand today as they have stood for seven or eight hundred years. Of Europe's 180 or so Gothic cathedrals, 80 of which are in France and 35 in England, all of them are giant churches of astounding symmetry and beauty, in their entirety and in every tiny detail.

It was in France that the first examples of Gothic architecture arose. In Paris the magnificent Notre-Dame was commenced in 1163, and throughout France the creative explosion quickly followed – with names like Beauvais, Laon, Amiens, Reims, Chartres, Bourges. Each was different from the other – even to the stone used. Notre-Dame is white, Strasbourg pink, Reims bright yellow, Chartres a bluish-grey. In each there is an awe-inspiring impression of space and light when entering. Delicate, fluted arches, supporting the whole structure, leap to meet the carved vaults high above, and everywhere there is exquisite carving.

Not least impressive is the inventiveness that lay behind their erection. The problems relating to narrow roof spans, which had given so much trouble to the builders of the earlier Saxon churches, were triumphantly overcome by the development of the 'ribbed vault'. For the first time in architectural history, it was discovered that a pointed arch would support far greater loads than either the round arches used by the Romans or the Saxons' limited wooden beams.

Crossed arches became ribs able to support roofing structures of greater width, and with their flowering sections brought symmetry and lightness as a further enhancement. The first of all Gothic cathedrals, that of Saint-Denis in Paris, set the example which others enthusiastically followed.

Please try this, dear reader. Go, say, to Cambridge's King's College Chapel, so called because a king, King Henry VI, was responsible for its erection (as also for the erection of Eton's College Chapel). Stare at its ceiling so far above you, and at its walls, and marvel at how the one can be supported by the other, let alone how it could have been built in the first place, in those supposedly primitive Middle Ages. *Marvel even more when you realize that today the technical knowledge nowhere exists which would make erecting this building possible.* With all our machinery and computer technology, we cannot come close to putting together what was flung up again and again, in endless variety all over Europe, during little more than a century, by people using only hand-tools, following the directions of architects of evidently stupendous learning, but most of whose names were not even thought worth preserving for posterity. No wonder massive books in profusion are published on those cathedrals year after year, on how the seemingly impossible was done.

Consider too the technical schools that must have existed to make such buildings possible. During the thirteenth century, every single important town throughout the whole of England was erecting a cathedral, each town trying to rival all the others in the grandeur of the cathedral itself and of the ancillary buildings needed by it. The towns did not lend each other's architects and workmen to each other. Instead there was a local pride in achieving what was best for one's own town.

THE CREATOR OF THE MIDDLE AGES

AS WE STARE AT THAT CHAPEL IN CAMBRIDGE AND wonder over such buildings, an obvious question is prompted. What sort of society was it that, apparently almost effortlessly, and certainly without ever making a mistake (no instances are recorded of such edifices, once started, having to be pulled down and started again), threw up such buildings anywhere that was thought appropriate, always in tune with the locality, always significantly different in appearance, but always of similar basic design?

First things first. To make sure we gain a proper understanding of the society we are going to have a look at, it is as well to start off by looking at the organization which, single-handed, created it, and produced in the process an extraordinary unity all over Europe while nevertheless at the same time encouraging and allowing an almost infinite variety of local cultures.

The Catholic Church was that organization, headed always by one man (even though it was occasionally not completely certain who that one man was), who was head of the Church of England, of the Church of Scotland, of the Church of France, of the Church of Spain, of the Church of Portugal, and of the Church of all the other countries and states of Europe, by virtue of being Bishop of Rome.

To give an account of the Catholic Church that is both adequate and useful for our purposes, I shall choose an author who, a solidly Protestant member of the Church of England all his life, cannot possibly be justifiably accused of prejudice in favour of the Catholic Church, and who also is arguably the best and most spectacular writer of English ever to go into print (and I have *not* forgotten the existence of Shakespeare!).

William Cobbett, who lived from 1766 to 1823, is the author in question – his important book dealing with our subject is his *History of the Protestant Reformation in England and Ireland*, never out of print since its publication and indeed existing in more than one edition today. Near the beginning of the book he writes:

Before we proceed further, let us clearly understand the meaning of these words:- Catholic, Protestant, and Reformation. Catholic means universal, and the religion which takes this epithet was called universal because all Christian people of every nation acknowledged it to be the only true religion, and because they all acknowledged one and the same head of the Church, and this was the Pope, who, though he generally resided at Rome, was the head of the Church in England, in France, in Spain, and, in short, in every part of the world where the Christian religion was professed. But there came a time, when some nations, or rather, parts of some nations, cast off the authority of the Pope, and of course no longer acknowledged him as the head of the Christian Church. These nations, or parts of nations, declared, or protested, against the authority of their former head, and also against the doctrines of that Church, which until now had been the only

Christian Church. They therefore called themselves Protestors or Protestants; and this is now the appellation given to all who are not Catholics. As to the word Reformation, it means an alteration for the better ...

Now, my friends, a fair and honest inquiry will teach us that this was an alteration greatly for the worse; that the 'Reformation', as it is called, was engendered in lust, brought forth in hypocrisy and perfidy, and cherished and fed by plunder, devastation, and by rivers of innocent English and Irish blood; and that as to its more remote consequences, they are, some of them, now before us, in that misery, that beggary, that nakedness, that hunger, that everlasting wrangling and spite, which now stare us in the face, and stun our ears at every turn, and which the 'Reformation' has given us in exchange for the ease, and happiness, and harmony, and Christian charity, enjoyed so abundantly and for so many ages by our Catholic forefathers ...

Ease, happiness, harmony and Christian charity? Can Cobbett be talking about the *Middle Ages*? Yes indeed; and he goes even further! – describing the England of those days as 'the happiest country, perhaps, that the world had ever seen'.

It was not a 'reformation', but a 'devastation', of England, which was, at the time when this event took place, the happiest country, perhaps, that the world had ever seen, a devastation which impoverished and degraded the main body of the people. But, in order that you may see this devastation in its true light, and that you may feel a just portion of indignation against the devastators and against their eulogists of the present day, it is necessary, first, that you take a correct view of the things on which their devastating powers were exercised.

The Catholic Church originated with Jesus Christ Himself. He selected Peter to be head of His Church. This Apostle's name was Simon, but his Master called him Peter, which means a stone or rock; and He said, 'On this rock will I build my Church.' Look at the Gospel of Saint Matthew 16:18,19, and at that of Saint John

21:15, and onward; and you will see that we must deny the truth of the Scriptures, or acknowledge that there was a head of the Church promised for all generations.

Saint Peter died a martyr at Rome in about 60 years after the birth of Christ. But another supplied his place; and there is the most satisfactory evidence that the chain of succession has remained unbroken from that day to this ...

Of later date, the Chief Bishop has been called in our language, the Pope. In the Latin he is called *Papa*, uniting and abbreviating the two Latin words, *Pater Patrum*, meaning Father of Fathers ...

The office of Pope continued in existence through all the great and repeated revolutions of kingdoms and empires ... At the time when the devastation, commonly called the "Reformation" of England, began, there had been, during the fifteen hundred years, about two hundred and sixty Popes, following each other in due and unbroken succession.

A mere look at the history of the Church in England, down to the time of the 'Reformation', a bare sketch of the principal facts, will show how false, how unjust, how ungrateful those have been who have vilified the Catholic Church, its Popes, its monks and its priests. It is supposed by some, with good authorities on their side, that the Christian religion was partly introduced into England as early as the second century after Christ. What we know for a certainty is that it was introduced effectually in the year 596, 923 years before Henry VIII began to destroy it.

The people of the whole country were pagans. Yes, pagans; they worshipped gods made with hands; and they sacrificed children on the altars of their idols. In this state England was when the Pope of that day, Gregory I, sent forty monks, with a monk of the name of Augustine at their head, to preach the Gospel to the English ...

The Protestant writers have been strangely embarrassed in their endeavours to make it out, that up to this year 596, or thereabouts, the Catholic Church was pure and trod in the steps of the Apostles; but that after this time that Church became corrupt. They applaud the character and acts of Pope Gregory; they do the same with regard to Augustine … but still they want to make out that there was no pure Christian religion after the Pope came to be the visible and acknowledged head and to have supreme authority. None of them can deny that it was the Roman Catholic religion that was introduced into England in the year 596, with all its dogmas, rites, ceremonies and observances, just as they all continued to exist at the time of the 'Reformation' … Whence it clearly follows, that if the Catholic Church were corrupt at the time of the 'Reformation', it was so in 596…

Bear in mind, that it was the Catholic faith, as now held, that was introduced into England by Pope Gregory the Great; and bearing this in mind, let us see what were the effects of this, and how that faith worked its way, in spite of wars, invasions, tyrannies, and political revolutions.

Saint Augustine, upon his arrival, applied to the Saxon king. He obtained leave to preach to the people, with great and immediate success. He converted the king himself, who was very gracious to him and his brethren, and provided dwellings and other necessaries for them at Canterbury. Saint Augustine and his brethren, being monks, lived together in common, and from there went forth over the country, preaching the Gospel. In time the number in the community was greatly augmented by new members. A church was built at Canterbury. Saint Augustine, the Bishop, or Head Priest, was succeeded by other bishops. As Christianity spread over the island, other communities, like that at Canterbury, were founded in other cities where there are now Cathedrals, or Bishops' churches. Hence, in process of time arose those majestic and venerable edifices, which we boast of as the work of our forefathers, while we have the folly, injustice and inconsistency to brand the memory of those very forefathers with the charge of grovelling ignorance, superstition and idolatry…

The clergy in those times were supported by oblations or free gifts, and sometimes by tithes, which land-owners paid themselves or ordered their tenants to pay. In this collective state the clergy remained for many years. But, in time, as the land-owners became converted to Christianity, they desired to have priests settled near to them, always ready to perform the offices of religion. The land-owners, therefore, built churches on their estates, and generally near their own houses, for the benefit of themselves, their vassals, and tenants. When they built the churches, they also built a house for the priest, which we now call the parsonage-house; and, in most cases, they attached some plough-land, or meadow-land, or both, to the priest's house, for his use; and this was called his glebe. Besides these, the land-owners endowed the churches with the tithe – one tenth – of the produce of their estates.

Hence parishes – priestships – arose. The great man's estate now became a parish. He retained the right of appointing the priest, whenever a vacancy happened; but he could not displace a priest, when once appointed; and the whole of the endowment became the property of the Church, independent of his control. But to this possession of so much property by the Church certain important conditions were attached; to which it behoves us to pay particular attention ...

When Christianity, the very basis of which is charity, became established, the taking care of the needy was deposited in the hands of the clergy. Upon the very face of it, it appears monstrous that a house, a small farm, and the tenth part of the produce of a large estate, should have been given to a priest who could have no family. But the grants were for other purposes as well as for the support of the priests. Typically the produce of the benefice was to be employed thus: 'Let the priests receive the tithes of the people and keep a written account of all that have paid them; and divide them in the presence of such as fear God, according to canonical authority. Let them set apart the first share for the repairs and ornaments of the church; let them distribute the second to the poor and the stranger, with their own hands, in mercy and humility; and reserve the third part for themselves.' Always two-fourths, at the least, of the annual produce of the benefice to be given to the needy, and to be employed in the repairing or in the ornamenting of the church.

Thus the providing for the poor became one of the great duties and uses of the Church. This duty could be lodged in no hands so fitly as in those of the clergy; for thus the work of charity, the feeding of the hungry, the clothing of the naked, the administering to the sick, the comforting of the widow, the fostering of the fatherless, came always in company with the performance of services to God. In place of the uncertain disposition of the rich, for their occasional and sometimes capricious charity, was substituted the certain, the steady, the impartial hand of a constantly resident and unmarried administrator of bodily as well as of spiritual comfort to the poor, the unfortunate, and the stranger.

Monastery means a place of residence for monks. There were monks, friars, and nuns. The word friar, from the French word fren, means brother. The word nun, from the French none, means a sister in religion, a virgin separated from the world. The persons, whether male or female, composing one of these religious communities, were called a convent; the place where monks lived a monastery; that where friars lived, a friary; that where nuns lived, a nunnery...

Some of these were abbeys and some priories – the former of a rank superior to the latter. An abbey had an abbot, or an abbess; a priory, a prior, or a prioress. Then there were different orders of monks, friars, and nuns ...

The persons belonging to a monastery lived in common, in one and the same building; they could possess no property individually; when they entered the walls of the monastery, they left the world wholly behind them; they made a solemn vow of celibacy; they could devise nothing by will; each had a life-interest only in the revenues of the community. Some of the monks and friars were also priests, though not all; and the business of the whole was to say masses and prayers, and to do deeds of hospitality and charity.

England, more, perhaps, than any other country in Europe, abounded in such institutions. In England there was, on an average, more than twenty of those establishments to a county! Here was a prize for an unjust and cruel tyrant to lay his lawless hands upon, and for 'Reformation' gentry to share amongst them! Here was enough to make robbers on a grand scale cry out against 'monkish ignorance and superstition'! No wonder that the bowels of Cranmer, Knox, and all the rest, yearned so piteously as they did, when they cast their pious eyes on all the farms and manors, and on all the silver and gold ornaments belonging to these communities! We shall see by-and-by with what alacrity they ousted, plundered, and pulled down: we shall see them robbing, under the basest pretences, even the altars of the country parish churches, down to the very smallest of those churches, and down to the value of five shillings ...

Now, let us put a plain question or two to ourselves, and to these our teachers; and we shall quickly be able to form a just estimate of the modesty, sincerity, and consistency of revilers of the Catholic religion. They cannot deny that this religion was the only Christian religion in the world for fifteen hundred years after the death of Christ. Whatever they may claim as to the first three hundred years, they cannot deny that for twelve hundred years there had been a Pope seated at Rome; and during that period all the nations of Europe, and some part of America, had become Christian, and all acknowledged the Pope as their head in religious matters; and, in short, there was no other Christian Church known in the world, nor had any other ever been thought of.

Can we believe then that Christ, who died to save sinners, who sent forth His Gospel as the means of their salvation, would have suffered a false Christian religion, and no other than a false Christian religion, to be known amongst men all this while? Will these modest assailants of the faith of their and our ancestors assert to our faces, that, for twelve hundred years at least, there were no true Christians in the world? Will they tell us that Christ, who promised to be with the teachers of His word to the end of the world, wholly left them, and gave up hundreds upon hundreds of millions of people to be led in darkness to their eternal perdition, by one whom His inspired followers had denominated the 'man of sin' and the 'scarlet whore'? Will they, indeed, dare to tell us that Christ gave up the world wholly to 'Antichrist' for twelve hundred years? Yet this they must do, they must thus stand forward with bold and unblushing blasphemy or they must confess themselves guilty of the most atrocious calumny against the Catholic religion.

Coming nearer home, our ancestors became Christians about six hundred years after the death of Christ. And how did they become Christians? Who first pronounced the name of Christ to this land? Who converted the English from paganism to Christianity? Some Protestant saint? No, no. The work was begun, continued and ended by the Popes, one of whom sent over some monks who settled at Canterbury, and from whose beginnings the Christian religion spread, like the grain of mustard-seed, rapidly over the land. Whatever therefore any other part of the world might have known of Christianity before the Pope became the settled and acknowledged head of the Church, England at any rate never had known of any Christian religion other than that at the head of which was the Pope; and in this religion, with the Pope at its head, England continued to be firmly fixed for nine hundred years.

In the foregoing, William Cobbett has covered a lot of ground and argued his case, I suggest, very satisfactorily. To supplement what he has told us, let us now examine in closer detail just what life was really like for the people of those days, and particularly for 'ordinary' people. 'Nasty, brutish, and short'? – or, as Cobbett would have it, abundant as never before or since in 'ease, and happiness, and harmony, and Christian charity'?

EDUCATION

SINCE, NO MATTER WHERE OR WHEN PEOPLE LIVE, THEY are inescapably the result of their upbringing to a large extent, it is surely right to start with the general run of education of those days, which we are often told was very much for the privileged few, and limited in what it covered even for them.

Oh my goodness! As readers by now will surely be expecting me to say in relation to just about every topic I address in these pages, the contrary is so much the case that it could hardly be more so. As to the extent of education's availability, any families who wanted their children educated, which was the vast majority of families in those days, could have them educated, *at no cost at all*, at either the nearest cathedral school or the nearest monastery; and nowhere was a monastery more than three or four miles distant from another one. And as to what education embraced ...

I say without hesitation that never in the history of the world, whether before or after the high point in the Middle Ages that was the thirteenth century, was education as profound, as all-embracing and as excellent in every respect as it was then. Evidence to this effect abounds.

In the first place, all the most important universities in Europe were founded during that period. The idea of a university had never even been thought of before; and, but for the Catholic Church, it can safely be said that it never would have been. In England, both the Oxford and the Cambridge that we know today was founded in the thirteenth century. And so on, throughout most of Europe.

What did they learn at those Catholic schools and universities?

We must go into this in some detail in order properly to appreciate it, not least because adequate treatments of the subject are not easy to come by.

The basic education consisted of the Liberal Arts. The term, though not the arts themselves, was lifted from classical antiquity, when the 'liberal arts' denoted the education proper to a free man ('*liber*' means free in Latin), by contrast with the education suitable for a slave.

The Liberal Arts were divided into two main parts: the *Trivium* and the *Quadrivium*, both of which date from the Middle Ages. Looking at the *Trivium* and the *Quadrivium* more closely ...

The *Trivium* consisted of logic, grammar, and rhetoric.

Logic is the art of thinking. Grammar is the art of using and combining words, spoken and written, to express thought. Rhetoric is the art of *communicating* thought from one person's mind to another person's mind.

The *Quadrivium* consisted of Arithmetic, Music, Geometry and Astronomy. But those four subject-headings are 'short-hand' rather than even remotely adequate descriptions of what was taught.

Arithmetic and music were about *individual numbers* and *quantities*, as opposed to *duration of time* and *extension of space*. Arithmetic was about the theory of *number*. Music was an *application* of the theory of number, with specific reference to measuring individual quantities *in motion*.

Geometry and Astronomy are about *continuous quantity* or *extension in space*. Geometry is the *theory of space*; Astronomy about *applying* the theory of space.

After these seven general arts of the Liberal education, there were further, more specialist arts that could be undertaken, and were undertaken by many – in two main categories.

One category was the Utilitarian Arts, for the production of utilities that serve the wants of mankind. Examples included carpentry, masonry, plumbing, law, medicine, and even, under this heading, the care of souls.

The other is the Fine Arts, of which there were seven: architecture, instrumental music, sculpture, painting, literature, the drama, and the dance. Their purpose was not merely for decoration and enjoyment, but also to elevate the human spirit – to *improve* mankind.

That was an education. First, it was learning, in the greatest depth, to think, to communicate, and to reckon with numbers and measurements. Then, with the mind properly trained, it was studying how best to use these abilities for the most useful and satisfying purposes. With the resources available in those days, the structure and content of education simply could not have been improved upon; we can indeed safely say that, if it could have been improved upon, it would have been.

Now, surely, it becomes clearer how it was that there existed in the Middle Ages large quantities of people all over England, and indeed all over Europe, who were capable of devising and organising the erection of those unimaginably complex and beautiful cathedrals and other buildings – for instance, a parish Church to every four square miles in England – that I used as our starting point for examining the Middle Ages.

But it takes more than devising and supervising to erect a huge building. What about the labour forces who did the hugely laborious work of quarrying, bricklaying and all the rest? When we remembered that almost none of the machinery that we take for granted today had yet been invented, is it not clear that erecting such buildings depended on a massive available labour force consisting of the virtual slaves known as serfs, villeins and whatever.

It is true that those involved in every detail of the building of those cathedrals received no pay, and the cathedrals, astonishingly, cost virtually nothing to build. But they were unpaid because they did not wish to be paid. Effectively, they built them in their spare time, as a sort of consecrated leisure activity.

ECONOMIC CONDITIONS

SPARE TIME? YES, EVEN THE LOWEST-BORN CITIZEN HAD an almost endless supply of it. No need to take my word for this. According to Professor Thorold Rogers, Professor of Political Economy at Oxford University in the mid-nineteenth century and an important enough scholar to rate an entry in *Encyclopaedia Britannica*, a labourer – yes a *labourer* – could provide all the necessities for his family for a year by working for no more than *fourteen* weeks, just over a quarter of the year. Another source of leisure, even in the periods that work was actually necessary, was the Catholic Church's feast days, of which our five or so bank holidays are the modern equivalent. Equivalent? The famous German economist and historian of his day Professor Werner Sombart (1863–1941), in a study of agricultural conditions in Central Europe in the fourteenth century, found literally hundreds of communities whose public holidays ranged from 160 to 180 days a year – very nearly half the year.

Time now to quote one of the most oft-quoted and authoritatively weighty passages of all by those who defend the reality of the Middle Ages – from the book *De Laudibus Legum Angliae* ('In Praise of the Laws of England') by Sir John Fortescue (1394–1476). And although Fortescue is writing of a period over a century later than the thirteenth century on which we are particularly focusing, that period is still very much in the Middle Ages. I shall let Cobbett introduce him:

Fortescue was Lord Chief Justice for nearly forty years, appointed Lord Chancellor by Henry VI. Being later in exile as a result of the wars between the Houses of York and Lancaster [the Wars of the Roses], with the king's son, Prince Edward, in exile with him, Fortescue wrote a series of letters to the prince to explain to him the nature and effect of the laws of England, and to induce him to study them and uphold them. *De Laudibus Legum Angliae* is a book of law authority quoted frequently in our courts today. No man can doubt the truth of the facts in it. It was written by a famous lawyer for a prince, intended to be read by other contemporary lawyers, and by all lawyers in future. The passage that I am about to quote, relating to the state of the English, was purely incidental, not intended to answer any temporary purpose. It must have been a true account.

From chapter 36 of Fortescue's book, the passage that so excites Cobbett and other authors:

The king [of England] cannot by himself lay taxes, subsidies or any imposition, of any kind, upon the subject; he cannot alter the laws or make new ones without the express consent of the whole kingdom in Parliament assembled; every inhabitant is at full liberty to use and enjoy whatever his farm produces; all the improvements he makes are his own to use and enjoy without the hindrance, interruption or denial of any; if he be in any wise injured, or oppressed, he shall have his amends and satisfaction against the party offending. Hence it is that the inhabitants are rich in gold, silver, and in all the necessaries and conveniences of life. They drink no water, unless upon a religious score, and by way of doing penance. They are fed, in great abundance, with all sorts of flesh and fish, of which they have plenty everywhere; they are clothed throughout in good woollens; their bedding and other furnitures in their houses are of wool, and in great store; they are also well provided with all other sorts of household goods and necessary implements for husbandry; every one, according to his rank, hath all things which conduce to make life easy and happy.

Remember, too: such people as were ever, for whatever reason, destitute had no more onerous problem to face than of finding their way to the nearest monastery.

Professor Thorold Rogers again, on the Middle Ages just before the 'Reformation' struck, on pages ix and 23 of volume 4 of his *History of Agriculture and Prices in England*:

> The prosperity of the nation remained unbroken ... The English nation, I mean those who worked and slaved, were singularly prosperous during the period on which I am dwelling ... There was solid, substantial unbroken prosperity. The fifteenth century, and the early years of the sixteenth, were the golden age of the English husbandman, the artisan and the labourer.

'Everyone, according to his rank, hath all things which conduce to make him happy,' declared Sir John Fortescue, writing at the time. 'The golden age of the English husbandman, the artisan and the labourer,' declared Professor Rogers some four centuries later, from detailed comparisons over a 600-year period. Would anyone dare write the same about our own day, anywhere?

Does anyone not believe Fortescue, Rogers, Cobbett, Macaulay and March (all non-Catholic except Fortescue), and many other authors I could quote to the same effect? Then ask yourself: to which period of English history does the phrase 'Merrie England' occur? Even on the simple answer to that alone, I can surely rest my case.

SOCIAL CONDITIONS

IT IS AGAINST THAT BACKGROUND THAT CULTURE FLOURished, not only in architecture, visible and dramatic as the evidence of it is, but in every field that culture can exist. Nor was it only culture that flourished. Cultural inventiveness did too; indeed inventiveness as such. 'Dark and primitive', many historians – disgracing that title – would have the Middle Ages to be. Once more I shall use Frederic March and Lord Macaulay, this time to help us look just a little further at the astonishing heights which the human race reached in those 'barbaric' days, and from which it has fallen since.

On architecture we need by now say no more, other than perhaps to remind ourselves that the architectural techniques the medievals invented were so advanced that they are no longer within our reach.

Universities we have already covered too. Under much the same heading we can now include hospitals. The concept of hospitals of a sort was not completely unknown before the Middle Ages, but the modern city hospital, caring for both the ill and the injured, is an entirely thirteenth-century invention. (The Catholic Church's contribution in this field is of course still honoured implicitly, though largely unconsciously, in the profusion of hospitals called after Catholic saints, including possibly London's greatest medical institution of all, Saint Thomas's Hospital, founded in 1213.)

Mention of hospitals should certainly include reference to hygiene, an area in which the medievals have perhaps been more insulted than in any other. Let us first start with what a medieval hospital actually looked like from inside. Fortunately, a late-thirteenth century hospital existed in Tanierre in France in a reasonable state of preservation, at least until recently; and our same Professor Walsh, in an appendix in *The Thirteenth: Greatest of Centuries*, quotes a modern architect of his day, a Mr Arthur Dillon, on it:

> It was an admirable hospital in every way, and it is doubtful if we today surpass it. It had the advantage we often lose, of being but one storey high. Each patient had more space than we now afford.
>
> The ventilation by the great windows and ventilators in the ceiling was excellent; it was cheerfully lighted, and the arrangement of the gallery shielded the patients from dazzling light and from draughts from the windows, and afforded an easy means of supervision. The division by the roofless, low partitions isolated the sick, obviating the depression that comes from the sight of others in pain.
>
> It contrasted greatly with the cheerless white ward of today. The vaulted ceiling was very beautiful; the woodwork was richly carved; the great windows were filled with coloured glass. Altogether, it was one of the best examples of the best period of Gothic architecture.

The standard of hygiene in this hospital and elsewhere? Professor Walsh again:

> It has been declared that the history of Europe from the fifth to the fifteenth century might be summed up as a thousand years without a bath. The more we know about this period, however, the less reason do we find to believe it. Mr. Cram, in *Ruined Abbeys of Great Britain* (Pott & Co., N.Y., 1907), has described wonderful arrangements within the monasteries for conducting water from long distances for all toilet purposes. There was much more attention to sanitary details than has been supposed. Mr. Cram, in describing what was by no means one of the greatest of the English abbeys of the thirteenth century, says:
>
> 'Here at Beaulieu the water was brought by an underground conduit from an unfailing spring a mile away, and this served for drinking, washing and bathing, the supply of the fish ponds, and for a constant flushing of the elaborate system of drainage. In sanitary matters, the monks were as far in advance of the rest of society as they were in learning and agriculture.'

In politics? Macaulay has already mentioned 'that constitution of which all the other free constitutions in the world are copies', which was structured to reduce as far as humanly possible the danger of legal tyranny. He has also mentioned the thirteenth century Magna Carta, important enough still to be one of the official constitutional documents in countries in many parts of the world. At the same time, trial by juries of twelve, with no one found guilty unless the verdict was unanimous, was properly established. Perhaps more important still, the Common Law was painstakingly perfected – the Common Law that is one of the only two great secular systems of law of the Christian era (the other being the Roman Law), the only one to have actually come out of the Christian centuries, and so precious to all with experience of it that even today it is clung to by America and all its states except one; Canada outside Quebec; Australia; New Zealand; India; South Africa; Ireland; and many others.

To help appreciate the marvel of the Common Law, I quote

probably the best twentieth-century author on the subject, Richard
O'Sullivan, Q.C., in his *The Spirit of the Common Law*, pages 95ff:

> One of the great conceptions of the Common Law is the 'free and
> law-abiding man; by virtue of his nature man is free'... This very
> idea is the creation of a common law, strengthening the bonds of
> society by administering equal justice to all its members ...
>
> The Common Law has a kindly concept of the nature of
> Everyman. Everyman is presumed to be a good man until the
> contrary is proved by lawful evidence. The Common Law has no
> hint of the radical corruption of human nature, no trace of the
> theory of Luther or of Hobbes (or of Hitler), which degrades
> human personality and necessarily exalts the power of the State –
> if human nature is radically corrupt, it needs the coalition of
> external power to lead it to decent ways of living.

Crucially important: under the Common Law, even properly enacted
laws were subject to reason, and any law or custom contrary to 'right
reason' was considered to be non-existent. O'Sullivan again:

> The duty of the King, or as we should say today the State, is to do
> justice to all manner of man. The King is under God and the law.
> He is no King when will and not law is the principle of his rule.
> Law is a rule of reason, and not a mere command of a superior.
> Against this law (of reason and of nature), neither prescription
> nor statute nor customer may prevail. And if any may be brought
> in against this law of reason and nature, they would not be pre-
> scriptions, statutes to this one. They would be things void and
> against justice.

I should not close this brief examination of the Common Law without
reference to how close we now are to losing completely and permanently this precious inheritance of ours. A famous judge of his time,
Lord Macmillan, sounded this warning as far back as 1948 (reported in
The Times, 6th April):

> The lover of our ancient laws and institutions ... cannot but look

with some dismay at the customary common law of the land, which has served us so well in the past, being increasingly superseded by a system of laws with no regard for the usages and customs of the people, but dictated by 'ideological theories'.

There will soon be little of the common law left. The Statute Book and vast volumes of statutory rules and orders will replace it. Our courts are concerned increasingly with interpreting often unintelligible legislation, decreasingly with discussing and developing legal principles. [...] It is vitally important that the new policy, while promoting liberty by securing better living conditions for the people, should not interferingly deprive them of initiative and independence, once Britain's most valuable asset.

Already true in 1948, how many times truer today, six decades later, with more than 90 per cent of legislation now originating in Brussels, where the Common Law plays no part?

Closely connected with politics and law is economics. There was no National Debt bearing annual interest to be met by the taxpayers; indeed, legally no interest-bearing debt at all – no bank-loan interest, mortgage interest, hire-purchase interest, credit-card interest. Interest-charging and paying was actually *banned* by the Church. Yet sizeable commercial transactions could and did take place.

As to the economic conditions of the poor who sometimes needed temporary assistance ... Cardinal Gasquet in his *Parish Life in England before the Reformation*:

> The parish wardens had their duties towards their local poor. Often they were guardians of the common chest, out of which needy parishioners could obtain temporary, interest-free loans, secured by pledges and the security of other parishioners, to tide themselves over in difficulties.

Furthermore, there was almost never any inflation or deflation of the currency. What it cost to buy a pair of shoes or a nice fat sheep in one century was pretty well what it cost you a century before or after. (We know that because statutes of that period actually recorded the price of some wages and food.)

CULTURE

ETURNING, IN OUR SEARCH FOR MEDIEVAL INVENTIVE-
ness, to culture once more ...
Literature? The crucially important invention of books of
pages, in place of long rolls of skin or paper, the 'codex', actually dates
back to the Catholic Europe from which the Middle Ages arose.
Unquestionably medieval, however, is the movable-type printing
press. And if the modern world is unimaginable without that, equally
imaginable is it, surely, without the purely medieval Catholic invention of rhyming and scanning, which completely transformed song
and other poetry, and without which even today's television advert-
izing jingles would not exist.

Still on literature ... As Professor Walsh demonstrates, in epic
poetry, shorter poems and prose of all kinds, the thirteenth century is
at least the equal of any other age. *And* this period saw the introduction
of – yes, truly – circulating libraries.

The visual arts – painting, sculpture, carving? With too much to say
for me even to summarize here, I shall restrict myself to mentioning
just one undoubted medieval invention: the stained-glass window.
Stained glass as such dates back to Ancient Egypt and classical Rome,
but nothing like its use in the cathedrals, abbeys and churches of
the Middle Ages had even been imagined before. Indeed a visit to the
thirteenth-century Saint Louis IX Chapel in Paris would very probably be enough to convince most people that the medieval standard will
never be seen again.

Music? Hmm. Does not all the best music start with Bach and
Handel in the early eighteenth century?

Lifting my head above the parapet, and braving the snorts of contempt which may well greet my next few words, no, I by no means
concede it. Indeed the medievals themselves would have been *repelled*
by it, under no fewer than three headings. First, as consistently and
gratingly out-of-tune (because of the all-but-universal use of so-called
'equal temperament' in the modern tuning of keyboard instruments).
Secondly, as utterly impoverished (because of the reduction of the
eight modes used by them in their compositions, to just *two* modes, our

Major and Minor keys, of which the Major key was seldom used, being considered degenerate; and (referred to as the '*modus lascivius*'). Thirdly, as suitable for children and savages rather than civilized grown-ups (because of its use, normally, of regular, measured rhythm, rather than the much more sophisticated free-flowing rhythms more ordinarily used before then).

You *like* classical and post-classical music of the last three centuries? I too. That proves nothing though. It *could* show that we have good taste; equally it could show that taste wretchedly corrupted by exposure to what is perverse. What is objectively beautiful in the Fine Arts is a matter for *analysis*, and must be *learnt*. Only in our present crazy era has it been commonly thought otherwise.

That said about music, and having perhaps opened up a subject for a future article, I shall now retire back behind the parapet.

SLAVERY, SERFDOM AND THE REST

LET US TAKE ONE LAST LOOK AT SOCIAL CONDITIONS IN 'Merrie England', with reference to this sentence by the legal expert Richard O'Sullivan that I quoted a little earlier: 'It is not necessary here to trace the slow assimilation of slave and serf and bondman into the status of the "free and law-abiding man."' Well, what about those serfs, bondmen and villeins then?

They existed, of course. To assess these statuses and conditions fairly, however, we must look at them against the background of what conditions were for the 'lower orders' before the Catholic Church 'conquered' Europe from the fourth century AD onwards.

From time immemorial, the lowest social order had of course been that of the slaves. Here is a description of the conditions of slaves throughout the Roman Empire as a whole taken from a superbly researched book published in 1892, *Lectures on Slavery and Freedom* by Canon W. R. Brownlow:

The law of Constantine the Great, regarded as a miracle of humanity toward the slave, gives us some idea of the hard condition of the slaves. The first Christian emperor enacted in AD319: 'If any master shall chastise his slaves with rods or thongs, or for safe keeping put him in chains, he shall incur no danger of a criminal charge if his slave die, whenever that death. He is, however, guilty of homicide if he slay him wilfully with a club or with stones, and if he use a weapon to inflict a deadly wound; if he order him to be hanged by a halter, if have him cast down a precipice; or if he have him poisoned, or his body flayed by public tortures, such as tearing open his sides with iron claws, or burning his limbs with red-hot plates ...'

Roman ladies treated their unfortunate handmaids equally cruelly. Surrounded by a multitude of slaves, the patrician lady undertook her toilet with a small stiletto always at hand to punish, with spiteful stabs, any failures in her tire-woman, and sometimes employed an executioner, paid annually, to flog slaves who had offended her ...

In Roman law a slave had no rights, were not persons. Seneca says they were used just as animals are. The jurist Ulpian classes them with cattle, 'a slave or other animal'.

The union between slaves, not dignified even with the name of 'marriage', was as much at the disposal of the master as the pairing of dogs, or horses, or pigs. A '*villicus*', a farm slave, was required to have a wife, to attach him more closely to the property. A cook, or confectioner, or a butler, was not allowed to marry. It made them idle, Cato observed. The 'marriage' could be broken, the husband and wife sold to different parties, and each obliged to contract another union.

The children of slaves were just as much the master's property as the fruit of his apple-trees or his flocks. Slave children belonged, not to their parents, but to their master ...

Apuleius thus describes those unfortunates condemned to grind flour: 'What poor wretches! – their skin livid and spotted with blows of the scourge; miserable rags cover their bruised backs, some clothed only by an apron round their loins, none have more than a tattered tunic to hide their nakedness. Branded on their brow, head half-shaven, feet shackled with a ring, bodies disfigured by fire, eyelids shrivelled by burning smoke and steaming heat, eyes almost sightless.

The philosopher Epictetus was a slave to a freedman. His brutal master once amused himself by twisting Epictetus' leg in an instrument of torture. Epictetus said: 'If you go on you will break it.' The wretch did go on, and did break it. Seneca, the best friend the slaves ever had among the pagans, seriously recommended suicide as the shortest remedy for their miseries. Suicide often became an epidemic among slaves.

No outrage against a female slave could be punished, and she was absolutely at her master's disposal. History gives instances of broken-down Roman nobles who supported themselves by the prostitution of their slaves.

Canon Brownlow has given us both a picture of slave conditions and also a clear picture of the philosophy among the pagan ruling class that the Catholic Church had to transform, a philosophy that was deeply engrained everywhere. Slavery, from time immemorial, was regarded as so much a part of the national order of things that not even philosophers such as Socrates and Aristotle, prepared to stand up for truth at the expense of unpopularity, thought it wrong. Given, too, the huge vested interests in slavery, if slavery had not been abolished in fact, surely one would have thought it impossible that it could have been.

Say what you like against the Catholic Church. What she accomplished would have seemed an impossible miracle to anyone, slaveowner or slave, who had lived before the Christian era. Even more impossibly miraculous, she did it without violence or economic disruption, without causing tension between master and slave, without inflaming resentment of the oppressed slaves, indeed while preaching to the slaves that they should be submissive and cheerfully obedient. Her method: by first insisting that their effective legal status be raised from that of, literally, animals to that of human beings, and, over a period as long as was necessary, consistently to permeate both masters and slaves with ideas and principles wholly inconsistent with the spirit of slavery, until, in every part of the world where the Church had complete sway, slavery changed from inevitable and ineradicable to inconceivable. And I think it is fair to ask: how could it possibly have been skilfully and wisely and tactfully and delicately and, above all, comprehensively done?

Many Protestant historians have generously credited the Catholic Church's achievement with slavery. Quoting Macaulay once again (*History...* volume 1, chapter 1, pages 22–23):

> A change infinitely more momentous than the acquisition or loss of any province: slavery and its accompanying evils were fast disappearing.

Remarkably, the revolution ending slavery was silently and imperceptibly effected. It surprised no contemporary observers, and has received very scanty attention from historians. Brought about neither by laws nor by physical force, moral causes noiselessly effaced the distinction between master and slave. It is only just to acknowledge that the chief agent was religion ... Christian morality is undoubtedly averse to distinctions of caste, and to the Catholic Church such distinctions are peculiarly odious."

Moreover no one can justly deny what the Catholic Church showed *by example* in relation to such distinctions. From the outset, the position of a slave born or received into the Church was complete equality with free citizens and Roman nobles, barred from no position whatever in the Church's hierarchy. In many other religions there is a priestly caste, at least in practice, but never in the Catholic Church, in theory or in practice. Even two of her popes, St Pius I in the first century and St Calixtus I in the second, were born slaves.

What is more, the Church had to accomplish the extermination of slavery *twice over*. First, it was abolished throughout the Roman Empire by early in the seventh century, less than three hundred years after the official adoption of Christianity. Soon afterwards, though, barbarian tribes brought about the empire's collapse, and re-established slavery wherever they conquered; and virtually England's entire population was subjected to slavery by invading Saxons. They too were eventually converted, however, and, as in other countries at the same time, the Church again gradually secured more rights and better living conditions for slaves and the poorest members of society. The eleventh-century Norman Conquest interrupted progress for a time (though the incidence of slavery did not increase), but gradually those conquerors too were absorbed into the population as a whole and England became, effectively, one people.

Well before the thirteenth century, slavery had for the most part again ceased to exist. It was indeed replaced by a form of servitude variously known as serfdom and villeinage; but if serfdom conjures up spectres of oppressed people in some readers' minds, well, serfdom was a very *modified* form of servitude. Granted, the serf was not legally equal to his master, but he was legally equal to everyone else, which slaves had never been. Nor was it long before serfdom became little more than a legal fiction with, for practical purposes, no onerous impositions on the serf at all. Professor Thorold Rogers, in his *History of Agriculture and Prices in England* (volume 1, pages 6–12 and 66–81):

> During Henry III's long reign (1216–1272) the mass of the English people passed from being serfs, perhaps even [in some cases] slaves, into becoming freemen ... In Henry's reign the baron is no longer the enemy, but the leader of the people ...
>
> The lot of the villeins was not so grievous as the expression suggests, or enquirers about our forefathers have concluded. It is held that that they themselves might be sold with their chattels at their lord's discretion ... But in the many thousands of accounts which I have investigated ... I have never found a trace of any transfer of villeins, or their services, to third parties ... So absolute a silence, I submit, is sufficient to prove that the legal theory of a villein's total lack of civil rights as against his lord had become antiquated before 1259 ...

And, anyway, by the end of the fifteenth century, for all practical purposes villeinage of any kind had had disappeared completely.

THE GUILDS

A NOTHER IMPORTANT SOCIAL FEATURE OF THE MIDDLE
Ages is the guilds. Religious-based, as was every institution
without exception of those times, they were a combination of
trade union, benefit club and religious fraternity. They regulated the
trade of craft with which they were concerned, ensured high standards
of workmanship from their members and adequate but not excessive
remuneration, and looked after those who got into difficulties, and also
engaged in special charitable projects that they chose, such as running
any hospital, almshouse or school that they had originally founded,
and keeping up bridges and roads. Some had no connection with the
trades or crafts at all, but had been set up purely for charitable purposes.

Protestant historians have acknowledged that it was characteristic of
the religious spirit of that period that, when any unusual distress
occurred in a community, people swiftly banded together to help.
Countless different guilds were fraternities for mutual comfort and
help, provided free, in sickness, old age, poverty, unjust imprisonment,
and losses by fire and shipwreck, all. Many built up substantial possessions for use in these charitable undertakings; and *that*, as the
Reformation took hold, and greedy cronies of Queen Elizabeth eyed
those possessions, was in due course to be their undoing.

THE CONDUCT OF WAR IN THE MIDDLE AGES

C AN WE FIND NO FAULT WITH THE MIDDLE AGES? HOW
about war? That was certainly not abolished. Indeed it was
more or less continuous in much of the fourteenth and
fifteenth centuries. The Hundred Years War lasted from 1337 to 1453,
and included its fair share of atrocities.

For the worst example that I can find, King Henry V's campaign
ending with England's victory at Agincourt, here is a modern histo-

rian, Desmond Seward, in his *Henry V as Warlord* (Sidgwick and Jackson, 1987, page xviii):

> The misery inflicted on the French by Henry's campaigns is indisputable, with many a town, a château, an abbey or a church sacked by his men. Life in the countryside became a nightmare. The English raiding enemy territory killed everything that moved, destroyed crops and food supplies and drove off livestock, trying to weaken their opponents by starving the civilian population. Occupied areas fared little better; villages had to pay extortionate dues in food and wine as well as money, or suffer executions and burnings.

And arguably Henry's ultimate atrocity, by civilized standards, was the massacre of all prisoners of war on the eve of Agincourt, as even Shakespeare, though setting out to glorify him in his play, records.

But that was not typical of the Middle Ages. Indeed, Henry's methods of warfare seems to have been unprecedented in Christian warfare. And they were not to be repeated until centuries later.

On the contrary, surely the Church's most astonishing achievement of all is how it *civilized* warfare. Realistically recognizing war, though a great evil, to be inevitable in a society which would always contain sinners as well as saints, it did what it could to reduce to the minimum its terrible effects, and succeeded to an extent that is unimaginable today. Some examples:

The introduction and constant encouragement of the notion of chivalry;

The so-called Peace of God, protecting from military hostilities clerics, monks, nuns, and even the poor, and pilgrims and merchants on a journey, and also creating the right of asylum in sanctuaries – all under pain of excommunication;

The so-called Truce of God, forbidding any acts of private warfare from Saturday night to Monday morning, from Wednesday night to Monday morning, and throughout Advent and Lent – again under pain of excommunication.

The Middle Ages in fact created the tradition of comradeship, courtesy, and various civilized conventions between soldiers of opposing sides, traces of which survived up to the beginning of the First World War. Perhaps more remarkably still, they were a time when a peasant could be ploughing tranquilly in the field while soldiers were killing each other in an important battle in the next field.

No, that is not fiction. Here is our hard-headed nineteenth-century economist Professor Thorold Rogers on the Wars of the Roses, hardly able to believe his eyes as he pored over the huge quantity of original documents while composing his *History of Agriculture and Prices in England from 1259 to 1793* (Preface to volume 4):

> Then came the civil war, the strangest civil war ever seen. No one suffered except the combatants. The people took no part in the strife. It was a long battle between two factions and their retainers ... A singular feature in this great war of succession is that it is a war of pitched battles, not of sieges. The partisans on either side seem to have made their way to some open heath and there to have fought out their quarrel. Still more singular is the silence of contemporary accounts about the struggle which was going on. In thousands of documents penned during the heat of the strife, I have found only two allusions to the character of the time in the wars. For the rest there is no sign of any interest in the combat ... Even those who took part were safe when out of the battle.

– a maxim that might as well never have been heard of by Elizabeth, Cromwell, William III, George II and 'Butcher' Cumberland, or any of the other heroes of the new era opened up by the Reformation and 'Glorious Revolution', or any of the wartime leaders of the last century or so of world history.

'But what about ... ?'

Thus the Middle Ages.

'But ...'

Do I hear objections? 'But what about historians' allegations that you have ignored? – the Spanish Inquisition of the end of the fifteenth century and later? – the Great Plague of the fourteenth century, reckoned to have killed about a third of Europe's population? – the scientific ignorance and naivity of these super-intelligent, super-logical, super-well-educated people, as you claim them to be, which made universal the belief that the earth was the fixed unchanging point of the entire universe and only about 6,000 years old, with Darwinian evolutionary theory unthought-of? – and ...?'

I do not shirk such objections. After all, it is I who have just raised them. And I certainly cannot skip past them. I claim for the thirteenth century, and its surrounding centuries, as close an approach to perfection as we humans can get to, and perfection demands an absence of serious imperfections as well as such excellences as we have been looking at. Perhaps I may be invited to address such objections in a future article. Here, because of the limited space allowed me, I shall simply say that, in my extensive studies of the period, I have come across no facts relating to the Middle Ages which contradict, or even weaken, my unqualified admiration of them. I say this, furthermore, without the least resistance to facing uncomfortable facts, if uncomfortable facts there should be; and if any reader, convinced differently, would like to refer me to facts showing me to be wrong here, it will be my pleasure to consider them for some future article if our editor will agree. [Not so fast son.]

DOWNHILL STEP BY STEP

MEANWHILE, THERE IS AN ARGUABLY MORE INTERESTing topic to close with. If the society of those days was as prosperous, productive and happy as I have been depicting, what happened to it? What transformed that earthly paradise into the world we know today?

Four events during the last 500 years were principally responsible.

First, Cobbett's 'so-called Reformation', set in motion in the early sixteenth century by King Henry VIII: whose title 'Defender of the Faith', bestowed by a Pope, has been hypocritically used by his anti-

Catholic successors up to today). Henry's motive; so that he could legally get adulterously married to Anne Boleyn, whom he, not long afterwards, judicially murdered by means of the executioner's axe. Henry's usurpation of spiritual authority from where it had been recognized for the previous 1,500 years in Europe, and nearly 1,000 in England, led swiftly to the stealing of some 2 million acres of monastery land, with such inevitable consequences as the abandonment of the poor and indigent, the closing of free hospitals and the free school that had been available to every child, and the end of the guilds from which craftsmen received skills and training, support when in difficulty and the equivalent of our old-age pensions on retirement. It even ruined the well-organized road system of those days, since one of the *many* social responsibilities of the monasteries was that of keeping the road in good order and repair.

The changes for the worse brought about by the 'Reformation' are so vast in scale that it is difficult to comprehend them. Here is Cobbett once more, to give us an example:

> Englishmen in general suppose that there were always poor-laws and paupers in England. They ought to remember that *for nine hundred years, under the Catholic religion, there were neither.*

Certainly there always were, and always have been, poor; but until the sixteenth century, relief for sick, starving and the otherwise needy was no further away than the nearest monastery. Indeed perhaps the most terrible aspect of the incredible sufferings of the poor during the reigns of Henry VIII, Edward VI and Elizabeth – see Cobbett again – is that it was the very stealing of the Church properties which *created* the paupers who suffered so horribly, *including being punished for being poor.* The land which was stolen from the Church amounted to about *one fifth* of the land in England; and *one third* of what the Church lands produced was *by law* for relieving the poor. Thus *one fifteenth of the property of England effectively belonged to the poor.* When Henry VIII, Edward VI's controllers and Elizabeth stole those lands for themselves and their courtiers, they were not *merely* robbing the Church, *merely* robbing all those of previous generations who had between them donated what the Church possessed. They were also, in a real sense, *robbing directly from the poor*.

Second event: the effective abolition of the monarchy as the head of the three-part constitution. This began with the execution of Charles I, continued with the deposition of James II, and was completed by the death of James's successor, William III, with the final knot tied at the accession of George I, who, unable to speak English, took virtually no part in political affairs. The monarchy gone, government was no longer led by members of a family, specially trained from birth for their role and motivated to take political decisions for long-term bene-fits. Henceforth it was led by people untrained for the most important job in the land and who, with very few exceptions, reached their pre-eminent political positions because they wanted them. 'The qualities needed to attain power by the democratic process are the exact oppo-site of the qualities needed to exercise power appropriately,' it has been wisely said.

Third: the setting up of the Bank of England in 1694 by stealth and deception. I do not exaggerate. The Act of Parliament producing this massive economic and political revolution was sneaked through, unde-bated, under the misleading title 'The Tunnage Act'. (The equally dis-honest description of the 'Tunnage Bill' put before Parliament represented it as a measure to tax ships and liquor 'for the Recompense and Advantages ... to such persons as shall Voluntarily Advance the sum of Fifteen Hundred Thousand Pounds towards Carrying on the War with France'.) Even more incredibly, the company founded to wield more than any other national organization in history ('Let me control credit of a nation,' Mayer Amschel Rothschild, the first English Rothschild, is supposed to have said, 'and I care not who makes its laws') was not owned by the nation, but by secret shareholders whose identity has never been disclosed, notwithstanding repeated requests, and whose accounts, even after that Bank's nationalization in 1948, have never once been audited. And what was the purpose and effect of this new secrecy-enveloped organization? No less than to make interest-bearing loans (previously largely outlawed as usurious and unjust) a permanent feature of our lives and, worse still, to bring money into existence by means of interest-bearing debt even though the money itself *was created out of nothing*.

The 'stealth and deception' were eventually exposed. For about 250 years this remarkable privilege of the Bank of England, to benefit secretly private shareholders who did not even need to be British, was unknown to the British public it purported to serve and even to the general run of financial experts.

That changed, however, in 1929. As a result of the devastating 1929 stock market crash, the then Labour government set up an official enquiry into 'banking, finance and credit' which in 1931 published its findings in a detailed document called the Macmillan Report.

Those findings were startling by any standards. Paragraph 74 of the Macmillan Report told its readers and the world (emphasis added):

> It is not unnatural to think of the deposits in a bank as being created by the public through the deposit of cash representing either savings or amounts which are not for the time being required to meet expenditure ... *But the bulk of the deposits arise out of the action of the banks themselves;* for, by granting loans, allowing money to be drawn on overdrafts, or purchasing securities, a bank creates a credit in its books which is the equivalent of a deposit.

Thus, too, in the banks all over the world. They create money out of nothing and then, unbelievably, shamefully and shamelessly, charge interest on it.

I did not exaggerate when saying that this information became known for the first time, even by experts, in 1931. The lengthy article on 'Money' in the eleventh to thirteenth editions of *Encyclopaedia Britannica* showed complete ignorance of these crucial facts about 'modern money'. For proof of that, turn to the fourteenth edition, published in 1933, *after* publication of the Macmillan Report in 1931. There an entirely new article on 'Money' *completely contradicts the previous edition*. (The Federal Reserve System, which has equivalent Central Bank control in the United States, was set up with similar 'cunning and stealth' in 1913.)

The final turning point in the gradual triumph of secularism, capitalism and socialism over the civilization perfected in the Middle Ages was the 1862 Companies Act, confirmed in its grossly immoral implications in the landmark legal case, *Salomon* v *Salomon & Co Ltd* in 1897. This established that a company was a completely different legal entity from its owners – a legal person in its own right. This meant, not only that the owners were not responsible for any debts they ran up in the company's name, but that the whole ethic of doing business changed fatally and for ever. *People* have souls, codes of ethics and consciences. *Companies* have none. A great man or woman is one who is remarkable for such qualities as wisdom, humanity and charity, who perhaps might be prepared to sacrifice his or her life for country or for truth of some kind. A great company is known only by the salability of its products or services and by the figures in its periodic profit-and-loss account and balance sheet. The sole ethic of a company is profit, and within the limits of the law of the land and the documents which govern a company's existence, 'anything goes.' And, all too frequently, anything very much *does* go, as anyone who takes a glance at corporate history will see depressingly clearly.

★

Farewell then, Middle Ages, civilization's highest point. And farewell too, before very much longer, to the final remnants of what the Middle Ages gave to the world as still somehow survives to the present day (such as bits of the Common Law, including trial by jury, some of our institutions and of course some of our buildings). Only the organization that created the Middle Ages could bring real civilization back.

☙

A fuller version of this article can be found at
www.nmgwynne.net/articles.htm

IDLE MARKET

IDLER BOOKS

THE IDLE PARENT (Penguin) Signed paperback copy.
by Tom Hodgkinson. 'A godsend to parents,' *Sunday Times*.   £8.99

THE IDLE PARENT (Hamish Hamilton)   £9.99 (rrp £14.99)
by Tom Hodgkinson. Signed hardback copy.

THE IDLER'S GLOSSARY (Biblioasis)   £12.95
by Joshua Glenn and Mark Kingwell. US book which is destined
to become the *Devil's Dictionary* for the idling classes.

THE BOOK OF IDLE PLEASURES (Ebury)   £10.99
edited by Tom Hodgkinson & Dan Kieran with fine illustrations by
Ged Wells. A sumptuous hardback anthology of pleasures that aims to
prove the best things in life really are free.
'Lovely book,' Mark Radcliffe, Radio 2.

HOW TO BE FREE (Penguin)   £7.99
by Tom Hodgkinson. 'Essential!' *Time Out*. Signed paperback copy.

HOW TO BE IDLE (Penguin)   £8.99
by Tom Hodgkinson. Signed paperback copy.

**WE WANT EVERYONE: FACEBOOK
AND THE NEW AMERICAN RIGHT** (Bracketpress)   £5.00
by Tom Hodgkinson. Describing the political ideology of the
founders of Facebook. Signed limited edition. Bracketpress pamphlet
with letterpress printed cover. Third edition.

THE IDLER BOOK OF CRAP HOLIDAYS (Boxtree)   £5.00 (rrp £10)
edited by Dan Kieran. Readers' accounts of their worst holidays in the sun.

**ON THE VISIONARY WORK AND REVOLUTIONARY
LIFE OF AN IDLE IDOL: WILLIAM MORRIS** (Bracketpress) £25.00
by John Mitchinson. Letterpress printed essay with frontispiece by
Edward Burne-Jones and Kelmscott borders, hand-bound limited edition.

IDLER BACK ISSUES

WORK WORK WORK No.3 – January/February 1994   £8
Bertrand Russell, Charles Handy

SKINT No.24 – September/October 1995   £8
Keith Allen, Louis Theroux, Charles Handy

MAN'S RUIN No.25 – Winter 1999   £15
The first book-format Idler, featuring Louis Theroux's Sick Notes, Will Self,
Howard Marks, Adam and Joe, and Ken Kesey

THE LOVE ISSUE No.30 – Summer 2002   £10
Louis Theroux meets Colin Wilson, Johnny Ball on Descartes, Crap Towns, Devon
Retreat, Chris Yates interview, Marchesa Casati

WAR ON WORK No.35 – Spring 2005   £10
Keith Allen's A to Z of life, Raoul Vaneigem interview, Jeremy Deller's Folk Art,
Dan Kieran's Seven Steps to the Idle Life, Chris Donald, Peter Doherty
and more Crap Jobs

YOUR MONEY OR YOUR LIFE No.36 – Winter 2005   £10
Mutoid Waste Company, Edward Chancellor on credit, Penny Rimbaud,
Jay Griffiths, A Hitch Hiker's Guide, The Guilds, Chris Donald

CHILDISH THINGS No.37 – Spring 2005   £10
Childcare for the Lazy, Michael Palin, Bertrand Russell, Free Range Education,
Running Away to Join the Circus

THE GREEN MAN No.38 – Winter 2006   £10.99
Stephen Harding on why doing less is the way forward, Richard Benson tries to sow a
meadow, In conversation with Jamie Reid, John Michell on Cobbett, plus ukulele special

LIE BACK & PROTEST No.39 – Spring 2007   £10.99
Penny Rimbaud on The Meaning of Life, Jay Griffiths eats missionaries for breakfast,
Ronald Hutton, Green Gartside, L. A. Rowland explains why we shouldn't bother
going to university

CARNAL KNOWLEDGE No.40 – Winter 2008   £10.99
Damien Hirst cover, Esther Perel on the sex drought, Neil Boorman, Nick Lezard,
Michael Bywater, Sarah Janes and Kevin Godley

SMASH THE SYSTEM No.42 – Summer 2009   £18.99
The first hardback Idler, bound in cloth. With essays by Alain de Botton,
Penny Rimbaud, Paul Kingsnorth and many more. Interviews with Oliver James,
Jaz Coleman and Youth.

IDLER CLOTHING

T-shirts are £15 and are available in XL, L and M and in girl's fit L and M. Designs include Snail, Work Kills, Do Less, Smash the System. Hoodies are £35 and feature the Idler Snail. All designed and produced by Ged Wells. Send cheque and size and we will choose design. Or check on the website for availability. Colours and designs change constantly.

IDLER SUBSCRIPTIONS

UK subscription	£36.00
Europe subscription	£45.00
Rest of the world subscription	£55.00

New subscribers will receive a hand-printed personalized card welcoming them into the Grand Order of Idlers

Go to www.idler.co.uk and order online, or write your order and send with a cheque payable to 'The Idler' and send it to:
The Idler, PO Box 280, Barnstaple, EX31 4QT, UK.

You must include post & packing costs as follows:
Issues 1–24: £1 per issue. Issues 25–34: £2.50 per issue.
T-shirts and hoodies: £2 per item.
For European Community, add 50%.
For rest of the world, add 100%

A downloadable order form is available from the Idler website
www.idler.co.uk

THE HISTORY of the book jacket is a strange one. The wretched thing started as a piece of plain paper, wrapped around the book to protect it during its sojourn in the bookseller's shop; but it has become this important, elaborate, not to say costly and embarrassing affair, that we know today, and of which we sometimes deplore the very existence. How much better might this mint of money, that is emptied on these ephemeral wrappers – little works of art though many of them may be – be spent upon improving the quality of the materials that are used in the making of the book itself?

– Richard de la Mare
6th Dent Memorial Lecture 1936